LUDWIG MIES VAN DER ROHE

Acknowledgments

The author thanks those who contributed to the preparation of this work, initially published in 1994, in a series conceived by Éric Hazan and designed by Roman Cieslewicz. The early research received the support of Pierre Adler and Terence Riley at the Museum of Modern Art in New York, and Cristina C. Carbone at the Prints and Photographic Division of the Library of Congress in Washington, D.C. The majority of articles cited in the text were collected by Petra Marguc, Hasan Dolan, and Ariela Katz. The generosity of Lord Palumbo made it possible for the author to visit the Farnsworth House, which was then closed to the public. Philip Johnson kindly shared with the author his memories of Germany in the 1930s.

The development of this edition, revised and greatly expanded in 2007, which was reprinted here, is due to the initiative of Jean-François Barrielle. The ground was laid for it during a seminar held at the Institute of Fine Arts at New York University in the fall of 1997. The 2007 edition took into account the wise comments of Phyllis Lambert, which had been included in translations of the first edition, as well as stimulating exchanges with Claire Zimmerman and Dietrich Neumann. The text also took up aspects of an essay published in 2001, at the request of Barry Bergdoll and Terence Riley, in *Mies in Berlin*. The bibliography was updated with the help of Anna Jozefacka. Some of the many new illustrations were added thanks to Louise Désy and Howard Shubert at the Canadian Centre for Architecture in Montreal. Finally, the 2007 book benefited from the efficient editorial coordination of Emmanuelle Levesque.

The text of this third edition, which has been made possible by the unfailing support of Ria Stein at Birkhäuser, and the help of Jérôme Gille at Editions Hazan, has been left mostly unchanged. Some footnotes have been updated or added, and the bibliography substantially expanded.

GRAPHIC DESIGN: Sylvie Milliet with Marie Donzelli, Vanves
LAYOUT OF THE ENGLISH EDITION: Alexandra Zöller, Berlin
COVER DESIGN: Jean-Marc Barrier, Vanves, adapted for the English edition by Alexandra Zöller, Berlin
EDITORIAL COORDINATION: Emmanuelle Levesque with Anne Chapoutot, Vanves
TRANSLATION FROM FRENCH: Elizabeth Kugler, Wayland, MA
COORDINATION OF THE ENGLISH AND GERMAN EDITION: Ria Stein, Berlin
PRODUCTION: Amelie Solbrig, Berlin
LITHOGRAPHY: Reproscan, Orio al Serio
PAPER: Magno matt, 150 g/m²
PRINTING: Beltz Grafische Betriebe GmbH

Library of Congress Control Number: 2018946879

Bibliographic information published by Die Deutsche Bibliothek
Die Deutsche Bibliothek lists this publication in the Deutsche Nationalbibliografie; detailed bibliographic data is available in the Internet at http://dnb.ddb.de.

Original title "MIES VAN DER ROHE," written by Jean-Louis Cohen, published by Editions Hazan, 2007
© Editions Hazan, Paris, 1994
© Editions Hazan, Paris, 2007

English edition:
© 2018 Birkhäuser Verlag GmbH, Basel
P.O. Box 44, 4009 Basel, Switzerland
Part of Walter de Gruyter GmbH, Berlin/Boston

This publication is also available as an e-book (ISBN PDF 978-3-0356-1681-1) and in a German language edition (ISBN 978-3-0356-1665-1).

Printed on acid-free paper produced from chlorine-free pulp. TCF ∞

Printed in Germany

ISBN 978-3-0356-1664-4

9 8 7 6 5 4 3 2 1

www.birkhauser.com

Jean-Louis Cohen

Ludwig **Mies van der Rohe**

Third and updated edition

Birkhäuser
Basel

CONTENTS

PREFACE 6

1. CHILDHOOD IN THE RHINELAND AND EARLY DAYS IN BERLIN (1886–1914) 10
Impressions from Aachen 11
Peter Behrens and the Architecture of Industry 17
The Kröller-Müller Project 22

2. THEORETICAL PROJECTS FOR THE METROPOLIS (1918–24) 26
The Friedrichstraße Skyscraper 27
G and the Concrete Office Building 34
The Concrete Country House 36
The Brick Country House 38

3. FOUNDATIONS OF A NEW DOMESTIC SPACE (1925–30) 44
Mies and Weimar Politics 45
Two Houses in Krefeld 56
The Barcelona Feat 64
Luxury at the Tugendhats 72

4. FROM THE BAUHAUS TO THE THIRD REICH (1930–38) 84
Mies and the National Socialists 90

5. CHICAGO AND AMERICAN PARADIGMS (1938–56) 98
Mies and the Illinois Institute of Technology 99
The Farnsworth House 110
Crown Hall 118
Lake Shore Drive: The Steel Towers 125

6. INDUSTRIAL CLASSICISM (1956–69) 140
The Seagram Stele 141
The Skyscraper Variation 146
Return to Berlin: The Neue Nationalgalerie 160
The Poetics of Modernization 165

NOTES 168
BIOGRAPHY 176
PRINCIPAL PROJECTS 179
BIBLIOGRAPHY 182
INDEX OF PERSONS AND PROJECTS 189
ILLUSTRATION CREDITS 192

Opposite:
Ludwig Mies van der Rohe,
Berlin, 1934.

PREFACE

Mies Today

The following pages might have seemed presumptuous when the first edition of this book was published in 1994. To try to convey in such a slender volume the depth and scope of Ludwig Mies van der Rohe's contribution to the architecture of the twentieth century was no easy task. It is no less difficult a dozen years later. After decades of bland criticism, the architect's doctrinal positions, biography, and conceptual work have been elucidated by the publications that accompanied or followed the centennial of his birth, celebrated in 1986 in Europe and in the United States.[1] Previously, apart from the occasional creative aperçu, the accepted image of Mies van der Rohe's work was based on a small number of buildings and a collection of aphorisms worn out by repetitive use or misuse.

Of course, Mies never went through the purgatory sometimes required for artistic or literary giants to become the father figures that are customarily conjured. Despite several vigorous critiques, such as the one by Robert Venturi, his stature was not lowered during the high season of Postmodernism. However, the "Mies effect" relied on simplifications and shortcuts even more schematic than those which were just beginning to be discredited in the study of Le Corbusier. But if the initial foundations of the historical mausoleum raised to glorify the German-American architect were often built upon textual and visual falsifica-

tions, the paucity of source material was in no way compensated for by the accumulation of clichés and shallow half-truths. The flood of details and anecdotes brought on by the opening of the archives has, fortunately, been accompanied by a body of refreshing reinterpretations, virtually erasing decades of generalizations.[2] And the two major exhibitions – "Mies in Berlin" and "Mies in America," mounted in 2001 by the Musuem of Modern Art in New York and the Canadian Centre for Architecture in Montreal – marked the high point in a research campaign that became more collective in anticipation of a new generation of monographs made possible by this research.[3]

Thus began a true rediscovery of Mies van der Rohe, clearing away the generalizations and factual errors, but also accompanied by new interpretations of his thinking and architectural approach. The sources of his work now appear more numerous and more diffuse. His early work in Berlin escapes the mythification of the figure of Behrens, who used to dominate, and the intellectual milieux that he frequented before 1914 come into new relief.[4] Formerly neglected, the exterior spaces and the urban developments conceived by Mies are now better known. The German and American sponsors become more concrete figures in their often enduring fidelity toward Mies. Without the persistence of Hermann Lange or Herbert Greenwald, his built work would not have been able to take on its full dimension either in Germany or in the United States. With such clients, Mies's professional practice, long nebulous or rather reduced to a sort of black box, reveals its collective dimension through the testimonies given by his former collaborators.

As was the case with Le Corbusier, the images produced or used by Mies were studied in their mode of production and use. These privileged mediums for project work and for the dissemination of his oeuvre now appear as documents developed between Mies and his collaborators, often drawing on issues of artistic modernity, as in the case of the collages. Mies was very aware of the stakes of representation of his work, and the relationships he maintained with photographers are also greatly elucidated, at least with regard to the German phase of his work.[5] Even more surprising for an architect whose creations have nothing immaterial about them, the corpus of his built work continues to grow with the discovery of archival documents attesting to the construction of projects considered unfinished, such as the Warnholtz House, whose destruction went as unnoticed as its construction.... Moreover, as buildings partially or entirely attributable to Mies – such as the Heusgen and Ryder Houses and a modest expansion of a school in Potsdam – come to light, they reveal the existence of works that were often hybrid, carried out in the margins of his canonical production.

Mies always had the greatest difficulty in writing texts more than half a page long, and he never completed the only book project that he ever planned, a work entitled *Baukunst*, commissioned in 1925.[6] Since the 1930s Mies's relatively few words left open the space for a mythic discourse that was substantiated by first-hand witnesses such as Philip Johnson, then by historians such as Arthur Drexler and by former staff members at his Chicago office. This rendered still more deafening the silence of Sigfried Giedion, who omitted Mies from several successive editions of *Space, Time and Architecture*, that monumental chronicle of the Modern Movement.[7] It was the very holes in the fabric of knowledge that afforded such scope to sensational analyses concerning, for example, Mies's relationship with the Nazi regime;[8] new interpretations started to appear in the mid-1970s, and their authenticity was put to the test at the centennial. The most outspoken of the sworn enemies of the Modern Movement saw in the work of an architect who "wanted to bee free – new every morning" the "spirit of the triumphant industrial world,"[9] even though most research tends to support the image of a Mies who profoundly respected the great edifices of European history.

A study of his correspondence and designs reveals a new picture of the architect, with his intellectual, philosophical, and religious outlook more clearly defined.[10] It is this view of Mies – as seen through his daily work, his professional strategies, his philosophical reflections, and his private person – that makes possible an undertaking such as the present book. Whereas his architecture was once reduced to a closed set of icons, he now appears as a more cultivated figure than Philip Johnson was prepared to admit when he sarcastically alluded to the three thousand books that Mies said he had left behind in Germany.[11] Mies's desire to be considered a profound thinker and his propensity for aphorisms and sententious statements have been unfairly interpreted as indicative of "a deep, pervasive, and lifelong insecurity about his intellectual qualifications,"[12] but now that his philosophical and literary contacts and interests are better known, the picture becomes more complex. The philosophical and scientific material that his patrons in Berlin and no doubt his wife encouraged him to read makes it possible to better understand the essential ideas and expressions in his discourse, and his artistic reading matter gives a useful index to interpret the guiding features of some of his projects.

His architectural work, built and unbuilt, designed over six decades of professional activity, has often been reduced to clichés about the "open plan" or "modern space" or an obsession with structural engineering. As we now see, this body of work is in fact shaped by a philosophy of construction and the definition of new spaces, which is inseparable from a concern for order, both structural and monumental. A solitary figure whose work was rooted in the technology and ethos of the second machine age, Mies was no nihilist. The direction of his work cannot be explained simply by his own experiences; it is inseparable from explicit and implicit relationships established with several generations of architects – as is shown by the notes written in 1959 for his acceptance speech for the RIBA gold medal, in which he lists the inspirations in his initial quest for an understanding of architecture: Messel, Behrens, Olbrich, Berlage, Lutyens, Voysey, Baillie Scott, and Mackintosh.[13] In fact, beyond the figures of his elders, Berlage and Behrens, Mies never lost sight of either Viollet-le-Duc (with his precept that "any form that is not determined by structure must be rejected") or Schinkel, whom he considered "the greatest classicist we had."[14]

Further back in history, Mies always maintained an intellectual affinity with medieval architecture and with Greece, which (unlike Rome) was a world of culture and not of mere civilization.[15] For the same reasons as Auguste Perret, he offered a new interpretation of the ideal of a "Graeco-Gothic" architecture, as expressed by the French rationalists of the nineteenth century. Unlike Perret, he did this by integrating the issues of modern art into his work.

His relationships with his contemporaries remained more complex: Mies never missed an opportunity to point out everything that separated him from individuals like Walter Gropius, Frank Lloyd Wright, and Le Corbusier and from avant-garde groups such as De Stijl and the Constructivists.[16] Presenting himself, in the interviews that he gave at the end of his life, as a solitary hero who rebelled against passing fashions, and reproaching his contemporaries for their obsession with the present, Mies emphasized the distinction between the meaning of continuity and mere historicism, conscientiously applying the slogan formulated in his manifesto of 1924, "Baukunst und Zeitwille!" (Construction and Contemporaneity!), which states: "It is not possible to go forward while looking back."[17] One year earlier, he had confirmed his strong desire to free *Bauerei* – "buildery," we might say, as distinct from architecture – from aesthetic fancy, to give the word *Bauen* (to build) its full force.[18]

Drawn toward constructive rationality on the one hand, and, on the other, toward the search for a *firmitas* that would be more institutional than physical, Mies always saw architecture as the expression of a certain *Zeitwille* (will of the age). The refined expression is based on those unchanging values that can be read in a Platonic perspective.[19] The monoliths of steel and glass built in American cities reflect this inclination toward *Bauen*: building using a lim-

ited repertoire of forms devoid of aesthetic intention and intended to serve rather than to interpret.

Mies van der Rohe's belief in Order and Truth, independent of human circumstances, evolved over many years and found its expression in his personal relationships with his clients and with those closest to him. There has been much talk – sometimes too much – of his lack of interest in some clients' expectations. As he said in 1964, he "never sought commissions," but always "let the clients come to [him]": "He who comes to me knows what he will have: the true Mies. And this is simplest and best, at least for the client himself."[20] If the Farnsworth House is not uninhabitable, as some have suggested,[21] it is true that the Esters sweltered behind the glass of their fully south-facing house. Trivial by comparison with the daily tribulations of the inhabitants of houses built by Le Corbusier or Frank Lloyd Wright, these clients' troubles were accepted by Mies with a certain amused condescension. In 1930 he imposed on the Tugendhats, in their Brno villa, a whole set of furniture that, he said, they "must learn to like"; in 1959 he declared, "We should treat our clients as children, not as architects."[22]

Here we see his character. Distant with his family, reserved with regard to feelings – "Everybody has emotions and this is the hell of our time" – he had, by his own admission, nothing of the sentimentalist about him.[23] A monolithic figure clad in wool and silk, he was rendered still more of an immovable object late in life, when arthritis struck; this elegant massiveness in some way served as a human metaphor for his American architecture.

What, then, can be the role of this book in the face of Mies's monumental achievement? It is no longer possible to restrict a commentary to the finished work of his "major" buildings alone, as in the compact monographs published from the 1960s onward; but at the same time, the limitations of this series, conceived by Éric Hazan, make it impossible to cover all the ramifications of ten years' research. I have therefore decided to concentrate on a limited number of designs and structures and to discuss them in depth, with full reference to their specific historical and biographical significance. In particular, I have tried to let Mies speak for himself, something he did more often than people might think. His own comments on his work, often retrospective, will in this way give a personal resonance to the places that he created – a resonance that he would no doubt have wanted to eliminate, but without which his comments are difficult to understand.

The 2007 edition did not contradict the original approach, but rather consolidated it in some ways. It corrected the blunders and slips scattered in the original edition, introduced more

in-depth analyses of buildings that had been inexplicably neglected, such as the Esters and Lange Houses and the Toronto Dominion Center, and it offered a more generous visual survey, thanks to the new format of the book. Some of the initial hunches have been replaced by more developed arguments that I have had the opportunity to make, especially with regard to Mies's relationship with America before his exile. Other reflections, which were too brief, have been clarified thanks to 'Miesologues' on both sides of the Atlantic, to whom I offer a brotherly tribute.

This third edition remains substantially unchanged, while listing the overabundant literature published since 2007.[24] The scholarly production by Barry Bergdoll, "Fifteen Years of Publication on Mies van der Rohe (2000–2015)," published 2014 in *Architectura,* which has been rich in new interpretation, has brought to the light several unknown buildings of Mies built during the Weimar period and early Nazi Germany.[25] Other practices of Mies, such as film, and the design of wallpapers, have been investigated.[26] The new contributions have been listed in an expanded bibliography. Some footnotes indicate relevant new sources.

Paris, June 2018

1. CHILDHOOD IN THE RHINELAND AND EARLY DAYS IN BERLIN (1886–1914)

Opposite:
Hugo Perls House, Berlin-
Zehlendorf, 1911, garden
façade.

Above:
Peter Behrens, German
Embassy, St. Petersburg,
1912.

Impressions from Aachen

Ludwig Mies built his first house at the age of twenty, in Neubabelsberg, a very middle-class residential suburb of Berlin. Like the chalets that the young Charles-Édouard Jeanneret built at La Chaux-de-Fonds and then meticulously deleted from his oeuvre in spite of the favorable publicity they attracted upon their completion, Mies's early creations would remain absent from major exhibitions and publications on his work until the 1980s. And yet his early career led him in just a few years from a provincial childhood and adolescence in the Rhineland to Berlin, where he became a fashionable success.

The impression left by his early life in Aachen remained strong. He often claimed that his Catholic family had Celtic origins.[1] His father, Michael Mies, was a mason and stonecutter, and Ludwig was steeped in the building trade from the outset. The youngest of five children of Michael Mies and Amalie Rohe, he would remain the lifelong friend of his older brother Ewald. But the negative connotations of his surname (in German *mies* means wretched) would lead him to coin a new one for himself by borrowing the name of his mother (Rohe is the Germanized version of the Walloon Roé)[2]: starting in 1921, he would call himself Miës (van der) Rohe, adding a diaeresis to his legal name.

In a town transformed by growth and modernization, Michael Mies built fireplaces, main-

tained the cathedral masonry, and built many tombs in partnership with his brother. The young Ludwig would remember the traditional houses that were progressively replaced by speculative apartment blocks, as well as the impression of strength of the cathedral and the Palatine Chapel, built by Charlemagne between 796 and 805:

"I remember seeing many old buildings in my hometown when I was young. Few of them were important buildings. They were mostly very simple, but very clear. I was impressed by the strength of these buildings because they did not belong to any epoch. They had been there for over a thousand years and were still impressive, and nothing could change that. All the great styles passed, but they were still there. They didn't lose anything and they were still as good as on the day they were built. They were medieval buildings, not with any special character but they were really *built*."[3]

Mies attended the Catholic Cathedral School from 1896 to 1899, then the Craft Day School from 1899 to 1901. Following this technical and vocational training, quite different from the classical curriculum at the Gymnasium (which he attended for two years), he completed his education with evening classes in building, civil engineering, mathematics, and life drawing.[4] Often enlisted by his father to carve inscriptions on headstones, he worked for a year as an unpaid apprentice bricklayer on local build-

Below left:
Bruno Paul, Westend
House, Berlin-
Charlottenburg, 1906.

Below right:
Bruno Paul, tennis club,
Berlin-Grunewald, 1908.

ing sites. Reminiscing in later life about brick-work, he would stress the difficulties involved in making angles and copings, but he insisted on the value of the experience in teaching him the details of construction.[5]

The Aachen cathedral, whose silhouette dominates the city, was only a symbolic center for the young Mies, who said he went there quite regularly with his mother.[6] The Palatine Chapel, built on an octagonal plan that called to mind the Basilica of San Vitale in Ravenna, could not but make an impression on him during the services. Its columns clad in slabs of landscape marble seem to anticipate the great onyx walls of the Barcelona Pavilion and the Tugendhat House. The importance of these columns is all the greater because their surface treatment took place just as Mies joined his father's stonecutting business. The Swiss Cipollino marble cladding, which was in fact conceived by the Hanover architect Hermann Schaper for the visit of the Kaiser in 1902, sparked a revolt among German architects and historians against a regrettable "disfiguration."[7] It is a safe bet that the job was assigned to Michael Mies and, even if he did not do the work himself, it is certain that the matter would have been discussed during meals at the family house… With the juxtaposition of its Carolingian columns covered in marble and its High Gothic stained-glass windows, the cathedral at Aachen announces two main themes of Mies's work: wall treatment and transparency.

The young Ludwig acquired practical experience both with craftsmen and architects. He was apprenticed to Max Fischer, a maker of plaster moldings, where he used vertical drawing boards, a habit he retained for a long time. Then, working for the architects Goebbels and (later) Albert Schneider, he became a draftsman valued for his skill in decorative ornament.[8]

While working in Schneider's office on the Tietz department store building, he found a copy of the literary review *Die Zukunft*, edited by Maximilian Harden; he continued to read more on his visits to the municipal library.[9] Having thus whetted his interest in the intellectual life of the capital, he let himself be persuaded by Dulow, one of the architects in the practice, to

apply for jobs in Berlin advertised in *Die Bauwelt*. And so he left his native city in 1905 to start work as a draftsman in the municipal architecture department of the urban district of Rixdorf, southwest of Berlin, run by John Martens. There, under Reinhold Kiehl, he designed the paneling of the council chamber of the town hall – not without some difficulty, for up until then he had worked only with masonry.[10]

His time in the Kaiser's army was extremely short: he was discharged after a case of bronchitis that flared up following a collective punishment of his unit. Back in civilian life, he met the architect Bruno Paul in early 1906, when the latter was moving his practice from

Munich to Berlin. It was a decisive meeting. Mies became both a draftsman in Paul's office and a pupil at the two institutions where Paul taught, enrolling in the school of the Museum of Arts and Crafts (Kunstgewerbemuseum) and at the school of Fine Arts (Hochschule für bildende Künste) from the summer term of 1906 to the summer term of 1908.[11] He had a special position in the practice on account of his previous practical experience in construction. He specialized in furniture design. Paul had long been a successful caricaturist in the satirical magazine *Simplicissimus*; over the next few years he expanded his work in Berlin, building blocks of flats and town houses and even fitting out the interiors of a number of German transatlantic liners.[12]

In 1906 Joseph Popp, an assistant to the artist Emil Orlik, in whose studio Mies was studying engraving, recommended the young architect to the wife of Alois Riehl, a professor of philosophy at the Friedrich Wilhelm University in Berlin and a leading expert on Nietzsche. The Riehls were looking for a young architect to design a weekend and vacation house. From them, Mies obtained his first commission at the age of twenty; he insisted on carrying out the work unaided, refusing all offers of advice from Bruno Paul.[13] It was completed in 1910 in an area of detached houses on a wooded slope in Neubabelsberg, an urban district later annexed by Potsdam; Mies was to design many other projects there, including the Urbig and Mosler Houses. Klösterli (the "Little Cloister") was built in 1907, a house of rendered brick with a steep roof.[14] The end wall overlooking Lake Griebnitzsee opens into a loggia, which reproduces the rhythms used by Bruno Paul in his Westend House, built at the same time.

The interior of the house has a rectangular plan, which centers on a large hall, opening onto two lateral alcoves and onto a loggia similar to the one at Paul's Berlin Tennis Club, which Mies must have studied while working in Paul's office.[15] The appearance of the end wall and that of the loggia perched on a long retaining parapet wall also recall the crematorium built the year before by Peter Behrens in the Ruhr, several dozen kilometers from Aachen.

A degree of English influence, received by way of Hermann Muthesius,[16] appears in the design of the hall, whose paneling has a finesse that characterizes all of the interior detailing of this remarkably compact interior, right down to the alcoves on the second floor. The kitchen, the bookcases, and the radiator grilles reflect Mies's interest in built-in furniture. The layout of the house is dominated by the right angle between the axis of entry and the downhill view, with the lateral extension of the building treated as a platform, overlooked by a façade that seems somewhat compressed by the top-heavy bulk of the roof. The detailing is faithful to the Prussian Biedermeier tradition of the early nineteenth century, which Paul Mebes praised in his successful book *Um 1800*, first published in 1908; from Mebes's book, the Stuckshof, next to the Langfuhr (today Wrzeszcz, outside Gdansk), seems to have given Mies the design motif for the main façade.[17]

This building, remarkably mature for such a young architect, was favorably received in

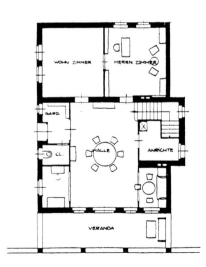

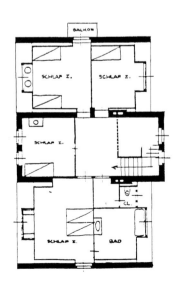

At left:
Alois Riehl House, side
façade in 1992.

Above:
Stuckshof farm, Langfuhr,
early nineteenth century.
Photograph published in
Paul Mebes, *Um 1800*
(1908).

the architectural press, which stressed the "skill" shown by an "irreproachable" work that gave a lesson in "balance" to Mies's older colleagues.[18] Hermann Muthesius paid homage to the quality of Mies's project by including it in a new edition of his book *Landhaus und Garten*,[19] for he recognized, in its relationship with the site and in the treatment of exterior spaces with arbors and low walls, a good response to the "architectonic garden" program, which constitutes one of the essential themes of his Wohnungsreform (housing reform) initiative.[20] A shot of the house would appear in 1924 on the cover of a book by the landscape architect Karl Foerster, hired by the Riehls to work on the garden.[21]

Delighted with Mies's talents and with his company, Alois and Sofie Riehl brought him into their social circle, where he met some of the founders of modern Germany, such as the industrialist Walther Rathenau, the philologue Werner Jaeger, the philosophers Eduard Spranger and Max Dessoir, and the art histo-

rian Heinrich Wölfflin, as is shown in the guest-book of the house, rediscovered by Fritz Neumeyer. In his company, Mies was prompted to reflect on the notion of space through the work of Riehl himself, and on the question of the spiritual legacy of Greek classicism, explored by Jaeger, whose theses on a "third humanism" of the modern age Mies read.[22] The key intellectual issues uncovered after the soirées at the Riehls would remain of fundamental importance to Mies for decades.

Mies matured with growing freedom in this world where he met the clients of his future houses, the Gerickes, Noldes, Dexels, Wolfs, and Eliats. Only Riehl's death in 1924 brought an end to the relationship, which Mies commemorated by designing the philosopher's gravestone in the Neubabelsberg cemetery. This friendship gave him access to the ideas of Nietzsche, for whom Riehl was a well-known proponent.[23] His frequent visits to the Riehl household also threw him into the arms of Ada Bruhn, the daughter of a former Danish officer

turned manufacturer of measuring instruments. After breaking off her engagement with Heinrich Wölfflin, she became a pupil at the Émile Jacques-Dalcroze dance school in Hellerau garden city, which Albert Jeanneret, the brother of Le Corbusier, also attended. Meanwhile, in 1908, the Riehls gave Mies a grant that enabled him to take a six-week trip to Munich, Rome, Florence, and Vicenza in the company of Joseph Popp. Mies was especially struck by the Pitti Palace and the villas of Palladio – "not only La Rotonda, which is very formal, but also the others, which are more free," he was to say sixty years later. On his return from Italy, however, he noticed that the details of Alfred Messel's houses in Wannsee, which he discovered while he was in Rixdorf, were "more delicate than those of Palladio.".... Mies also mentioned the admiration he felt for Messel's "wonderful" Wertheim department store, with its glass façade overlooking Potsdamer Platz.[24]

Peter Behrens and the Architecture of Industry

Impressed by the qualities of the Riehl House, Paul Thiersch, manager of Bruno Paul's firm, advised Mies to introduce himself to Peter Behrens, who took him on in October 1908. Behrens had been appointed the previous year by Emil Rathenau's AEG concern to create a corporate identity for its buildings, products, and advertising. He had made his name in 1901 by building his own house in the artists' colony of Darmstadt, and later by his teaching and his architectural work in Düsseldorf.[25]

On one of his last trips to Berlin, Mies was to announce that he himself had designed the courtyard façade of Behrens's AEG-Turbinenhalle, which was simply defined by the plate-glass wall, the profile of the metal piers in a double T-shape, and the brick base: "Behrens didn't realize what he was doing," said Mies, for, intending to build a factory, he "resolved all the problems of architecture."[26] In addi-

Below:
Peter Behrens,
Kleinmotorenfabrik for the
AEG, Berlin-Wedding,
1910–13 (photograph
published in Fritz Hoeber,
Peter Behrens, 1913).

At right:
Peter Behrens,
Turbinenhalle for the AEG,
Berlin-Moabit, 1909
(photograph published
in Fritz Hoeber, *Peter
Behrens*, 1913).

At left:
Competition project for a
monument to Bismarck,
Elisenhöhe, Bingen,
1910, perspective view of
the main courtyard
(autograph, Mies van der
Rohe Archives, Museum
of Modern Art, New York).

Above:
Competition project for a
monument to Bismarck,
Elisenhöhe, Bingen, 1910,
side elevation (autograph,
Mies van der Rohe
Archives, Museum of
Modern Art, New York).

tion to this contribution, which foreshadowed the buildings of the Illinois Institute of Technology, Mies collaborated on the small motor factory (Kleinmotorenfabrik) in the Wedding section of Berlin.[27] For Mies and other young architects in the practice – including Walter Gropius, his future partner Adolf Meyer, and Charles-Édouard Jeanneret, whom Mies remembered having "met in a doorway"[28] – Behrens was the archetype of the Nietzschean artist who had sealed an alliance with modern industry. But Behrens was also responsible for Mies's lifelong passion for the architecture of Karl Friedrich Schinkel.[29]

Behrens took his young colleagues to look at some of Schinkel's buildings near the office in Neubabelsberg, including the mansion and garden buildings in Glienicke park and the gardener's house and the Roman baths of Charlottenhof, in Potsdam. Mies's interest in

Schinkel – recorded in 1927 by Paul Westheim, who spoke of the "amazing feeling" the two architects shared for "the mass, the relationships, the rhythms, and the harmony of forms" – sprang from these visits.[30]

Mies wasted no time in turning his interest in Schinkel into practice. In 1910 he entered a competition for a monument in Bingen intended for the centenary celebrations of the birth of Bismarck, which were planned for 1915. All German architects were invited to participate, and the event constitutes an essential episode in the rejection of historicism.[31] Mies visualized a stone bastion, built against the Elisenhöhe hillside overlooking the Rhine, on which a colonnade framed a rectangular space before a statue of the Iron Chancellor, to be designed by Mies's brother Ewald. There are striking affinities between the situation of this colonnade and that of the palace that

Schinkel designed for the tsar at Orianda, in the Crimea.[32] Nevertheless, Mies felt no nostalgia for the graphic techniques of the nineteenth century and used in his submission a large collage of a photograph of the model on a photograph of the site, thus pioneering the architectural use of montage, a technique that he would turn to on many subsequent occasions.[33] Entitled "Germany's Gratitude," his entry was on the shortlist of 40 selected out of 379 for more detailed study, but the evident cost of its foundations meant that it was set aside. The competition provoked lively debates, and in the end it was Wilhelm Kreis who was given the commission, after an initial vote in favor of a more modern project by German Bestelmeyer.[34]

The love of Schinkel brought Mies his second commission, from the wealthy lawyer Hugo Perls, a collector of contemporary art and a fel-

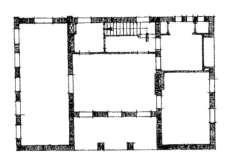

Top:
Hugo Perls House,
Berlin-Zehlendorf, 1911,
garden façade.

Bottom left:
Hugo Perls House,
Berlin-Zehlendorf,
ground floor plan.

Bottom center:
Hugo Perls House,
Berlin-Zehlendorf,
detail of the cornice.

Bottom right:
Peter Behrens,
Wiegand House,
Berlin-Dahlem, 1912,
detail of the cornice.

CHILDHOOD IN THE RHINELAND AND EARLY DAYS IN BERLIN (1886–1914)

Above:
Peter Behrens, Wiegand
House, Berlin-Dahlem,
1912, entrance.

Opposite page:
Peter Behrens,
Mannesmann headquarters,
Düsseldorf, perspective
(published in Fritz Hoeber,
Peter Behrens, 1913).

low enthusiast for the work of the great Prussian architect. In 1910 Perls hired Mies, whom he had met at one of the artistic soirées that he organized, to build him a house at Zehlendorf. Mies worked on it with Ferries Goebbels, one of his friends from Behrens's firm. The relationship between the main block of the house and the roof is very different from that in the Riehl House. The ground floor, intended for Perls's art collection – comprising works by Picasso, Matisse, and Munch – centers on a dining room that was to feature frescoes by Max Pechstein, a painter from the artists' group Die Brücke.[35] It opens onto a loggia fronted by two columns, like that of

Schinkel's pavilion at Charlottenburg, but brought down to ground level. On one side of the dining room is a study and on the other a library/music room, with the bedrooms relegated to the second floor of this compact building of stuccoed brick.[36] Other echoes of Schinkel are present in the ochre color of the exterior and in the layout of the geometrical gardens that surround the house.

The Perls House reflects not only the relationship that Mies had forged with Schinkel but also the reinterpretation of Schinkel's work attempted by Behrens in the large house that he built the very same year at Dahlem for

Theodor Wiegand, an archaeologist and the director of the Imperial Museums in Berlin.[37] Schinkel's spirit was transposed into the system of colonnades, into the relationship to the site with its platforms and foundations, and into the design of the cornices of the main building, built in gray limestone. Mies does not seem to have worked on this project; his main job with Behrens at that time was the German embassy in Saint Petersburg, and, in a marginal way, the Mannesmann offices.

For the administrative headquarters of Mannesmann Röhren-Werke, partners of AEG, Behrens's approach was remarkable in that he started from the base unit, which was the office, and went toward the building as a whole, paying particular attention to the modularity of the ensemble and to the quality of natural light.[38] This large building block with a metal structure clad in stone evokes Florentine palazzi, so much that its publication in Hoeber's monograph on Behrens is accompanied by a citation taken from Jacob Burckhardt's *Civilization of the Renaissance in Italy*.[39] Mies worked on the entrance and on the staircase of this building, where the idea of a free plan was implemented.[40] He also supervised construction at the German embassy in Saint Petersburg, where he worked on-site in 1911–12.[41] But he later admitted that he had designed only one door handle for a building for which he seems to have cared little.[42]

"That was really a kind of palace, architecturally – Palladio or that sort of thing. But Behrens decided to use Finnish granite. That of course made all classicist details disappear. The character all the same was something like the Brandenburger Tor, something which conveys Berlin, and that suited Petersburg quite well … So under Behrens I learnt the grand form, if you see what I mean."[43]

The Kröller-Müller Project

In fact, Mies appears to have had some diffi-culty working at Behrens's firm, where, until Gropius's departure in 1910, he found him-self under the tutelage of an architect senior to himself, a man who also came from a priv-ileged social class. He stayed on the fringe of the Deutscher Werkbund, in which Gropius and Behrens were involved. It was with the commission for the Kröller-Müller House, in 1912, that the falling-out came. In the spring of 1911 Behrens had received the commis-sion for a residence that this factory-owning couple wanted to build on a piece of land near Otterlo, in the Netherlands, to house their collection of works by Van Gogh and other mod-ern artists. Assigned to work on the project, Mies designed for Behrens a building whose overly "long perspectives" were criticized by Hélène Kröller-Müller. She requested a full-size canvas mock-up, erected on-site in January 1912. The commission was then given directly to Mies, whom the client seems to have found more amenable to her ideas.[44]

Mies spent the summer in The Hague, working on the house at the company headquarters, in a room whose walls were covered with paint-ings by Van Gogh. This exhibition would affect his manner of drawing certain color perspec-tives from 1920 to 1930. Moreover, he could not fail to see the Henny House by Berlage and especially the Berlage stock exchange in Amsterdam. Berlage would remain a funda-mental source for his overall approach, expos-ing the stone, brick, or steel simply as them-selves, without any dissimulation. After the practical education in stonecutting received at his father's firm, Mies glimpsed, in Berlage's buildings, the possibility of a rigorous approach to the design of building elements. Mies would say that he "never talked about architecture" with Berlage during their meetings, never for-got the lesson he got "just by looking at his buildings" during his stay in the Netherlands: "The construction was what made the strongest impression, you know, the use of brick, the honesty of materials, and so on."[45]

His relationship with Holland, which was intense during the summer of 1912, was natural in the so-called Dreiländereck – the region surround-ing Aachen, where Belgium, Germany, and the Netherlands meet – and would be as influ-ential as the Berlin experience. The diversion of the Kröller-Müller commission alienated Behrens even more firmly than did Mies's grow-ing veneration for Berlage, whom he cease-lessly praised for his "honesty," to the profound irritation of his employer:
"Berlage's Exchange (in Amsterdam) had impressed me enormously. Behrens was of the opinion that it was all passé, but I said to him: 'Well, if you aren't badly mistaken.' He was furi-ous; he looked as if he wanted to hit me. What interested me most in Berlage was his care-ful construction, honest to the bones. And his spiritual attitude had nothing to do with classicism, nothing with historic styles alto-gether. It was really a modern building."[46]
Taking over the Kröller-Müller project him-self, Mies transformed the original design. He enlarged the building, opened it out to the landscape by putting it up against the trees, and articulated its freely symmetrical recti-linear blocks by means of a colonnade. The lin-earity and the planar quality of this design explain why it was the only early work judged worthy of being shown in the Mies retrospec-tive at the Museum of Modern Art in New York in 1947. Mrs. Kröller's advisors, who seem to have had a penchant for Mies, nevertheless persuaded her to make him compete with Berlage. In spite of the support given to Mies's design by the critic Julius Meier-Graefe, Mrs. Kröller's advisor, Hendrik Peter Bremmer, con-trasted the "art" of Berlage with Mies's sup-posed lack of it. Another full-size mock-up was made, and Mies was eliminated.[47]

After his Dutch experience Mies set up an inde-pendent practice: he opened his own office in Steglitz, Berlin, in 1913, and married Ada Bruhn on 10 April of the same year. He lost no time in becoming absorbed in a series of plans for Berlin housing and was equally conscientious in evading the responsibilities of marital life.[48]

In 1912-13, on a plot adjacent to the Perls House in Zehlendorf, he built with Ferries Goebbels a residence for the engineer Ernst Werner. With its *Satteldach*, or hipped roof, his exterior design seemed to respond to the specifications formulated by Paul Mebes and Paul Schultze-Naumburg and based on a celebration of early-nineteenth-century houses. The house seemed to reproduce the Czarnikau castle, in the Polish province of Posen, held up by Schultze-Naumburg as an example to follow.[49] The house, on a rectangular plan, is symmetrical in layout, and Mies devoted himself to the study of each detail on the interior. The garden brings to mind both Schinkel's design at Charlottenhof in Potsdam and the Wiegand House by Behrens. Thus the ensemble betrayed Mies's effort to situate himself in relation both to the principles of his mentor's project and to the ideal of a return to a Prussian architecture, given that, as a native Rhinelander, he should express his faithfulness to the culture of Berlin.

In the same vein, in 1915 Mies built a house in Charlottenburg that was much more luxurious, but still embued with the spirit of the *Um 1800* movement. It was intended for Johann Warnholtz, head of the Deutsche Ost-Afrikanische Gesellschaft. Its two projecting wings on the garden side sheltered verandas and were compared with the Oppenheim House, built in 1908 by Alfred Messel, where certain echoes of the composition of Palladian villas are per-

Above:
Ernst Werner House,
Berlin-Zehlendorf, 1912–13,
garden façade.

Bottom left:
Ernst Werner House,
dining room.

Bottom right:
Ernst Werner House,
radiator cover.

Franz Urbig House, Neubabelsberg, 1917, view from the riverbank.

ceptible; this would not have escaped Mies, as we have seen.[50] It is significant that critics later contrasted this house to the "excesses" of the radical moderns.[51]

Between 1913 and 1915, in Neubabelsberg, Mies built a villa with solemn, cold interiors for the banker Franz Urbig and his wife, friends and neighbors of the Riehls. Built at water level beside Lake Griebnitz, its large mass of traditional construction in rendered masonry occupies a rectangular ground plan, extended by a lakeside dining room. Mies's original design incorporated a virtually flat roof in the style of Schinkel, but Urbig objected and they agreed on a steeply sloped roof.[52] The garden, accentuating the precipice effect toward the lake, was developed in collaboration with the landscape gardener Karl Foerster, whom Mies met at the Riehls. Echoes of Frank Lloyd Wright's Winslow House are barely perceptible.[53]

Although a good ten years later than the Urbig House, the villa built nearby for the banker Georg Mosler in 1924 is comparable. Its masses are similar; it occupies a lakeside site below the Riehl House, with a massive loggia supported by three columns whose workmanship brings to mind Berlage (who no doubt knew the client, a man of Dutch origin); and its rectilinear lateral extension contains the kitchen. The plain surface of the brickwork is relieved by vertical windows with gray stone dressings; the thick mass of the walls conveys an impression of middle-class permanence that is reinforced by the trim of the rooms and the solidity of the main staircase.[54] After World War I Mies would build three houses in Berlin with identical themes in terms of their composition and their construction: the Kempner House in Charlottenburg, the Feldmann House in Grunewald, and the house for the bookseller Georg Eichstädt in Nikolassee, for whom he created his most complex garden.

In contrast to these buildings, which were in many respects more conservative than the Perls House, Mies designed a house for his own family in 1914, to be built on a plot of land that he and his wife had bought in Werder, west of Potsdam. Schinkel-esque in its relationship to the site, defined by platforms, this house with its two sharp-edged blocks and its flat roofs points to a radically different way of thinking. In fact, it was the forerunner of the new generation of projects that Mies was to design after the war.

Mies was not drafted until 1915, when he was stationed near Frankfurt-am-Main. After returning to Berlin for a time, he was sent in 1917 to Romania, where he spent the rest of the war. For him, the war was largely a latent period during which he assiduously sought out the company of the sculptor Wilhelm Lehmbruck without being able to put to productive use the considerable knowledge acquired during the early years of his practice: through his experience with Behrens, he had learned the importance of the connection with industry and the innovative field represented by the modern metropolis. But his successes in the world of collectors and patrons also suggested to him – and, to a certain extent, to the public – the possibility of a career oriented around the art world.

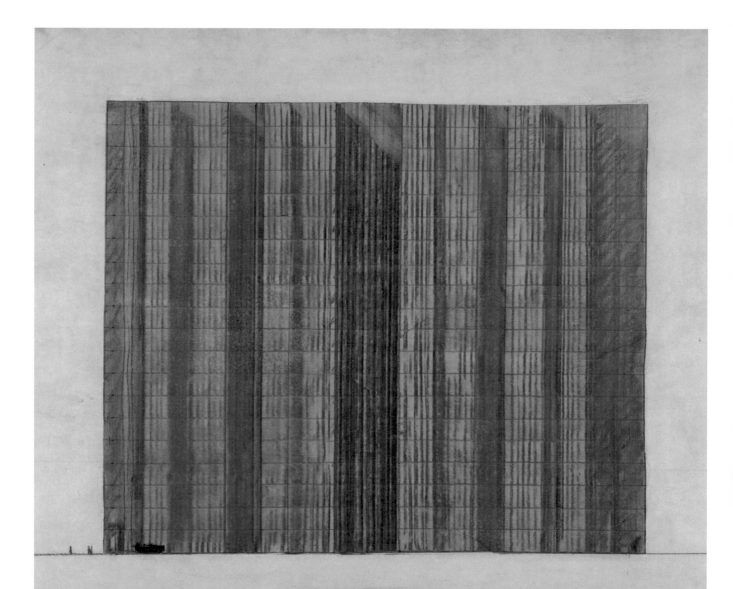

HOCH-HAUS
1:200

Jede ästhetische Spekulation,
jede Doktrin,
und jeden Formalismus
lehnen wir ab.

Baukunst ist raumgefaßter Zeitwille.
Lebendig. Wechselnd. Neu.

Nicht das Gestern, nicht das Morgen, nur das Heute ist formbar.
Nur dieses Bauen gestaltet.

Gestaltet die Form aus dem Wesen der Aufgabe mit den Mitteln unserer Zeit.

Das ist unsere Arbeit.

B Ü R O H A U S

Das Bürohaus ist ein Haus der Arbeit der Organisation der Klarheit der Okonomie.
Helle weite Arbeitsräume, übersichtlich, ungeteilt, nur gegliedert wie der Organismus des Betriebes. Größter Effekt mit geringstem Aufwand an Mitteln.

Die Materialien sind Beton Eisen Glas.

Eisenbetonbauten sind ihrem Wesen nach Skelettbauten. Keine Teigwaren noch Panzertürme. Bei tragender Binderkonstruktion eine nichttragende Wand. Also Haut- und Knochenbauten.

Die zweckmäßigste Einteilung der Arbeitsplätze war für die Raumtiefe maßgebend; diese beträgt 16 m. Ein zweistieliger Rahmen von 8 m Spannweite mit beiderseitiger Konsolauskragung von 4 m Länge wurde als das ökonomischste Konstruktionsprinzip ermittelt. Die Binderentfernung beträgt 5 m. Dieses Bindersystem trägt die Deckenplatte, die am Ende der Kragarme senkrecht hochgewinkelt Außenhaut wird und als Rückwand der Regale dient, die aus dem Rauminnern der Übersichtlichkeit wegen in die Außenwände verlegt wurden. Über den 2 m hohen Regalen liegt ein bis zur Decke reichendes durchlaufendes Fensterband.

Berlin, Mai 1923

Mies v. d. Rohe

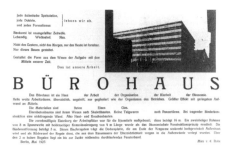

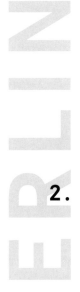

BERLIN

2. THEORETICAL PROJECTS FOR THE METROPOLIS (1918–24)

The Friedrichstraße Skyscraper

In 1927, when Paul Westheim published the first comprehensive view of Mies's work under the subtitle "Development of an Architect," he deliberately excluded most of the pre-1914 projects, with the exception of the Kröller-Müller House and the design for a house at Werder. In both of these early works he recognized the stamp of Schinkel, and he stressed their continuity with Mies's postwar work.[1] Such a suggestion no doubt surprised readers of the time because a quartet of unbuilt designs from the immediate postwar period seemed to mark an absolute break with the past: the Glass Skyscraper (in its two successive versions), the Concrete Office Building, and the Concrete and Brick Country Houses certainly showed a very different profile. This new cycle began in 1921, three years after the Republican Revolution of November 1918, to which Mies seems to have been indifferent. Moreover, his initial relations with the utopian groups emerging in a Germany buzzing with new ideas were difficult, since the Kröller-Müller project, which he was later to designate as the turning point of his career, was condemned by Gropius, who in 1919 organized the "Exhibition of Unknown Architects" in Berlin under the auspices of the Arbeitsrat für Kunst. There is no doubt that this led to a certain bitterness on Mies's part toward his former colleague from the Behrens office.[2]

Opposite:
Competition project for an Office Skyscraper, Friedrichstraße, Berlin, 1921, perspective of the whole building in charcoal (autograph, Mies van der Rohe Archives, Museum of Modern Art, New York).

Above:
Project for the Concrete Office Building, 1922, published in *G*, July 1923.

Kurt Szafranski,
cover of the
brochure *Berlins
Dritte Dimension*,
1912.

BERLINS DRITTE DIMENSION

The entry of Miës van der Rohe – by this time he had embellished his name with an aristocratic flourish by adding a diaeresis, a particule, and the surname of his mother – to the competition for the Friedrichstraße skyscraper, submitted in late January 1922, revealed the originality of his thinking and should be repositioned as part of the intense debate that had been taking place in Berlin for the past ten years. In 1912 the *Berliner Morgenpost* had raised the issue of a "third dimension" that was essential if the capital was to become a truly global metropolis.[3] The newspaper interviewed three people of great importance in Berlin culture – Peter Behrens, Bruno Möhring, and Walther Rathenau – on the conditions for an introduction in Berlin of the kind of buildings that had been appearing since the 1890s in Chicago and New York. The head of the Allgemeine Elektrizitäts-Gesellschaft (AEG) and a regular at the Riehls' salon, Rathenau confirmed that, "since the Middle Ages, nothing as imposing as the City of New York had been created… For the first time, the creation of these façades that rise to attack the sky illustrates the birth of a new constructive thought process in architecture." Rathenau contrasted this radically new thinking with the "compromises" of the buildings constructed in Berlin at the same time.[4]

Möhring, an architect familiar with the New World, thought that "the composition of the soil in Berlin was not at all a handicap for buildings regardless of their height."[5] It was precisely by launching the Friedrichstraße skyscraper competition that Möhring would put his ideas to work. In 1920, six years after he had proposed the construction of a tall building on a triangular site bounded by the Spree, the Friedrichstraße, and the train station of the same name, he again encouraged the professional organizations to pressure the Prussian minister of the interior into authorizing exemptions to the building height restrictions in Berlin, which were strictly set at twenty-two meters. On 1 November 1922 the Turmhaus Aktiengesellschaft (Tower House Company), established for the purpose, launched a competition for a building eighty meters tall, housing offices and a number of public facilities. Recalling his own reactions to America, Peter Behrens explained in 1912:

"What made the greatest impression on me in America, in terms of aesthetics and in general, was without doubt the very tall commercial buildings. In a country that shows few original artistic developments, whose official buildings are frozen in an insipid classicism and whose country houses imitate almost without exception the style of English cottages or the colonial American style, the commercial buildings, with their audacious structure, hold the seeds of a new architecture."[6]

For Behrens, the skyscraper goes beyond architectural aesthetics because, even more than the public squares or isolated buildings, it presents the problem of "horizontal territory" in the metropolis, which "calls for a medium, a body that cannot be found except through the insertion of compact, vertical masses."

Another fundamental discourse on the new urban spaces was formulated by August Endell in *Die Schönheit der großen Stadt*, published in 1908. Without doubt, Mies van der Rohe read the passage devoted to the Friedrichstraße train station, with the "play of light on large glass panes" that led to the glass skyscraper.[7] Endell also found accents of Nietzsche's Zarathoustra to condemn the depravity of the metropolis. But he recognized that "the big city [...] is a marvel of beauty and poetry to anyone who is willing to look, a fairy-tale, brighter, more colourful, more diverse than anything ever invented by a poet, a home, a mother, who daily bestows new happiness and great abundance over her children."[8] From all the "thousand beauties" that he counted, Endell heralded both the aesthetics of futurism and that of expressionism. In any case, he praised the "crystalline forms" of the large modern business and the "beauty of work" that would be illustrated by Weimar culture and then by Nazi culture.

From the time of the Friedrichstraße competition onward, Mies devoted himself to the creation of the "rationally built city," on which the critic Karl Scheffler pinned his hopes in *Die Architektur der Großstadt*.[9] As in the American business centers, and in contrast to the theories of Bruno Taut, the "crown of the city" did not consist of communal buildings bringing together the threatened community, but of tall, anonymous corporate offices.[10] From this point of view, even the decision to put the project under the sign of the "hive," since that is the motto that Mies chose, is not at all innocent. It refers to the glass partitions used in beekeepers' hives.[11] The urbanist Martin Mächler saw in this type of building the "economic center" of a living and working community.[12] The issue was discussed in major international newspapers and journals, where critics such as Siegfried Kracauer denounced the "ugliness of New York." In his eyes, the "Turmhaus" incorporated "the spirit of materialism and capitalist exploitation." The completion of the projects proposed in various competitions of the

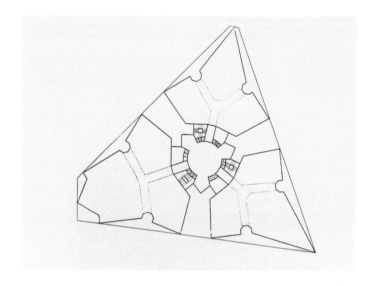

moment would depend not only on the "creative force of our architects, but also on the social conscience, on the aspiration of all our people to form a community."[13]

Among the great variety of projects submitted to the competition, Mies's project, entitled "Beehive," stood out for its rejection of any contextualization and of any visible hierarchical distinction between stories with different functions. In that respect, his entry was different from all the others, except that of his friend Hugo Häring. A triangular steel-framed glass prism twenty stories tall, with no definition at the base or the top, as though the roof had been sliced off, it occupied the entire triangular site. Three deep recesses afforded ground-floor access to the elevators while also allowing light to reach the three wings of the building, which were connected by a triangular central core. Two buildings in New York

seem to have served as the basis of Mies's project. The sharp angle of his building cannot fail to bring to mind the Flatiron Building, built by Daniel Burnham in 1903. In an extraordinary photograph of the "Dada Fair" that was held in Berlin in 1920, Johannes Baader shows Mies a copy of the journal *Neue Jugend* from June 1917, which reproduced a photograph of the Flatiron.[14] Moreover, the narrow passages of the Equitable Building by Ernest Graham – a building so contested that, in 1916, it precipitated the adoption of legislation regulating the height of skyscrapers – heralded the canyons in Mies's project. This building had been published in 1920 by Ludwig Hilberseimer and Udo Rukser, who emphasized the vertical articulation of the mass and the "change in the signification of windows" introduced by the American architect in his play on repetition.[15] Mies shed light on his intentions in Bruno Taut's magazine, *Frühlicht*:

"In my design […], intended for a triangular site, a prismatic form corresponding to the triangle appeared to offer the right solution for this building, and I angled the respective façade fronts slightly toward each other to avoid the danger of an effect of lifelessness that often occurs if one employs large glass panels. My experiments with a glass model helped me along the way and I soon recognized that by employing glass, it is not an effect of light and shadow one wants to achieve but a rich interplay of light reflections."[16]

This critique of the play of light and shadow implies a break with the architectural approach of Behrens. Not only did Mies do away with any vertical differentiation; he entirely bypassed the problem of the articulation of the load-bearing elements and infills on the façade by using an unbroken plate-glass surface.

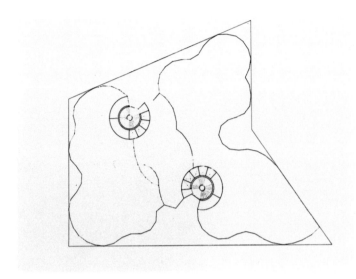

Opposite page, left:
Competition project
for an Office Skyscraper,
Friedrichstraße, Berlin,
1921, photomontage.

Opposite page, right:
Competition project
for an Office Skyscraper,
typical floor plan.

At left:
Project for a Glass
Skyscraper, 1922,
typical floor plan.

The echo of the essays and novels of Paul Scheerbart, and especially the echo of the aphorisms of his 1914 work *Glass Architecture*,[17] are felt in this large volume, the first to be built since Bruno Taut's pavilion at the Cologne Werkbund exhibition of 1914.[18] The volume does not respond to the respective qualities of the sides of the site, as is indicated in the increasingly decontextualized versions of the successive photomontages made by Mies. This has enabled Francesco Dal Co and Manfredo Tafuri to assert that "Mies's windows take away the image of the city," creating "impenetrable screens."[19] His projects would, in any case, occupy a prominent place in Arthur Korn's comprehensive analysis of the architectonic potential of glass, published in 1929.[20]

Mies was not among the thirty-seven German architects who participated in the 1922 Chicago Tribune competition.[21] Nor did he approve of all the projects for the vertical city, even when the skyscraper debate resumed, in the late 1920s, thanks to economic stabilization.[22] In the spring of 1922, however, he developed a second version of the skyscraper, based on research that extended the theme of the competition. This time the site was not specified, although Mies probably had in mind a particular location in the center of Berlin. Between the first and second versions, the lobby changes, becoming more sculptural in its design. Carl Gottfried stressed the "dematerialization" and the "timelessness" of Mies's two glass skyscrapers, embued with a sort of "Gothic force."[23] Mies himself insisted on the empirical nature of his approach, suggesting painstaking adjustments to the curves of the plan, achieved by manipulating the glass sides of the model on a clay base. The lines have nothing to do with Hans Arp or the expressionists, as was later suggested:[24]

"At first glance the contour of the ground plan appears arbitrary, but in reality it is the result of many experiments on the glass model. The curves were determined by the need to illuminate the interior, the effect of the building mass in the urban context, and finally the play of the desired light reflection. Ground plan contours in which the curves were calculated from the point of view of light and shadow revealed themselves on the model, if glass was employed, as totally unsuitable. The only fixed points in the ground plan are the stairs and the elevator shafts."[25]

For the model shown at the Große Berliner Kunstausstellung of 1923, the inclusion of the second project in the Berlin site is evoked by a row of Berlin apartment houses in clay surrounding the transparent tower. Created by the sculptor Oswald Herzog, this context serves both as a foil and as a "straight man" for the

At left:
Competition project
for an Office Skyscraper,
Friedrichstraße, Berlin,
1921, charcoal elevation
(autograph, Mies van der
Rohe Archive, Museum of
Modern Art, New York).

Opposite:
Project for a Glass
Skyscraper, 1922,
view of the model.

tower, in a game that could have been likened to the strategies of expressionist cinema.[26] One cannot but think of the struggle against "compromise" that was denounced by Walther Rathenau in 1912 when he critiqued everyday buildings:
"These buildings, crossbreeds of offices and residences, whose fourth floors are crammed with bow windows, are difficult to address architectonically. By contrast, the tower, as exemplified in American cities, actually makes possible new solutions satisfying all the requirements for air and light."[27]

Mies's model seems to pick up directly on the intention of the politician, who was assassinated in 1922. Unlike the traditionalist skyscrapers envisaged by several German architects before 1914, Mies's two projects refer back to the glass structures that already existed in Berlin, such as the concourses of the Friedrichstraße and Zoologischer Garten railway stations, which, according to Scheffler, expressed "heroic monumentality"[28] even more

than Behrens's Turbinenhalle or Gropius and Meyer's Fagus Works. But the structure that supported these vertical glass prisms was not explicit. The model was supported by posts with a circular section, but none of the floor plans clearly showed the configuration of the supports. If these cylindrical posts actually represented the proposed structure, their connection to the floor slabs remains quite mysterious. One columnist for the *Journal of the American Institute of Architects* would see in the skyscraper plan of 1923 "a picture of a Nude Building falling down stairs," in response to Walter Curt Behrendt's proposed analysis of the projects, especially the one by Mies. He added, "German architects have evinced rather remarkable creative originality, and have perhaps surpassed the American models by experimenting in various and entirely new directions."[29]

This structural vagueness is all the more surprising given that Mies's main grievance with "Constructivist formalism" and the "artistic

confusion" of the organizers of the Internationale Architekturausstellung (International Architectural Exhibition) in Weimar (where, in 1923, he exhibited the model of the second glass skyscraper, which went missing on that occasion) was their acceptance of a "play with forms."[30] Mies's new associations were apparent in his connection with the De Stijl group after a 1921 meeting with its founder and coordinator, Theo van Doesburg, and his appearance in Berlin under the aegis of the Novembergruppe. Affiliated with this organization, whose doctrinal radicalism had mellowed somewhat, he came into contact with the core members of the Berlin Dada group – Raoul Hausmann, Hanna Höch, and Kurt Schwitters – and with the founders of the short-lived Constructivist International – Hans Richter, El Lissitzky, and Theo van Doesburg, who had all signed a common declaration at the International Congress of Progressive Artists in Düsseldorf in May 1922.[31]

THEORETICAL PROJECTS FOR THE METROPOLIS (1918–24)

G and the Concrete Office Building

In July 1923, Richter, Lissitzky, and Werner Graeff, who had attended Van Doesburg's lectures at the Bauhaus, published the first issue of *G – Material für elementare Gestaltung*.[32] Like *L'Esprit nouveau*, founded three years earlier, and like *Sovremennaya Arkhitektura*, three years later, this magazine showed images from the world of technology and derived from them a scientific approach to architecture, rooted in the principle of economy and detached from any explicit connection with social reform, in spite of the radical political views of Lissitzky and Richter. The latter insisted in his memoirs on Mies's essential role in the journal: "His person, his work, and his active participation were more influential and indispensable for *G* than those of all the others."[33]

In its pages Mies settled some old scores, using a crossed-out image of a house by Bruno Paul to assert that the "fundamental reorganization of the building trades is urgent."[34] In its first issue, *G* published an article on Mies's Concrete Office Building, which was in many ways different from his previous towers. The loss of the

original model, which is known only from a poor photograph taken at the time of its presentation at Weimar in 1923, does not prevent an analysis of the structure of the building, which is fairly clear from a charcoal drawing that is almost three meters long. Two other drawings of the building were shown at the exhibition "Les architectes du groupe De Stijl," which marked the first appearance of Mies's work in Paris.[35]

The length of the building can be estimated only by assuming that the visible entrance is placed on an axis of symmetry. This idea was put forward in 1969 by Ludwig Glaeser, who also hypothesized a central courtyard.[36] The floor slabs are supported by two orthogonal sets of reinforced-concrete columns; their clarity and rigor inspired Mies to assert in *G* that they had nothing in common with the "noodles" used for contemporary office blocks in Berlin. The interaxis of columns is five meters, with an eight-meter unsupported span between the rows and a four-meter cantilever at each end. The building seems to float, being raised

Industrielles Bauen
Von Mies v. d. Rohe

Die Notwendigkeit einer Industrialisierung des Bauwesens wurde noch vor kurzer Zeit von fast allen beteiligten Kreisen bestritten und ich betrachte es als einen Fortschritt, daß diese Frage jetzt von einem größeren Kreise ernsthaft erörtert wird, wenn auch wenige hiervon wirklich überzeugt sind. Die fortschreitende Industrialisierung auf allen Gebieten hätte auch das Baugewerbe ohne Rücksicht auf veraltete Anschauungen und Gefühlswerte ergriffen, wenn hier nicht besondere Umstände hindernd den Weg versperrten. In der Industrialisierung des Bauwesens sehe ich das Kernproblem des Bauens unserer Zeit. Gelingt es uns, diese Industrialisierung durchzuführen dann werden sich die sozialen, wirtschaftlichen, technischen und auch künstlerischen Fragen leicht lösen lassen. Die Frage, wie die Industrialisierung durchzuführen ist, läßt sich vielleicht dann beantworten, wenn wir festzustellen versuchen, was hier hindernd bisher im Wege stand. Die Vermutung, daß rückständige Betriebsformen Ursache hierzu seien, trifft nicht zu. Sie sind nicht Ursache, sondern Wirkung eines Zustandes und sie stehen in keinem Gegensatz zu dem Charakter der alten Bauwirtschaft. Der Versuch zu neuen Betriebsformen ist wiederholt unternommen worden und hat nur die Teile des Bauwesens erfaßt, die eine Industrialisierung zuließen. Auch wird der Montagecharakter des heutigen Bauens zweifellos überschätzt. Er ist fast nur bei Hallenbauten für die Industrie und die Landwirtschaft durchgeführt worden und zwar waren es

Deutsche Zollbau G. m. b. H., Berlin-Lichterfelde

above the ground by a line of windows; by way of cornice, a slab, similar to the others, crowns a floor of reduced height. Each story's perimeter enclosure consists of a solid wall to a height of at least two meters, surmounted by a ribbon window that is set back, probably to shelter it from the rain.[37] There is no indication of internal partitioning, except in the entrance lobby, which is separated from the rest of the ground floor by a glass wall. Mies stressed the fact that the way in which the floor slabs turn up around the perimeter to become high parapet walls allows for the installation of a filing system under the windows, leaving the floors completely unobstructed.[38]

In contrast to the two glass skyscrapers, which offered exterior views, this was a kind of multistory factory, faithfully expressing *G*'s decision to celebrate industrial objects and spaces as such. It is not inappropriate to compare this plan, based on a concrete framework, with the Dom-ino House designed by Charles-Édouard Jeanneret in 1914; no doubt Mies was acquainted with it.[39] Unlike the Dom-ino space,

which is certainly not subdivided inside but is limited by the size of the floor slabs and by the different infill components that can, at times, block out the full height of the story, the open space of the Bürohaus (Concrete Office Building) is sliced in two horizontally by the plane defined by the top of the parapet walls. Below this plane, the expanse of offices stretches out, without a view to the outside; above, a swathe of air connects the space to the outside with no interruption except the diaphragm of the windows. To accompany this scheme, Mies produced a manifesto simply entitled "Bürohaus," the first expression of his theoretical thinking: "We reject any aesthetic speculation, any doctrine and any formalism. Building art is the spatially apprehended will of the epoch. Alive. Changing. New."[40]

In a longer text, written in July for the *Deutsche Allgemeine Zeitung*,[41] he revealed the degree to which his architectural doctrine was rooted in the theories of the structural rationalists, from Viollet-le-Duc to Karl Scheffler and Hermann Sörgel.[42] He also reflected on the office

workspace, where as early as 1912 Behrens had envisioned leaving whole floors of offices without partitions.[43] Moreover, his project seems to respond, point by point, to the experience with the Mannesmann Building in Düsseldorf, whose modularity, symmetry, and to a certain extent, monumentality are preserved, but whose roof, vertical openings, and partitions are abandoned:

"The office building is a building of work, of organization, of clarity, and of economy. Bright wide workrooms, uncluttered, undivided, only articulated according to the organism of the firm. The greatest effect with the least expenditure of means. The materials are concrete, iron, glass. Ferroconcrete buildings are essentially skeletal structures. Neither pastry nor tank turrets. Supporting girder construction with a nonsupporting wall."[44]

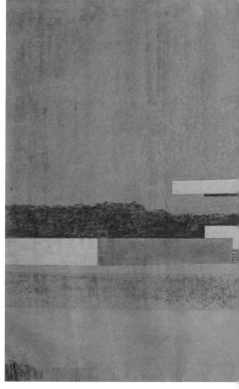

Project for the Concrete
Country House, 1922,
model.

The Concrete Country House

In the second issue of *G*, Mies published one of his most significant texts, "Bauen," in which he asserted, "We know no forms, only building problems."[45] This remark accompanied a second exploration of the potential of reinforced-concrete construction. This was the Concrete Country House, which was in total contrast to Mies's early domestic architectural work. It was exhibited at the Große Berliner Kunstausstellung of May 1923, a few meters away from Lissitzky's famous Prounen-Raum. The suggested setting for the house was Potsdam, and one might suppose that the eventual owner would be none other than the architect himself,[46] but the absence of context and explicit identification of the site made these aspects of secondary importance. All that remains today are the colored charcoal drawings, probably made at a later date, and the photographs of the lost model, a central feature of the project. The plan and all the preparatory sketches have been lost, including the drawing shown by Van Doesburg at the Galerie de l'Effort Moderne in 1923 and at the Nancy-Paris exhibition of 1926.[47]

The Concrete Country House, like the Concrete Office Building, uses load-bearing columns, but it does not have a regular grid. Thus, openings could be introduced at will – "a thin concrete skin […] forms both walls and roof," in Mies's words[48] – and the partitions could be positioned with total freedom, for he was able to "concentrate the supports and reinforcements in a few building locations,"[49] Werner Oechslin found, in this approach, the echo of the theories on the expected effects of reinforced-concrete technology, put forth starting in 1910 by the industrialist Karl Ernst Osthaus.[50] Whereas the office buildings are single units, the house, by contrast, is divided across the site, as if to cover and enclose as much of it

Project for the Concrete
Country House, 1922,
perspective (autograph,
Mies van der Rohe Archive,
Museum of Modern Art,
New York).

as possible. The main entrance, on the wall of the entrance courtyard, is marked by a staircase similar to that of the Concrete Office Building and by a projecting canopy. It leads straight into an entrance lobby, connected on the corner to a U reminiscent of the 1914 project for Mies's house at Werder. One arm of the U leads to the almost detached mass of the living room, which is dominated by a huge fireplace and lit by large horizontal windows; the other contains one or more bedrooms. Both arms of the U are linked to a large room of undefined purpose. The kitchen is in the basement, accessible from the outside by a service entrance marked by a canopy at the corner of the house. It is lit by a horizontal strip of windows similar to the window on the ground floor of the Concrete Office Building.

The abstract appearance of the model in photographs has led certain critics, perhaps unwisely, to see this design as an unprecedented demonstration of self-referential architecture.[51] In fact, the horizontal deployment of these rectilinear blocks reveals Mies's knowledge of the first Proun by Lissitzky, as well as echoes of Wright's Prairie Houses. But unlike Wright's first solutions, the divided plan of the house lacks a visible hierarchy, and the modeling of the platforms and floors continues the layouts of the Wiegand and Kröller-Müller Houses and can thus be related to the architecture of Schinkel. As for the precedents this house might have set, another remark is in order: the detached arrangement of its volumes is based on the differentiation of functions. Walter Gropius would expand on this theme explicitly in the Dessau Bauhaus of 1925.[52]

The Brick Country House

Situated this time, without ambiguity, on a site near Neubabelsberg, an area that was well known to Mies and was where he wanted to live himself, the Brick Country House was exhibited at the Große Berliner Kunstausstellung of 1924. Only the photographs survive of the two original drawings, which were a charcoal perspective drawn by Mies shortly before the opening of the exhibition and a plan, of which later versions appeared, with variations in the pattern of the brick fireplaces. The notable differences between the plan and the perspective suggest that the perspective was drawn earlier.[53] The project shows the effects both of the work seen at the Bauhaus exhibition at Weimar and of the work of De Stijl, a movement into which Mies had been hastily assimilated during the exhibition at the Galerie de l'Effort Moderne in Paris. Designed at exactly the same time as the Mosler House, which demonstrated Mies's skill in brickwork, the Brick Country House used the same material but relied on very different principles of composition, even though the Mosler House's cube-shaped kitchen, which was right up against the main volume of the house, gives an indication as to the appearance the building might have had. The vocabulary used in the Brick Country House consists of elementary forms and includes brick walls of two varying heights,

with two blocks containing a fireplace, flat roofs with slight overhangs, and vertical expanses of glass. The walls are screens that do not intersect but touch at their extremities. Mies stressed the contrast between this work and the Concrete Country House: "In the ground plan of this house, I have abandoned the usual concept of enclosed rooms and striven for a series of spatial effects rather than a row of individual rooms. The wall looses its enclosing character and serves only to articulate the house organism."[54]

Thus the space is fluid and continuous, inviting movement and offering controlled openings to the landscape. The designs envisioned for the openings themselves remain mysterious, for they require lintels of a length "totally incompatible with the construction possibilities of traditional buildings in brick," as Wolf Tegethoff has observed.[55] The function of the rooms is not specified, which troubled some of Mies's prospective clients, who asked him to "put a name to the different spaces of the house."[56] Rather than being strictly centered, the plan focuses more on two areas of increased density; this fundamentally distinguishes it from

Theo van Doesburg's painting *Rhythm of a Russian Dance* (1918), with which it has been so frequently compared.[57] If there is any Russian dance involved, it is more likely to be that of Lissitzky's Prouns, whose spatial development links linear elements resembling the walls of a house with denser agglomerations. Another possible source could be Hans Richter's "Filmmomente," spatial compositions with autonomous plans that the film director published in 1923 in *De Stijl*.[58] Moreover, Richter describes his discovery of Mies through Van Doesburg, who had said of Mies "that the plans of his houses resembled the designs of Mondrian or rather those on your rolls [of film]." He would see in Mies's designs "more than a plan, a new language, precisely the one that seemed to win over our generation."[59]

The relationship with the Dutch movement thus seemed to involve Mies's expansion of the visual field of the rooms of the house, which is comparable with Piet Mondrian's ideas on the limits of his canvases.[60] On the other hand, the relationship between the fluidity of the interior spaces and the investigations of Frank Lloyd Wright is incontestable. Already obvious

in the undetermined interior of the Concrete Office Building, which was informed by the layout of the Larkin Building, this relationship is quite clear here. Moreover, in 1940 Mies let it be known that his debt to Wright dated back to 1910:

"At this moment, so critical for us, there came to Berlin the exhibition of the work of Frank Lloyd Wright. This comprehensive display and the extensive publications of his works enabled us really to become acquainted with the achievement of this architect. The encounter was destined to prove of great significance to the development of architecture in Europe. The work of this great master revealed an architectural world of unexpected force and clarity of language, and also a disconcerting richness of form. Here finally was a master-builder drawing upon the veritable fountainhead of architecture, who with true originality lifted his architectural creations into the light. Here, again, at last, genuine organic architecture flowered."[61]

At this point, almost fifteen years after leaving Behrens's office, Mies seems to have rooted his own approach in a personal synthesis of

Schinkel-esque and Wrightian experiments, reinterpreted in terms of the geometric networks explored by his own avant-garde contemporaries. But at the same time, he successfully elaborated a theoretical position that supplemented and expanded the previous comments that he had made on specific projects. In his lecture in December 1923 on "Resolved Problems," Mies remained faithful to the stances of *G* with regard to the rejection of issues of form and the exclusive concern with structure and materials, based on "a new attitude toward construction," presenting as examples tepees, igloos, and huts made out of branches.[62] This interest in primitive dwellings did not come from reading Marc-Antoine Laugier, but from the study of works by German geographers and anthropologists such as Leo Frobenius.[63] At the same time, in an article in *G*, Mies called for the industrialization of building, prophesying total prefabrication in factories, following the model by Ford, whom the Germans found fascinating and to whom Mies paid tribute in 1924.[64] On a more theoretical level, his text of 1924, "Baukunst und Zeitwille!" (Architecture and the Will of the Epoch), echoed the affirmation inscribed on the endpaper of the 1913 monograph on Peter Behrens, ac-cording to which "architecture embodies the rhythmic expression of the spirit of the time."[65] But his desire for a split has incontestable Nietzschean accents. The idea of the eternal return, but also of a new art extending throughout life, was derived from it, as was the idea of beauty as the child of necessity, a concept formulated by Nietzsche in *The Gay Science*. Discussing Mies's projects in the 1960s, and specifically the vertical windows of the Concrete Office Building, Ludwig Hilberseimer would cite the "salutation" of Zarathustra, who spoke of beings "with orthogonal bodies and souls."[66]

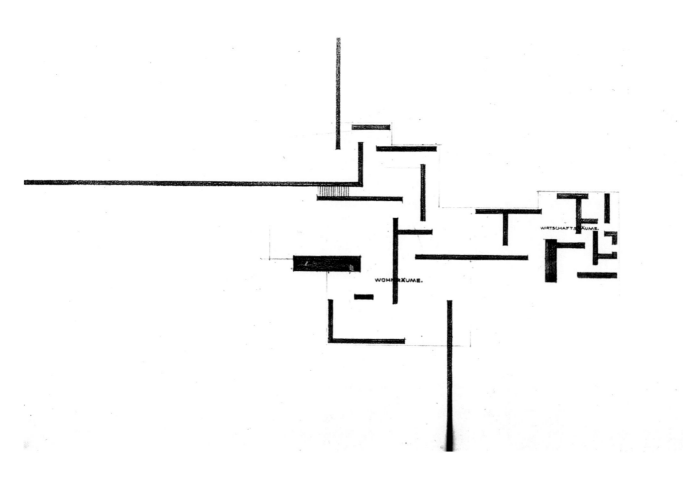

Mies's reading also encompassed history, medieval art, and popular science, particularly the works of Raoul Heinrich Francé on botany and natural harmony.[67] There are echoes of Oswald Spengler in this text, but the fact is that references, whether tacit or overt, to *The Decline of the West* are commonplace in all the architectural writing of the time, including that of the Russian Constructivists.

"The building art is always the spatially apprehended will of the epoch, nothing else. Only when this simple truth is clearly recognized can the struggle for the principles of a new building art be conducted purposefully and effectively. Until then it must remain a chaos of confusing forces. For this reason the question as to the nature of the building art is of decisive importance. One will have to understand that all building art arises out of its own epoch and can only manifest itself in addressing vital tasks with the means of its own time. It has never been otherwise."[68]

Well before Spengler, this subject – the attunement of architecture to the themes of the epoch – had been the central argument of a little book by Otto Wagner, entitled *Moderne Architektur*, first published in 1896.[69] This argument is taken up again by one of the founders of *G*, the Dadaist Hans Richter, who in 1925 sought to define the profile of the "new builder" working in an "internationally organized" space that required of him both a "new sensuality" and the capacity to respond to a "more practical and less sentimental" society, in a world of "rapid mobility" and "precise calculation."[70] He had no doubt that the concrete figure of this new *Baumeister* was none other than Ludwig Mies van der Rohe…

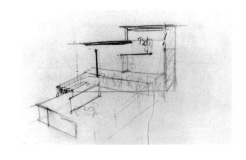

NEW HOUSING

3. FOUNDATIONS OF A NEW DOMESTIC SPACE (1925–30)

Mies and Weimar Politics

By the mid-1920s Mies van der Rohe was recognized as one of the uncontested leaders of modern architecture. He plunged into his professional life, and his commissions now gave him the freedom to abandon the language of conservatism, to which previous clients had bound him and to which he was still bound with the Mosler House. He finally joined the Deutscher Werkbund, becoming vice president, and in April 1924 he founded the Ring, an organization intended to combat, in the name of the ideals of modern architecture, the overly conservative Bund Deutscher Architekten (Association of German Architects). Having been a member of the regional board of the Bund since 1923, he resigned noisily in 1926. He directed the Ring activities in close collaboration with Hugo Häring, who was otherwise removed from Mies in terms of ideas.[1]

Although, from that moment on, clients accepted the new directions of his architecture, not all the projects went forward. The first client, in 1925, was the painter Walter Dexel, who was also director of the Kunstverein (Art Union) in Jena. Dexel had always encouraged the work of radical architects, but he immediately quarreled with Mies, who required a schedule that was, in Dexel's opinion, overly long.[2] Drafted in several weeks, the project is one of simplest and clearest of the new cycle inaugurated by the theoretical houses.

That same year, Mies designed a house for the banker Ernst Eliat on a site at Nedlitz, near Dessau. In this design he attempted to reconcile the principles of the Concrete Country House with the limitations of a real program, enclosing his sprawling plan within rather thick cement-block walls. In the only known perspective drawing,[3] the cubic envelope of the house also reveals affinities with Wright's Californian house designs, which were shown a few months earlier in the Dutch journal *Wendingen*.

In the end, it was the house built in the small Silesian town of Guben for the industrialist Erich Wolf, who had been won over by his visit to the Kempner House, that presented the first tangible evidence of Mies's new direction. No photographic record survives of the furniture designed for this house, which was built between 1925 and 1927 and destroyed during World War II.[4] Mies set his house on the crest of the narrow site that sloped down toward the Neisse Valley. The ground floor opened onto a terrace. The plan developed the layout of the Eliat House, and the internal spaces were arranged around this terrace. The front and street elevations were strongly emphasized by the contrast between the planes of brickwork, with the bond clearly visible, and the door and window openings. But, seen from the bottom of the slope, the house was partly obscured by the terrace wall – an arrangement that was reminiscent of the Riehl House. Thus the terrace became a kind of horizontal layer similar to the retaining wall of the garden and offering from the bottom of the slope a view so spectacular that the house became, as Barry Bergdoll has noted, a "local icon."[5] With its

cubist volumes, the garden shows the displacement of Mies's visual horizon, from the rigorously structured gardens prior to 1914 toward an overall approach that was close to Constructivist forms.

Mies van der Rohe continued his architectural experiments with bricks when he received an unexpected commission for a monument in the Friedrichsfelde cemetery, Berlin, to commemorate the assassination of Karl Liebknecht and Rosa Luxemburg. Up to that point, he had hardly expressed himself in the political arena, and this work would long remain a burdensome testimony. In 1926 Mies met Eduard Fuchs, who was then living in the Perls House.[6] A former compositor turned manager of the daily Social Democrat newspaper *Vorwärts*, Fuchs had published several works on cultural history and sexual customs and possessed a considerable collection of etchings, including six thousand lithographs by Daumier.[7] According to Perls, Liebknecht promised Mies, whom he met at his house before 1918, that he would make sure to give him some work after the socialists' victory.[8]

Top:
Erich Wolf House, Guben,
1925–27, view from the
Neisse Valley.

Bottom:
Monument to Karl
Liebknecht and Rosa
Luxemburg, Friedrichsfelde
cemetery, Berlin, 1926,
general view.

Mies was horrified by the official columned monument that was planned by the German Communist Party (KPD); he told him "it would be a fine monument for a banker" and said to Fuchs that, in his opinion, "as most of these people were shot in front of a wall, a brick wall would what [he] would build as a monument."[9] Sergius Ruegenberg, a draftsman in Mies's firm from 1925 to 1934, imagined a collection of basalt blocks.[10] But it certainly appears that the communist leader Wilhelm Pieck had already planned to build a wall, like that Mur des Fédérés (Communards' Wall) at the Père-Lachaise cemetery, in front of which a relief by Rodin was to have been installed.[11] The image of Paul Moreau-Vauthier's built monument commemorating the repression of the Paris Commune obviously comes to mind.[12]

Fuchs secured the commission for Mies, who built it in a few weeks with recycled bricks much coarser than those at Guben. He laid the bricks in slabs of stretchers, each with a course of headers at the bottom, with no concern for constructive realism: they were supported by

At left:
View of the monument
to Karl Liebknecht and
Rosa Luxemburg during a
ceremony (published by
the *Arbeiter-Illustrierte
Zeitung*).

Opposite page:
Social Housing Scheme,
Afrikanische Straße,
Berlin-Wedding, 1926–27,
street façade.

WIR SIND NICHT ZU VERBIETEN! Von KARL LIEBKNECHT

Trotz Zörgiebels Gummiknüppelattacke, trotz aller Demonstrationsverbote erkämpfte sich die Berliner Arbeiterschaft die Straße, um in der Lenin-Liebknecht-Luxemburg-Woche für die Ideen ihrer großen Toten zu demonstrieren

Und wenn Ihr uns verboten habt,
Wir sind nicht zu bezwingen,
Wir regen doch, den Adlern gleich
Nur kräftiger die Schwingen.
Und habt Ihr uns auch tot gesagt,
Wir kämpfen weiter, unverzagt,
Wir sind nicht zu verbieten!

Wir sind der Sturm, wir sind die Glut!
Wir sind des Volkes Stimme.
Wir stürmen wie des Wassers Flut
Und trotzen Eurem Grimme!
Wir sind des Volkes Rachegeist,
Der Euch doch endlich niederreißt,
Wir sind nicht zu verbieten!

Rechts: An der Lichtensteinbrücke, von der Rosa Luxemburg in den Landwehrkanal geworfen wurde, legen die Arbeiter Kränze nieder

63

a concrete core and steel rods. Their expressive force is more evocative of the approach used by the expressionists from northern Germany than that of the artists who gathered around *G*. The large star placed in front of the blocks was made of pieces of steel designed by the sculptor Herbert Garbe and ordered from Krupp, but they had to be found elsewhere owing to the refusal of the industrialist to participate in so subversive an undertaking. The inscription "Ich war, ich bin, ich werde sein!" (I was, I am, I will be!) was taken from an article by Rosa Luxemburg and was initially planned for the left side, but it was not included. As much as it was a monument – with an impressive frontal mass some fifteen meters wide, underlined by shadows – it was also a platform for oratory, which was used at important communist demonstrations, in accordance with a symbolism that the "Rhineland revolutionary" (as Mies called himself) was to recall forty years later:

"[I gave it] a square shape. Clarity and truth were to join forces against the fog that had descended and was killing all hopes – the hopes, as we rightly perceived at the time, of a lasting German republic."[13]

In his American exile, Mies tried to make it appear as if the commission for the monument had been fortuitous. The fact is, however, that in 1926 he also belonged to the Society of the Friends of New Russia, as did his colleagues Bruno Taut and Erich Mendelsohn.[14] In addition to the monument, Mies's friendship with Eduard Fuchs also brought him the work on an addition to Perls House, where in 1928 the collector could install his engravings.

Committed, at least implicitly, on the side of the Left, Mies nonetheless refused to take over Taut's position as city architect of Magdeburg in 1925, so as not to be entangled in party conflict. Thus, as Richard Pommer has pointed out,

his political position at that time was similar to that of the right wing of the German Democratic Party, which generally favored modern architecture,[15] whereas he drifted toward a kind of idealism under the influence of the Quickborn (fountain of youth) movement, whose theoretician, the Catholic priest Romano Guardini, published texts calling for the irresistible power of industry to submit to an ideal force linking Plato and Nietzsche.[16] A new and more spiritual dimension thus began to appear in Mies's discourse, as is revealed, for example, in a lecture given in 1926:

"Building art is not the realization of specific formal problems, no matter how much they may be contained therein. But it is always, I repeat, the spatial execution of spiritual decisions."[17]

The rather laborious attention that Mies devoted to the books by Guardini, Friedrich Dessauer, and the Cologne-based architect

At left:
Social Housing Scheme,
Afrikanische Straße,
partial view of the
street façade.

Above:
Social Housing Scheme,
Afrikanische Straße,
courtyard façade.

Rudolf Schwarz on the philosophy of technology is evident in his reading notes for the years 1927-28, which are now housed at the Museum of Modern Art in New York.[18] He remained on cordial terms with Schwarz, whose antifunctionalist modernism was never very similar to his own.[19] At that time, Mies obtained his only commission for public housing (a flourishing sector in Weimar Germany). In Berlin, between late 1925 and 1927, he built four apartment houses along Afrikanische Straße, in the working-class area of Wedding. It was a commission from the Primus company, of largely conservative taste, but whose policy evolved with the arrival of Martin Wagner in the urbanism sector of Berlin, where he encouraged innovative projects. Disliked by Mies himself, this project was the first major undertaking that he had ever realized.[20]

This development is similar to certain projects of Bruno Taut from the same era, particularly in the repetition of long, smooth blocks broken by standardized windows. But, as Fritz Neumeyer points out, with their cubic volumes, the buildings also evoke the "houses in rough

Below:
Model estate
of the Deutscher
Werkbund at the
Weißenhof, Stuttgart,
1927, general view.

At right:
Model estate
of the Deutscher
Werkbund at the
Weißenhof, model
of the first version.

Below:
Model estate
of the Deutscher
Werkbund at the
Weißenhof, Stuttgart,
1927, general view.

At right:
Model estate
of the Deutscher
Werkbund at the
Weißenhof, model
of the first version.

concrete" published by Le Corbusier in *Vers une architecture*. (Mies owned a copy of the 1924 edition of that work, as well as the German translation.)[21] The buildings are austere with their ochre surface and reasonably well equipped for affordable housing. The main blocks, which are aligned with the street and suggest a break with regard to the morphology of closed-courtyard housing blocks in Berlin, connect at each end to lower lateral wings, providing a pattern of autonomous and repetitive units; only the final one is distinguished by the inclusion of a shop. The slab blocks facing the street are joined by their corners to the return wings, which look like separate cubes wearing loggias like masks, by three balconies, one above the other inserted in reflex angles – the only curved elements in an otherwise orthogonal design.[22] The apartments are grouped in pairs on each landing, with each block including three stairwells on the street and one on each wing.

The experimental Weißenhofsiedlung in Stuttgart in 1927 was at the center of European attention. Mies van der Rohe's appointment as director conferred on him the status of an organizer and urban planner, coupled with that of an innovator in collective housing, which the Afrikanische Straße development would never have achieved for him. The Württemberg branch of the Deutscher Werkbund had been planning a national housing exhibition since 1925; Mies, now a vice president of the Werkbund, found himself assigned to design a show housing estate at the Weißenhof, a district overlooking the Swabian metropolis, which had been under development since 1920. In contrast to the idea of a garden-city formulated in the initial

WERKBUNDAUSSTELLUNG
DIE **WOHNUNG**
STUTTGART
23. Juli bis 23. Oktober 1927

plan of municipal services, his first attempt was ready at the end of 1925, in the form of a model that topped the hill with a blanket of cubic houses. Their crystallized flow follows the hill's contour, and above them a cluster of apartment blocks form a sort of *Stadtkrone* (city crown). Mies would affirm that he tried "to avoid anything schematic" and was careful "to rule out everything that could constitute a restriction to free work process" of the participants.[23] His project, with its organic lines, looked like "the spatial rendering of the will of the epoch" on a grand scale, echoing the idea of an "organic" economy on which Walther Rathenau had pinned his hopes before his assassination in 1922. His design seemed to respond to "the boredom and lack of imagination of optimist rationalism" that his friend Rudolf Schwarz would critique in his 1928 text "The Metropolis as Fact and as Program."[24] The building that dominates the development brings to mind the studios built in 1901 by Joseph Maria Olbrich above the artists' colony in Darmstadt, which Mies knew well.

This design immediately aroused strong reactions from local architects, who could not bear to see this commission escape them. The traditionalist Paul Schmitthenner condemned Mies's plan for "dilettantism," and Paul Bonatz reproached him for his "romanticism." Under these circumstances, Mies had to revise his plan in July 1926, imposing an almost orthogonal geometry and simplifying the dominant verticals.[25]

In the final version of the overall project, the landscaping is greatly simplified. However, following the principles Mies used in his villas, it succeeds in unifying a development intended to accommodate twenty-one different buildings. Mies himself undertook the main apartment block and gave the other to Peter Behrens as a tribute, asking his former employer to add a building to those of a generation that he had helped to train, since three of his former draftsmen figure among the creators of the development. Among the architects invited to participate were Gropius, Bruno and Max

Taut, Oud, Mart Stam, Hans Scharoun, Ludwig Hilberseimer, and Le Corbusier, while Tessenow, Mendelsohn, and Häring, who had been approached initially, were ruled out.[26] Contact among the architects was maintained directly by Mies's Berlin office, while Richard Döcker, a local modernist, oversaw the work on-site.

Mies's apartment block dominates the development, with its four floors and four repeated units, each served by a stairwell leading to two apartments per landing, as in the Afrikanische Straße development.[27] For the first time, Mies used a steel frame; its stanchions at last permitted the openness and flexibility that had already been suggested by Behrens and to which Mies had long aspired. The framework is almost everywhere buried within the walls, however, with the white surfacing giving no hint of the play between the framework and the infill, although variations in the apartment layouts reveal the potential freedom offered by this construction system. Mies demonstrated this by installing mobile partitions in

certain apartments, convinced as he was that only the kitchens and the bathrooms should in the future remain fixed.[28] The joinery and the metal components evoke the world of industry, and the tubular chairs specially designed for the apartments launched a prolific series of furniture. The exhibition inspired a great deal of press in Germany and the rest of Europe; Mies's building was greeted with interest and was described by the trade paper *Deutsche Bauhütte* as "Bolshevik barracks."[29]

Away from the Weißenhofsiedlung, in the technical section of the Stuttgart exhibition, Mies built a "glass room" whose space was defined by partitions with different finishes and degrees of transparency; its tangential openings were a throwback to the Brick Country House of 1923. Above all, it fulfilled the ideal of a light without shadow radiating from the walls and seemed, in its fluidity, as Detlef Mertins noted, to embody the comments underlined by Mies in Henri Bergson's *Evolution créatrice*, according to which "the essential in life lies in the movement that conveys it."[30]

Basking in the public success of the exhibition, Mies took the opportunity offered by his numerous – and pithy – introductions to books devoted to his work to advance a new formu-

lation of his theoretical position. He insisted on the importance of the spiritual dimension in new architecture, rejecting points of view that were "unilateral and doctrinaire" with regard to rationalization and standardization, but also attacking the idea of form "as an end in itself."[31] On this point, he seems to have been in agreement with Le Corbusier, whom he met again in Stuttgart in 1926, sixteen years after their brief introduction at Behrens's firm. Impressed by Le Corbusier's houses at the Weißenhofsiedlung, which he featured prominently as the figurehead of the group and which he supported against the local authorities, Mies called upon Le Corbusier to witness to his anti-functionalist positions, and Le Corbusier, then fully embattled against the representatives of Sachlichkeit (objectivity), could but share them:
"In Germany, a country of organizers, above all, it seems to me necessary to underline with the greatest clarity that architecture cannot be reduced to crude functionalism. In Germany,

the fight against the rationalists will be harder than the fight against the Academy."[32]

For his part, Le Corbusier approached Mies in 1928, during the formation of the board of patrons of the first International Congress of Modern Architecture (CIAM).[33] As the Stuttgart model was taking shape, Mies began a long-lasting relationship with Lilly Reich, an interior designer and fashion stylist trained by Josef Hoffmann; their meeting would have a profound effect on his professional and personal life. Lilly Reich had known Mies since 1925 and had fully backed his application for the post of chief city planner in Frankfurt, which was finally given to Ernst May. Involved in the decisions and in the work of the firm, she was to take part in many of Mies's projects, in particular the interiors, exhibition design, and furniture. She also managed his daily life, as well as that of Ada and the girls.[34]

Two Houses in Krefeld

Lilly Reich introduced Mies to the industrialist Hermann Lange, owner of the Vereinigte Seidenwebereien A.G. (or Verseidag) silk-spinning mill and a very active collector of modern art, who had initially asked Theo van Doesburg to design his house. A member of the Deutscher Werkbund, Lange would support Mies's work for ten years, first hiring him to build a house at Krefeld, in the Ruhr (1927-30). To this commission was added one for the house next door, intended for Josef Esters, Lange's friend and joint shareholder. Mies seized this opportunity to renew the principles developed in the Wolf House, but using a steel construction system. The façades were made of several solid parts and very complex metal frames that allowed for the long span of the window lintels. They were covered in partially glazed Bockhorn brick, which were worked in meticulous calpinage at a scale of 1/20. The large windows that allowed for these pieces of technical prowess brought light from the south into the deepest rooms.

Joseph Esters House,
Krefeld, 1929, detail
of the garden façade.

Joseph Esters House,
garden façade,
with an installation
by Iñigo Manglano-Ovalle.

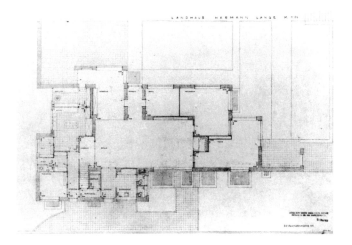

Above, left:
Hermann Lange House,
Krefeld, 1929, ground
floor plan (autograph,
Mies van der Rohe Archive,
Museum of Modern Art,
New York).

Above, right:
Hermann Lange House,
view of the ground floor.

Opposite page:
Joseph Esters House,
view of the ground floor.
The column is part
of Iñigo Manglano-Ovalle's
installation, shown in 2005.

In this calm neighborhood of luxurious, traditional villas shaded by trees, dark brick was already very much in use. The innovation introduced by Mies concerned the use of an industrial language for the volumes and the details. The two houses are parallel to the street, with canopies marking their entrances. The strips of windows on the first floor show no regard for a strict correspondence between plan and elevation, especially as the first sketches show the idea of façades made entirely of glass. The windows in the Lange House open onto a long corridor, whereas those of the Esters House light a series of separate rooms. Mies used accordion windows and retractable windows vertically in the wall. This arrangement, inspired by train cars, was tested by Berlage in his Saint Hubertus Lodge of 1919, which Mies had no doubt visited. On the inside, the door frames and openings in light wood give rhythm to the depth, with the continuity of the walls ensured notably by the recessing of the big radiators in the window aprons. The efficient display of Lange's exceptional collection of

cubist and expressionist works led the critic Walter Cohen to contrast this residence with other recent houses, where "the hostility toward the paintings [was] expressed by the architecture."[35]

On the garden side, the brick base of the Wolf House is repeated; more generous rectangular openings ensure the relationship with the interior, although by his own admission Mies would have liked "to make this house much more in glass."[36] One finds a certain contra-diction between the openness and the fluidity of the rooms on the ground floor. The play of walls and levels links the villas to the Brick Country House. Above all, the exterior work extends their architecture and gives them a broad foundation reminiscent of the Prairie Houses of Frank Lloyd Wright. Particularly striking is the contrast between the street side, shaped according to the trajectory of cars, and the vast stretches of grass shaded by big trees, toward the interior of the blocks.

The Barcelona Feat

After Stuttgart, Mies and Reich worked together for the fashion exhibition "Die Mode der Dame," which took place in Berlin in the autumn of 1927, where they built the Velvet and Silk Café. Its space was defined by fabric screens and furnished with chairs from the Weißenhofsiedlung. They worked together again in 1929, in the German section of the International Exhibition in Barcelona. Hermann Lange saw to it that the commission for the whole German section was given to Mies; its centerpiece was a pavilion that was not intended, as has often been written, as a model dwelling, but rather as a place arranged for and by the requirements of official ceremonies, in particular the formal reception for the king of Spain. In short, it was a building "without an obvious, tangible, or essential destination – a building devoted to representation, an empty space and thereby a space in itself."[37] Precisely because of that,

it was nevertheless a turning point in Mies's work and in the architecture of the twentieth century, thanks especially to Wilhelm Niemann, the owner of the Berliner Bild-Bericht firm, who photographed the pavilion under the supervision of Mies himself and distributed the pictures widely.[38]

Its reception was accompanied by a stream of clichés (and not only photographic ones) that have been appropriately analyzed by Juan Pablo Bonta.[39] The scrupulous reconstruction of the pavilion, completed in 1986, has added a new dimension to the modern perception of the building. The re-created color seems rather forced, given that the black-and-white photographs had taken on the aura of authenticity. In some way, this reverses Walter Benjamin's hypothesis on "the work of art in the era of technical reproducibility." However, the opportunity of passing through the re-created space of the pavilion makes two-dimensional reproductions pale by comparison.[40]

The pavilion was designed between November 1928 and February 1929 on a site that Mies himself chose after having refused the location proposed by the Spanish. From Mies's very first sketches – now lost – a demountable model showed two courtyards linked by a pavilion, itself resembling a covered courtyard. The disjunction of the load-bearing and space-dividing elements and the concentration on a cen-

Top:
German Pavilion at the
International Exhibition,
Barcelona, 1929, general
view of the reconstructed
pavilion.

At right:
German Pavilion at the
International Exhibition,
Barcelona, 1929, general
view in 1929.

Overleaf:
German Pavilion at the
International Exhibition,
Barcelona, 1929, interior of
the reconstructed pavilion.

FOUNDATIONS OF A NEW DOMESTIC SPACE (1925–30)

Top:
German Pavilion at the
International Exhibition,
Barcelona, 1929, interior
view in 1929.

Bottom:
German Pavilion at the
International Exhibition,
Barcelona, 1929, plan.

Opposite page, top:
German Pavilion at the
International Exhibition,
Barcelona, 1929, view of
the reconstructed pavilion
with the sculpture by Georg
Kolbe.

Opposite page, bottom:
German Pavilion at the
International Exhibition,
Barcelona, 1929,
reconstructed pavilion,
detail of the intersection of
a partition and a column
with the ceiling.

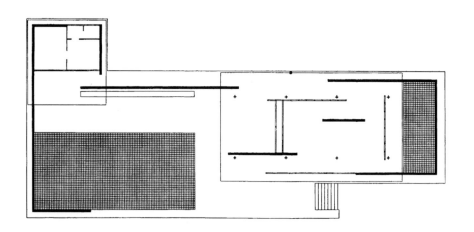

tral core emerged in the course of planning, although the single roof and the strip open toward the street did not emerge immediately. Preparatory drawings indicate the emphasis on walls enclosing space, as well as the late addition of eight metal columns. Furthermore, it was only after several attempts that the pool found its place in the corner. One of the controlling elements of the project was a single block of gold onyx from the Atlas Mountains, which alone represented a fifth of the total cost; Mies himself bought it during the winter of 1928 in Hamburg. It had been earmarked to make vases for a Norddeutsche Lloyd ocean liner and cut into slices three centimeters

thick.[41] In 1961 Mies asserted that the internal vertical dimensions of the pavilion were determined by the size of the stone:
"When I had the idea for this building I had to look around. There was not much time, very little time in fact. It was deep in winter, and you cannot move marble in from the quarry in winter because it is still wet inside and would easily freeze to pieces. So we had to find dry material. I looked around in huge marble depots, and in one I found an onyx block. This block had a certain size and, since I had only the possibility of taking this block, I made the Pavilion twice that height."[42]

This dividing of the wall into slabs of limited height can also be linked to the solutions adopted for the cladding of the Palatine Chapel, where panels of limited height were superimposed. But the pavilion was not based on any overall module predetermined by the onyx block, any more than it had an overall grid – as indicated in the working drawings.[43] The grid appeared only in a drawing published by Werner Blaser in 1965. After a building process complicated by the need to stabilize the slope, the pavilion offered a startling architectural journey, from the entrance at foundation level through a reversal of direction into the interior, and then toward the dominant onyx wall. Sergius Ruegenberg stresses Mies's attachment to the idea of putting the main scene of the pavilion against a wall, which sums up his affirmation: "I must have a wall behind me."[44] Set off behind this jewel box of stone are columns and glass partitions, one of which was internally lit, thus developing the theme of the Glasraum in Stuttgart.[45] Each interior space was matched, extended, and echoed by an exterior space whose presence was all the more vital as no artificial lighting was

installed. This essentially picturesque effect was to have been reinforced by the presence of several sculptures acting as perspectival focuses,[46] but the only one to be installed was the statue *Morning* by Georg Kolbe, to whom Mies had turned when he despaired of finding a work by his old friend Wilhelm Lehmbruck, who had died in 1919.

In this universe of transparencies and mineral and metal reflections, the colored planes stood out. The petrified landscape of the onyx wall set off the black carpet and the red curtains, and these three colors, which bring to mind those on the German Weimar flag, play on the white leather seats intended for the king and queen of Spain, who would never use them. It should be noted that, if the vertical columns were magnified by their stainless-steel sheaths, the horizontal structure of the roof was played down to the point that it gave the impression of being a homogeneous slab. This kind of process explains why Mies insisted that no photographs of his sites be published when the construction systems were improvised. In the unhierarchical space of the pavilion, open to

diagonal views and to movement, the only perceptible symmetry was that which rendered the plane of the floor visually identical to that of the ceiling – to the point that there are certain photographs of the pavilion that can be viewed upside down.[47] This symmetry was of course revealed only after one had stepped up onto the plinth – another quotation from Schinkel. The German officials seem to have recognized the qualities of the pavilion; note the appreciation voiced by the commissioner of the German delegation, Georg von Schnitzler: "We have wanted to show here what we can do, what we are and how we feel today. We do not want anything more than clarity, simplicity and integrity."[48]

It is difficult to define the relationship between the policies of the German industrialists and the decision by Mies to present his slender steel columns as if they were precious objects – a civilized and paradoxical echo of the skeletons of the African huts published in the books by Frobenius, which Mies consulted, according to Sergius Ruegenberg.[49] After projects dominated by glass, with no explicit structure to speak

At right:
German Pavilion at the
International Exhibition,
Barcelona, 1929,
reconstructed pavilion,
partial view with the Georg
Kolbe statue.

of, such as the second Glass Skyscraper or the Glasraum, or by concrete and brick, the pavilion was of a more general scope, addressing the idea of openness, which had already been explored in the Brick Country House, by introducing metal columns. Henceforth these were to delimit the interior of the building, liberating the vertical planes, which define the space, from the structure. The idea of the "open plan" which Le Corbusier had formulated when he built his houses in Stuttgart,[50] and that of wall treatments, extolled by Berlage, were thus solidly united.

The comments of some of those architects who inspired the pavilion revealed their lack of comprehension on this point. Wright, to whom Mies was indebted for the opposition between the solid central core and the light precise structure, said, "some day let's persuade Mies to get rid of those damned little steel posts that look so dangerous and interfering in his lovely designs."[51]

Opposite page, top:
Fritz and Grete Tugendhat
House, Brno, 1929–30,
view from the garden.

Opposite page, bottom:
Fritz and Grete Tugendhat
House, plan of the upper
and lower floors.

Luxury at the Tugendhats

Designed while the Barcelona Pavilion was being built, the Tugendhat House in Brno consolidated the architectural decisions made in Barcelona. The young American critic Philip Johnson told Oud of his admiration for this building in September 1930, when construction was almost complete:

"I wish I could communicate the feeling of seeing the Brünn [Brno] House of Mies. I have only had similar architectural experiences before [at] the Hoek and in old things like the Parthenon. Of course such things should not be talked about because there enters into them so much that is extraneous, such as having studied Greek or being acquainted with the prophetic nature of Mies' own character. In American slang, the Brünn House is swell."[52]

The recently married, wealthy couple Grete and Fritz Tugendhat were friends of Eduard Fuchs. They were doubtless disappointed if they expected Mies to design another Perls House. They went with their architect to visit the Krefeld and Guben houses. Contrary to the rather disparaging accounts that he liked to give of them afterward, the Tugendhats seem to have fully committed themselves to build-

ing a house that would unleash violent polemics even among the champions of Neues Bauen. In fact, the Tugendhat House was not a minimal, reproducible house, like Le Corbusier's house in the Weissenhofsiedlung (although it did have some affinities with that house and with the Villa Stein) but a positively luxurious residence. This was more than some critics could bear.

In September 1928, when he was designing the Barcelona Pavilion, Mies went to inspect the Tugendhats' plot of ground at Schwarzfeldgasse, overlooking the ancient Moravian city of Brno. It had been given to Grete Löw-Beer by her parents on the occasion of her marriage to Fritz Tugendhat. Both families were textile mill owners in an industrial center where modern architecture had strongly taken root.[53] A close echo of the pavilion in Barcelona, the house was criticized by Julius Bier in *Die Form* for being "showpiece architecture."[54] Some components – the onyx partition, the cruciform columns, and the large plate-glass windows – are identical to the Barcelona Pavilion, and the layout also echoes the pavilion in several respects, such as the conservatory along the end wall of the building, in the position occu-

pied in Barcelona by a small courtyard.[55] All in all, the house is the more complex and the more dramatic of the two because of the surprises it affords and its incorporation of the elements of the site, such as the large weeping willow that centers the façade on the downhill side.

The slope of the land, accessed from the top and facing southwest, made it possible to conceal the verticality of the three-story house: only the top floor is visible at street level. The opening between the garage and the bedrooms frames a view of the city, thus indicating the importance of the view in the design of the main rooms. From the entrance lobby, a staircase encased in frosted glass leads down to the reception rooms. Julius Posener drew attention to this arrangement, which goes against traditional rules; guests cut across the access route between the bedrooms and the living rooms.[56] From the foot of this staircase, the visitor sees the music room straight ahead and a view of the city diagonally ahead, framed on the right by a wooden cylindrical form and on the left by a polished onyx partition that reflects the outdoor light.

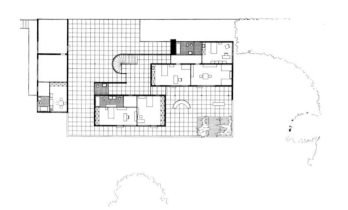

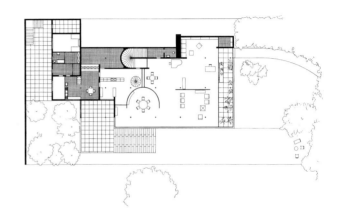

FOUNDATIONS OF A NEW DOMESTIC SPACE (1925–30)

Top:
Fritz and Grete Tugendhat
House, view from the
street.

Bottom:
Fritz and Grete Tugendhat
House, view of the
entrance.

The complexity of this large space reveals itself gradually. The degree of intimacy and visual protection increases from the glass wall on the valley side to the more enclosed library on the uphill side. The distance between the conservatory and the glass wall makes it possible to create an artificial landscape punctuated by slender columns – to the surprise of the Tugendhats, who had not understood the significance of the mysterious little crosses on their plans.[57] These columns have a different skin outdoors. Inside, they are chrome-plated, whereas their external counterparts are galvanized. The interplay between partitions, façades, and vertical columns is more difficult and more complex than in Barcelona because the main rooms are lit only on two sides. Behind the continuous glass wall, Mies defined the uses of his space by means of the sheltering macassar ebony hemicylinder – with a conversation corner tucked in behind its outer face – and the onyx screen. In a most germane way, Bruno Reichlin likened this plan by Mies to those by his friend Hugo Häring, despite differences in appearance. The likenesses can be seen in the comparison, suggested in 1927 by Walter Curt Behrendt, between the Brick Country House of the former and the organic plan of the latter.[58] He emphasizes how much, in the villas by Häring or Hans Scharoun, "each curve of the walls, each opening, each corner in the shadow, each armchair, each type or group of seats" reveals

Fritz and Grete Tugendhat
House, view of the corner.

FOUNDATIONS OF A NEW DOMESTIC SPACE (1925–30)

"about an activity, an ambience, a custom."[59] Everything unfolds as if, far from having wanted to design a priori a completely fluid space, Mies, who for the past two decades was very up-to-date on the customs in the middle-class residence, had first renewed the delimitation of various locations of domestic life before proceeding to remove the walls. In his 1927 article on Mies's approach, Paul Westheim already alluded to this procedure:

"Mies was among those who thought of the house as a unity. Not as a juxtaposition of rooms covered by a roof, but as a circulation leading from room to room, following the way of life. And, as in urbanism, it was a question of organizing the circulation in such a way that the domestic life which the building was to serve unfolded with the fewest possible obstacles. The overall residence was to be thought of as a kind of business that, like any other business, would be based on the principle of an articulation of various functions. No isolated room would be cut off from the others. Even more, continuity between the rooms would be sought. The entire space would be arranged organically according to its uses."[60]

The onyx wall defines a living room that opens onto the conservatory and onto thin air, while restricting the outside view from the library. The insertion of a curved form in this interior no doubt reflects Mies's interest in Le Corbusier's Villa Stein, a design that he had

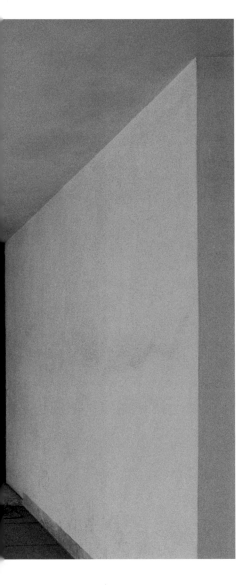

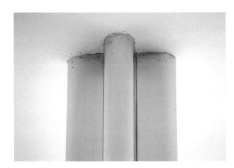

FOUNDATIONS OF A NEW DOMESTIC SPACE (1925-30)

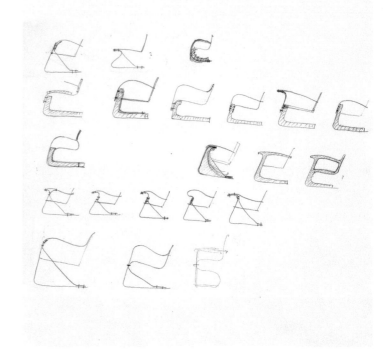

Above, left:
The Barcelona chair,
1929–30.

Above, right:
Study of cantilever chairs
seen in profile, circa
1935.

Opposite page:
Fritz and Grete
Tugendhat House,
living room and
winter garden.

carefully studied, as Ruegenberg noted. Fritz Tugendhat spoke of his pleasure in opening the great glass wall, which slid downward: "When there was frost, the lowered glass allows one to sit in the sun looking out over a snowy landscape, as at Davos."[61] The gabled window, which lights the conservatory, calls to mind the pierced opening on the ground floor of the Esters House, which offers a side view from the terrace.

Upstairs, the bedrooms line a well-lit corridor. Like first-class cabins on a transatlantic liner, they open onto the upper terrace, a gateway in midair. The parents' bedroom and bathroom is mirrored by the children's suite.[62] The garden is divided into two parts – planted terraced beds and a lawn. It continues the stepped pattern of the house, in an arrangement that is reminiscent of the Wolf House and in which the willow plays an essential role. The size and comfort of the Tugendhat House, emphasized

by Lilly Reich's decor and Mies's metal furniture (his third set of furniture, after Stuttgart and Barcelona) aroused reservations among critics linked to the Modern Movement; one of them, the Parisian leftist Roger Ginsburger, reproached him in *Die Form* for a "luxury" contrary to the ideas of the Neues Bauen.[63]

In 1929 Mies elaborated on part of the spatial configuration of the Tugendhat House when he designed a house for the painter Emil Nolde,

in Zehlendorf, Berlin. He had met Nolde in the Riehl circle, and designed for him a single-story building, stretching out along solid unbroken walls onto which the living room and studio backed, as at Brno. The suggested frame was of steel. But the project was abandoned shortly before ground was broken, and other, more ambitious projects responding to the problems of the German cities also came to nothing. In 1928 Mies returned to the office block program with a design for a bank in

Stuttgart and another for the Adam building, in Leipzigerstrasse in Berlin, abandoning the infill panels and the concrete structure to wrap the framework of the buildings in a wall of glass. In the Stuttgart building the wall supported commercial signs and advertisements in contrast to the stone portico of the Paul Bonatz train station opposite it.[64]

For the Adam department store project, at the corner of Leipziger Straße and Friedrichstraße

in Berlin, on a site that he had studied for a signal tower in 1925, Mies competed against Behrens, Poelzig, and Straumer. There, he gave an extremely clear image of the modern commercial building with a free plan. The angle subtly rounded by the block, as illustrated in the presentation photomontage, is a testament to how much the concept of the glass building had changed since 1923. In 1929 Mies would also return to the triangular site in the Friedrichstraße to compete, again unsuccessfully,

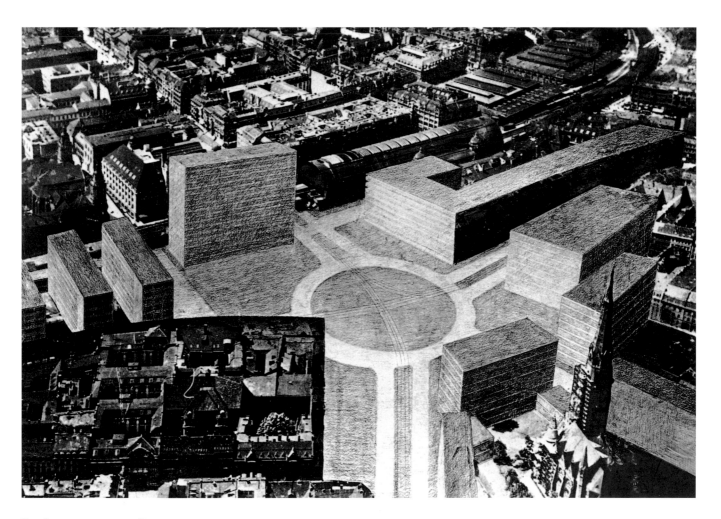

Opposite page:
Adam department store
project, Berlin, 1928,
photomontage.

Above:
Competition project for the
layout of the
Alexanderplatz, Berlin,
1929, photomontage.

for a new office block project. The vertical rise of the Glass Skyscrapers of 1921-22 was abandoned, but the principle of the central core was retained, now solidly set at the heart of three glass-walled, concave wings, giving the building as many façades on which were reflected the other disparate buildings of the neighborhood.

That same year in Berlin, Martin Wagner, who was in charge of urbanism in the capital, launched a competition for the redevelopment of the Alexanderplatz, for which Mies created a more complex metropolitan space, assembling his rectangular glass prisms according to a logic that was frontal (around the traffic roundabout that served as the central focus) and serial (based on the repetition of six slabs of gradually increasing length). Rejecting the idea of a symmetrical composition proposed by Wagner, Mies made the placement of the buildings independent of the design for the network of roads. Although the competition was won by the Luckhardt brothers and the final project handed over to Behrens, Ludwig Hilberseimer succeeded in making Mies's proposal a topic of discussion.[65] The imagined buildings go beyond both the Concrete Office Building and the Glass Skyscraper.

This project in Berlin epitomizes Mies's thinking on the metropolis. He connects considerations relating to the physical form of the city,

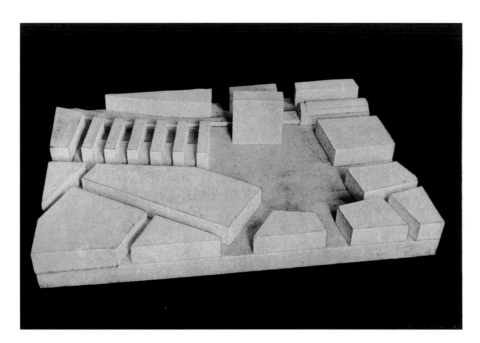

At left:
Competition project
for the layout of the
Alexanderplatz, Berlin,
1929, view of the model.

Opposite page:
Erich Mendelsohn, the
Brooklyn Bridge and the
Manhattan skyline
(illustration published in
*Amerika, das Bilderbuch
eines Architekten*, 1926).

in the sense of the Latin *urbs*, to its social space, in the sense of *civitas*, as Saint Augustine meant it in *The City of God*, a text that Mies knew well and that stresses the continuance of a Christian civitas despite the sac of Rome by the barbarians. The awareness of urban transformations in Germany, which Mies witnessed both in Aachen, where the expansion policy of the Second Reich had been implemented, and in Berlin, the prototype of the *Weltstadt* (world city) surfaced when, in 1926, not without epic accents, he became aware of the process of urbanization:

"The unified German empire achieved world power status. International traffic and international trade determine life from now on. Metropolises of immense proportions develop. The speed of development permits no reflection.

One builds streets upon streets in endless sequence. Industry experiences unexampled expansion. A new technology arises with unforeseen possibilities. Bold constructions never seen before are invented. Here, too, one knows no limits.

Traffic takes on immense dimensions and interferes in the organism of our cities with fierce brutality. Gigantic industrial complexes arise, yes, entire industrial cities."[66]

In his 1928 text "The Preconditions of Architectural Creation," illustrated by images of the skyline and streets of New York, Mies expanded his thinking to an almost global dimension, confirming, "The world shrinks more and more." His overarching concerns changed too, to the extent that it was not longer circulation or industry that, in his opinion, guided the urban transformations, but the overall economy: "Traffic serves economy. Economy becomes the great distributor, interferes in all domains, forces man into its service.

Economy begins to rule. Everything stands in the service of use. Profitability becomes law. Technology forces economic attitudes, transforms material into power, quantity into quality. The most effective use of power is consciously brought about."[67]

In these observations on the inexorable development of the metropolis, Mies van der Rohe echoed the thinking on the metropolis that was spreading through Berlin before 1914.[68] In 1913 Scheffler foreshadowed Mies's words when he wrote: "The Großstadt should contain the economy of the family as much as the economy of the city, to correspond perfectly to mod-

ern needs and to be a point of crystallization of interests directed toward an international economy." Internal specialization and internationalism are traits characteristic of the big city, that alone, in Scheffler's view, "can be the location where the struggle for a new architecture can be waged in all its forms."[69] The very practice of Mies van der Rohe brought him face to face with this disjunction between the dense center, where he designed his office buildings, and the residential area on the western periphery, where he designed his first villas. Immersed in contemporary analyses of American cities,[70] Mies compared the German concerns to the *Plan Voisin*, which Le Corbusier developed for Paris in 1925. Essentially, he reproached the Parisian architect for dealing only with the "problem of the form of metropolises": "Le Corbusier's plans can only be understood from the Parisian point of view. Paris is, on account of its historical development, a city of representation."[71]

It was as if Mies van der Rohe compared Le Corbusier's approach to an expression of an out-of-sync civilization that could be contrasted to the culture.[72] Mies seemed to speak for the interests of capitalism overall, to introduce an idea of control, and not for particular projects. Unlike Hilberseimer, he did not formulate a project to fix Berlin, no doubt because he recognized the value of the city as a fixed social capital… Nationwide in Germany, he deplored the absence of forethought, stressing the advantage of the experiment in regional planning that had been undertaken in the Ruhr.[73] In Bruno Taut's projects for the city of Magdeburg, Mies saw an alternative to the urbanism of representation in the *Plan Voisin*. In Taut's plan "one does not find anything fantastic or arbitrary. It has been designed in response to the landscape, the traffic, and with respect for the people that have to live and work there." For Mies it was "just because form was not striven for" that "this plan has obtained its significant and characteristic form."[74] It was also because of "the dominance of economic power over us" that a planning principle could be instituted, which would "lead to an organic form for our cities."[75] But, in 1930, lacking any opportunity to put his ideas into practice in the big city, Mies van der Rohe responded to an invitation from the academic world.

BAUHAUS

4. FROM THE BAUHAUS TO THE THIRD REICH (1930–38)

Opposite page:
Mies van der Rohe
reviewing student
drawings at the Dessau
Bauhaus, 1931.

Above:
Competition project for a
memorial inside Karl
Friedrich Schinkel's Neue
Wache, Berlin, 1930
(autograph, Mies van der
Rohe Archive, Museum of
Modern Art, New York).

Mies van der Rohe's attitude in the first months of the Nazi regime led Sybil Moholy-Nagy, thirty years later, to consider him a "traitor."[1] Ise Gropius reproached him for supposedly supporting the régime, forgetting the efforts that Walter Gropius made to stay in Germany.[2] What really was the relationship between Mies's career and German politics during the decade before his flight from Europe? The directorship of the Bauhaus, held by Walter Gropius since its foundation in Weimar in 1919, was first offered to Mies in 1928, and in the end was taken by Hannes Meyer. Two years later, after Meyer had been driven from the post for political reasons,[3] Mies accepted the renewed offer from Mayor Fritz Hesse of Dessau and from Gropius, who told him, "The school will break to pieces if you don't take it."[4] As it happens, philanthropic reasons seem to have counted for less than material ones, so slim were the economic prospects for Mies's practice: Germany had been stricken by economic crisis; his work in Barcelona and Brno was finished; and his competition entries failed to yield results. He was appointed for a five-year term on 5 August 1930.

The first encounter between Mies and his students was a disaster. The director called in the police to control the left-wing students, who were seething with resentment at the eviction of Meyer. Twenty of them were expelled. However, in a way Mies was only continuing

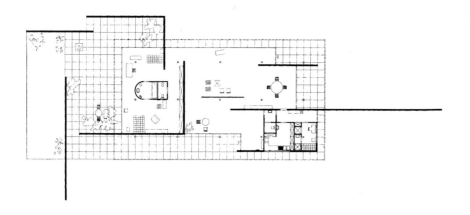

At left:
House for a Childless
Couple at the Berlin
Building Exposition,
Berlin, 1931, plan.

Opposite page, top left:
House for a Childless
Couple at the Berlin
Building Exposition,
axonometric (autograph,
Mies van der Rohe Archive,
Museum of Modern Art,
New York).

the policies of his predecessor. Meyer had initiated a process intended to make the Bauhaus a true school of architecture. Mies pursued this aim by giving more weight to the teaching of Ludwig Hilberseimer, whom Meyer had enlisted to teach urban planning,[5] and of the photographer Walter Peterhans. He assigned the textile studio to Lilly Reich, to whom he also committed a large part of the school's administration. He emphasized the distinction between workshop activity and instruction within the Bauhaus in order to concentrate on what constituted his first experience of teaching.[6]

The assignments that he gave to the students were limited in their scope. In particular he would require them to design courtyard houses, abandoning the collective housing projects of the Meyer era and urging them to develop their designs through a long succession of

sketches – up to a hundred of them – before making the finished drawings. The style of his corrections was often curt. As the American Bauhaus architect Howard Dearstyne recalled, the Miesian leitmotiv was "Try it again!"[7] Gradually distancing himself from the legacy of Gropius and Meyer, he limited the scale and the complexity of acceptable projects, introducing into the Bauhaus studios techniques similar to those used in his own firm. Mies would defend himself his whole life for having been an "architect of the Bauhaus," rejecting this label that applied to only three years of his life.[8]

It was also in 1930 that he met Philip Johnson, who arrived in Berlin with his mother, his sister, and his Cord convertible. The American dandy assiduously sought out the company of Mies and Lilly Reich, inviting them to picnics and commissioning the former to refurbish his

apartment at 24 West Fifty-second Street, New York. Mies was in raptures over the rationality of the floor plans of the apartment building and designed for the two-room apartment a fully demountable system of tables and shelves that could be transported across the Atlantic; to these he added a selection of chairs from Barcelona and Brno.[9] Upon his return to the U.S., Johnson embarked on preparations for an architecture exhibition at the Museum of Modern Art. He planned to entrust the exhibition design to Mies, who would also design a show house at the same time. In fact, Johnson's apartment was practically Mies's only commission in 1930, as he did not win the competition for the installation of a war memorial in the Neue Wache building, built by Karl Friedrich Schinkel on Unter den Linden. Simply entitled Raum (Space), his design defined a large volume with Tinos marble-clad walls, empty except for a thick black horizontal slab in the center

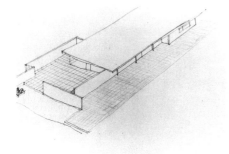

At right and bottom:
House for a Childless
Couple at the Berlin
Building Exposition,
interior view.

of the floor. His abstract approach offered a contrast to the customary rhetoric of commemorative monuments. In the end, the project would be built by Heinrich Tessenow. Also in 1918, Mies failed to secure the commission for the design of a golf clubhouse in Krefeld, to be inserted into an open landscape, where it would have formed a kind of belvedere.[10]

During these years, as the political atmosphere became more oppressive, Mies achieved his biggest success at the Building Exposition (Bauausstellung) in Berlin in 1931, which was held in a large exhibition hall. Mies, in charge of the section on contemporary dwellings, recruited the other participants, including Luckhardt, Häring, Gropius, Hilberseimer, and Lilly Reich.[11] He himself designed a "real construction project," a one-story house for a couple without children. Here, the evolution of the theme of the Barcelona Pavilion can be appre-

ciated in direct relation to the housing theme.[12] The regular arrangement of metal columns recalled the 1929 pavilion, but the walls that extended beyond the flat roof, opening out the internal space, were more reminiscent of the Brick Country House. The onyx partition also reappeared, but in the cylindrical form of the wooden screen in the Tugendhat House. One of the walls enclosing the dining corner was made of glass and could slide down into the floor, like the windows in Brno and in the Henke House expansion, which Mies had completed the previous year in Essen. There was no door between the living space and the two sleeping areas, which were separated by the block of the bathroom. The smaller of these bedrooms looked out over an ornamental pool, bordered by a statue by Kolbe. This ephemeral

building did not go unnoticed, and the American historian Henry-Russell Hitchcock noted that it "stands out like that of Schinkel in old Berlin."[13] Lilly Reich's house for a couple without children, in a more compact L shape, was connected to Mies's house by a courtyard and used the same furniture. Reich also fitted out an apartment in the collective building on pilotis which dominated the exhibition.

Shortly after this exhibition, Mies was invited by Herbert Gericke, the director of the German Academy in Rome, to take part in a competition to design the house he intended to build in Berlin-Wannsee. The design recalls the outline of the Brno house, certain elements of the golf clubhouse, and especially, in the development of its ramifications from a central core, the

projects of the early 1920s. The relationship with nature was fundamental: the whole living area, surrounded by floor-to-ceiling glass, was dominated by the landscape of the lake. Considered alongside this spacious and luxurious project, the one that Mies designed for the printer and art collector Karl Lemke on another lakeside site, on the shore of the Obersee in the Hohenschönhausen district of Berlin, is pale by comparison. After a series of designs involving almost completely enclosed variations around a courtyard, the Lemke House was actually built in 1932-33, the only completed project in a long series of designs for courtyard houses. Moreover, it remains practically intact today.[14]

FROM THE BAUHAUS TO THE THIRD REICH (1930–38)

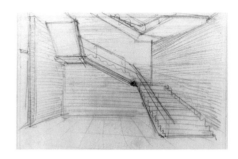

Factory for the Vereinigte
Seidenwebereien AG,
Krefeld, 1931–35, sketch of
the staircase (autograph,
Mies van der Rohe Archive,
Museum of Modern Art,
New York).

Mies and the National Socialists

Contemporaneous with this very modest work, the only building of any size that Mies succeeded in building was the Verseidag factory for hat linings at Krefeld, designed for his friends Lange and Esters. In 1930 he had received the commission for the dyeing works, which he carried out in two parts between 1931 and I935, combining a rigidly rectilinear slab with a low structure roofed by north lights. The steel staircase, wedged in the angle of the walls, constructed later by the research office of the factory, anticipated the solutions used ten years later at IIT.[15] The appearance of the building is similar to that of the Bauhaus in Dessau, but also to the apartment building in Stuttgart. In 1932, for the necktie manufacturer Heusgen, a friend of the Langes, Mies designed a house, since forgotten, whose realization partially followed his plans. It extended the principle of the Exhibition House of 1931.[16]

But in the meantime, the Bauhaus situation had deteriorated. On 22 August 1932, the school was expelled from Dessau. The town council, dominated by the Nazis, had called in the spokesman for the conservatives, the traditionalist architect Paul Schultze-Naumburg, to appraise the students' work. Mies agreed to confront Schultze-Naumburg publicly, convinced that he would succeed in convincing the Nazis of the apolitical nature of modern architecture.[17] He also began to prepare for his survival under a future regime dominated by the Nazis. When the Bauhaus reopened in Berlin-Steglitz on 25 October 1932, its status was no longer that of a public school, as it had been in Dessau, but of a private establishment owned by Mies, who advanced the 27,000 German marks needed to convert an old telephone factory, a building "less pretentious" and "much better," he would say, than the one by Gropius. In the move, he succeeded in eliminating student opposition to himself.[18]

It would not be long, in the words of Mies himself, recorded by a *Bauhausler*, before the "iron hand" that held Germany in its grip would crush the Bauhaus.[19] On 11 April 1933, little more than a month after the electoral victory of the Nazis, the police raided the Steglitz Bauhaus, on the pretext of a complaint from the authorities at Dessau. The students were taken in for questioning and the building was sealed, but Mies had already evacuated the archives to Switzerland.[20] Against the advice of Reich and Hilberseimer, he went to plead with Alfred Rosenberg, whose Nazi party newspaper, the *Völkischer Beobachter*, had upheld the action of Schultze-Naumburg, and who was then in rivalry with Joseph Goebbels for control of cultural policy. But this visit proved unproductive.

Under pressure from right-wing students, led by Helmut Heide, Mies went to the Gestapo in Berlin and met its leader, Rudolph Diels, at the end of May. Diels warned him about Kandinsky, but expressed no objection to the reopening of the school. The Dessau Nazis, who had launched the proceedings, were apparently placated. But on 20 July, when Mies learned of the conditions imposed by the regime for the reopening of the Bauhaus – notably the dismissal of Hilberseimer and Kandinsky – the faculty rejected the offer. In order not to leave this task to the Nazis, Mies said he would "himself shut down" the Bauhaus.[21]

Factory for the Vereinigte Seidenwebereien AG, general view. Only the two lower levels on the left were built by Mies.

The Nazi policy of *Gleichschaltung* (or bringing to heel) also applied to the Prussian Academy of Fine Arts, to which Mies had been admitted in 1931 in an attempt to co-opt the Modernists. The writer Heinrich Mann and the painter Käthe Kollwitz were forced out on 15 February 1933. The novelist Alfred Döblin and the urbanist Martin Wagner resigned in protest, but Mies remained. On 1 July 1933, the academy questioned Mies about his Aryan credentials. A few days earlier, a meeting of the association of Nazi students had praised the Modernists, including Mies. The exhibition that they had organized was closed. But on 1 September, at the Kulturtagung (Culture Session of the Party's Congress), Hitler combined a fierce criticism of the radical artistic tendencies that had flowered in the Weimar Republic with a degree of acceptance of what was called "a functionalism of crystalline clarity."[22] Mies's professional situation was not in fact desperate: in July he had been one of six finalists in the competition for the Reichsbank headquarters; in the autumn he took part in the German presentation at the Triennale in Milan, from which Gropius and Mendelsohn were excluded.

According to Philip Johnson, "There is only one man whom even the young men can defend and that is Mies van der Rohe."[23]

In fact, there was indeed no lack of support for the Modernists. Goebbels gave their champion, Hans Weidemann, important duties at the Ministry of Propaganda, and he pressed Mies to design an exhibition entitled "Deutsches Volk – Deutsche Arbeit" (German Nation – German Labour) and to be on the panel judging the young artists' competition that he planned to launch with the regime's leisure-activity organization, Kraft durch Freude (Strength Through Joy). "Deutsches Volk – Deutsche Arbeit" opened on 21 April 1934. Next to Gropius's contribution, Mies presented a section on mines, marked by the construction of two robust walls of coal and salt, delicately drawn – which Hitler disliked, according to Albert Speer.[24] The situation was very unstable. Alfred Rosenberg took control of the Kraft durch Freude and sidelined Weidemann, while Hitler replaced the president of the Reichsbank, Hans Luther, with Hjalmar Schacht and canceled the competition.

These setbacks coincided with new attempts by Mies to bring himself closer to the regime. He joined the Reichskulturkammer (Reich Chamber of Culture) and followed Schultze-Naumburg in signing a motion of support for the Führer on the occasion of the referendum of 19 August 1934,[25] no doubt because he feared becoming a "second-class German," to quote Ivano Panaggi, who wondered whether this was "necessity or ambition."[26] Still full of illusions, Gropius himself had pondered, five months earlier, the risks of "throw[ing] overboard the new architecture and its spiritual leaders, when there is nothing to replace them."[27] In January 1934 Gropius took part in the competition for the Haus der Arbeit (House of Labor), and later in the year he left Germany. Mies remained and gave another of his minimalist indications of support for the regime by joining the Volkswohlfahrt (People's Welfare) on 30 August. His position was then considered to be secure by foreign observers. The American George Nelson supposed, not without some naïveté, that he was the only Modernist to have any future;[28] but material – and financial – reality was more precarious.

"Deutsches Volk – Deutsche Arbeit" exhibition, Berlin, 1934, section on mining, drawing by Sergius Ruegenberg. An early version of Mies' walls is visible in the back.

Mies's great hope in the years 1933-34 had been to design the Reichsbank headquarters on a trapezoidal site bordering the Spree. He envisioned a large building consisting of a main core and three perpendicular wings whose side walls faced the Spree. Unlike the neighboring buildings, its smooth eight-story front façade traced a shallow curve similar to that of the Schocken department store, built by Mendelsohn in Chemnitz in 1929. At the rear, the building presented a symmetrical composition of three wings to the River Spree. It retained the autonomy of the projects of the early 1920s, but in a more monumental and rigorous vein.[29] The sketch for the German Pavilion at the 1935 exhibition in Brussels is closer to Mies's earlier approach. Presented by Mies as a representation of the "essence of German labor" and surmounted by a Teutonic eagle of modest size, the project is in no way a renunciation of the principles of Barcelona; on the contrary, it extends them on a square plan within an opaque enclosure wall. The contradiction between the fluidity of the forms conceived since Barcelona and the monumental requirements of the program, which led to a redis-covery of the solutions employed for the Neue Wache, is fairly clear in the extant drawings.[30] Following Hitler's intervention, it was the monumental project by Ludwig Ruff that was chosen – before Germany finally withdrew altogether from the exhibition.[31] A more concrete outrage was the demolition of the monument to Rosa Luxemburg and Karl Liebknecht, carried out on 9 January 1935.[32]

In the 1930s, Mies van der Rohe moved away from the model of the vertical city, and his more organic direction led him to become interested in other areas, such as the spatial definition of highways, whose program had been discussed since the early 1920s. He spoke on the question of landscape in the pages of the publication of *HaFraBA*, an organization created under Weimar to build the Hamburg-Frankfurt-Basel highway in the years before the Nazi program of 1933.[33] But his project for a standardized Autobahn service station never saw the light of day.

Mies's preoccupation with courtyard houses at this time, no doubt in response to a commission from Margarete Hubbe, could pass for a metaphor of the narrowing of his professional space, his only remaining resources being royalties on his furniture. (His daughter Georgia remembers his diet at the time consisting exclusively of spinach and eggs.[34]) As he developed ideas on the courtyard-house theme, first conceived at the Bauhaus with the Exhibition House of 1931, his sketches introduced variations in the proportions of roofed parts and courtyards and in the scale of the living area. This series was dominated by the House with Three Courts, for which he presented a perspective drawing in which a Braque reproduction indicated the material of a wall, and by a house with curved walls, in which the spatial tensions were the strongest. The pattern was now defined by blind enclosing walls, glass screens and slim metal columns, often in rectangular groupings. These houses make it possible to imagine a horizontal landscape of residential areas very different from the dense city, but also from the model neighborhoods of Weimar Germany, as Ludwig Hilberseimer defined them in his contemporaneous projects.

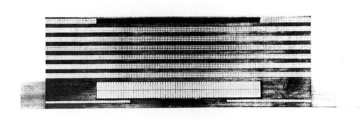

To this series were added two projects intended
for real sites, neither of which was built. In 1935
Mies designed for Margarete Hubbe, a member of the Deutsche Werkbund and a friend
of Nolde, a house on the banks of the Elbe in
Magdeburg, in which he repeated the theme
of the courtyard houses in order, he said, to
avoid a view which was "boring, not to say
annoying, towards the south." He explored
innumerable variations for a T-shaped building
inside an enclosing wall opening toward the
river. The house was not built, and the plot was
sold.[35] The second project was for the Langes,
who commissioned a house for their son Ulrich,
in Krefeld. In the first version, the single-story
house was divided into two wings, one of them
for services; later these were integrated into
a single T shape inside a brick wall. The focal
point of the living area was a sinuous wall, a
rather new element in Mies's vocabulary. But
the authorities rejected this project as "un-
German," although they then offered to approve
it if it was surrounded by an earthen wall; Mies
refused, thus forfeiting the only tangible commission he had at the time.

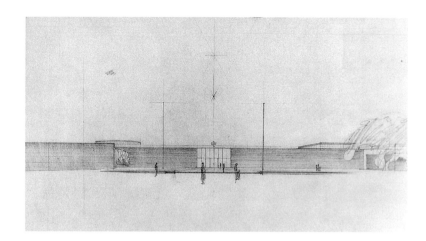

At left:
Competition project for the
German Pavilion at the
1935 International
Exhibition, Brussels, 1934,
elevation (autograph,
Mies van der Rohe Archive,
Museum of Modern Art,
New York).

Opposite page, left:
Study for a courtyard house
with garage, 1934.

Opposite page, right:
Study for a group of three
courtyard houses, 1938
(autograph, Mies van der
Rohe Archive, Museum of
Modern Art, New York).

Thanks to the active admiration of Philip Johnson, who had even suggested recruiting American students for the Dessau Bauhaus,[36] Mies had been one of the stars of the 1932 exhibition of modern architecture at the Museum of Modern Art, which traveled widely in the United States.[37] An attempt by Johnson to mount an exhibition by Mies's pupils failed owing to Mies's own reservations, but there were numerous invitations luring him across the Atlantic.[38] A first invitation to teach at Mills College in Oakland reached him in December 1935. After a month he turned it down, no doubt because of the new hopes aroused by the preparation of the German Textile Exhibition of 1937, which he had been asked to organize.

Celebrating his fiftieth birthday on 27 March 1936, Mies discussed with his friends an invitation from the Armour Institute in Chicago, and this time he left the door open.[39] On 20 June 1936, Alfred H. Barr, the director of the Museum of Modern Art, suggested that Mies work on the project for the museum building, as he did with Gropius and Oud.[40] In August,

Mies met Joseph Hudnut, the dean of Harvard, who had previously begun to modernize the curriculum of Columbia University according to a Miesian line by recruiting the former Bauhaus members Jan Ruhtenberg and William Turk Priestley.[41] In the end, Hudnut invited Gropius to Harvard, while Barr pursued the idea of giving the museum project to Mies, whose close friends and family pressed him daily to leave Germany, where the situation was becoming more and more difficult.

At the last moment the Textile Exhibition was placed under the patronage of Hermann Göring, who relieved Mies of his responsibilities and transferred them to Ernst Sagebiel, the architect of Tempelhof Airport. On 8 July 1937, the president of the academy asked Mies to hand in his resignation, which he did on the 19th. Assured of the probability of an American commission, he arrived in New York on 20 August.

In April 1938 House and Garden asked Mies to do a project on the theme of "the house of tomorrow."[42] But the American commission

that he pursued was the one for a vacation house in Wilson, west of Jackson Hole, Wyoming. It was intended for Stanley Burnet Resor, president of the Walter Thompson Co. advertising agency, and his wife, Helen Landsdowne, a trustee of the Museum of Modern Art, who was advised by Barr to approach Mies after a first submission from Philip Goodwin. Landsdowne, a copywriter, had put together a collection of works by European artists, and she was interested in modern architecture.[43] In 1937 Mies negotiated the terms of his contract with Resor.

Several weeks later, immediately upon his arrival in the United States, Mies went to Wyoming to see the site and the existing buildings, set in the foothills of the Grand Tetons. Passing through Chicago en route to and from Wyoming, he negotiated for the directorship of the Armour Institute's School of Architecture. He was shown around Chicago by John Barney Rodgers and two former pupils of the Bauhaus, Bertrand Goldberg and William Priestley, and he traveled to Taliesin, Wisconsin, to meet Frank

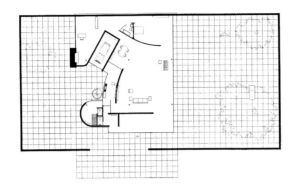

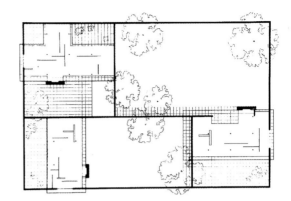

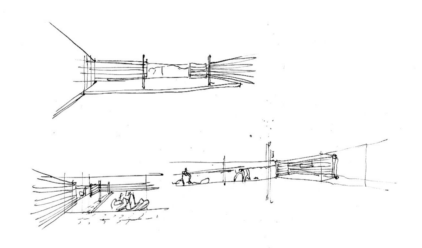

Lloyd Wright, who brought him to the construction site of the Johnson Wax offices in
Racine. Mies was so impressed by this visit
that he exclaimed: "Freedom! This is a king-
dom!"[44] He returned to Germany on 5 April
1938, after having finalized the Resor project.

In the design phase, which lasted until 1939,
Mies had to take into account the first structure and the foundations by Goodwin, which
had already been dug. Onto this Mies projected
his own ideas, formulated in the sketches of
1934, for a Glass House on a Hill. A large rectangle open in the center and set above Mill
Creek, the house connected a metal skeleton, whose section was identical to those in
Barcelona and Brno, and foundations of stone,
a material that was also used for the chim-
ney, the focal point of this project with rustic
accents. Mies used both large windows and
panels of cypress plywood manufactured in
America.

The courtyard houses were forgotten, and the
landscape in which the house was inscribed

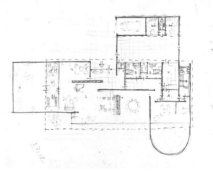

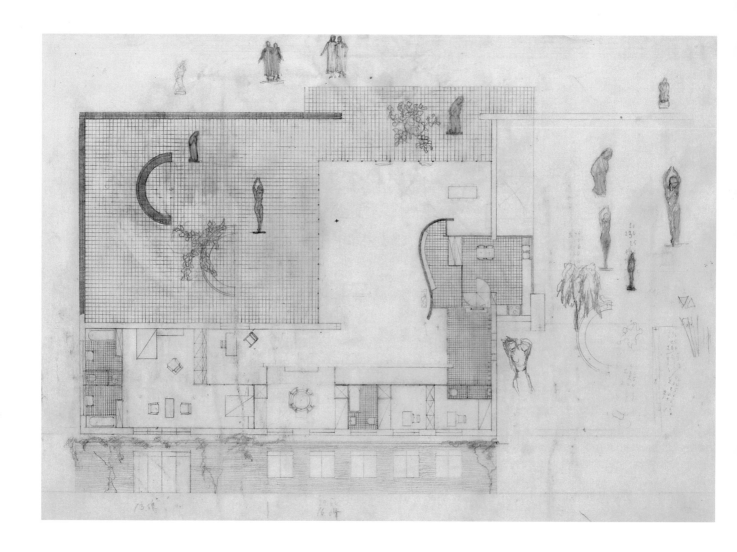

was an immense and distant horizon, hardly broken by the verticals of the posts and in which the framing was created by the partitions. This project, which set up a large frame around the view of the mountainous expanses, could not but bring to mind the adventures of Winnetou, published in little paperback volumes by Karl May; these were the reading matter for all little Germans at the turn of the century.[45] From this point of view, the Resor project could be considered as an instance

of acting out, a condensation of the latent vision of a house inscribed in the large spaces that May described, for example, in *The Treasure of the Rocky Mountains*.

Nostalgic for a friend left behind in Europe, Mies pasted onto one of the perspective montages, against the wide open spaces of the West, a reproduction of Paul Klee's painting *Bunte Mahlzeit* (1928), which Helen Resor had just acquired.[46] In 1938 he himself began to

build a collection of Klee's works through the Berlin dealer Karl Nierendorf, an émigré like Mies.[47] But during his return trip to Germany, Mies received a message from Stanley Resor telling him of the postponement of the project, which was deemed too expensive.[48] He took up the design again after returning to the United States, developing a more radical single-story version, which was finally abandoned during the war.

Opposite page:
Project for the Ulrich Lange
House, Krefeld, 1935,
furnished plan with figures
(autograph, Mies van der
Rohe Archive, Museum of
Modern Art, New York).

Above:
Project for the Stanley
Resor House, Jackson Hole,
Wyoming, 1937-38,
photomontage of the
interior with Paul Klee's
painting *Bunte Mahlzeit*
(Mies van der Rohe Archive,
Museum of Modern Art,
New York).

Mies left his country for good after spending several weeks on the final expression of confidence from Lange – a design for an administrative building for Verseidag, a project in which he returned to the trapezoidal configuration of the Reichsbank and explored a new principle of articulation of the main part of buildings by vertical circulations placed in autonomous volumes. The idea of a project for a Faculty of Law in Ankara did not go forward, and the Gestapo exerted increasing pressure.

According to Georgia van der Rohe, it was an interview during which Rosenberg is said to have asked Mies to be the figurehead for Hitler's projects, which led Mies to emigrate without delay.[49] Mies then decided to accept the invitation of the Armour Institute.[50] He left behind him his family and Lilly Reich, who succeeded in conveying a large part of the firm's archive to a place of safety.

CHICAGO

5. CHICAGO AND AMERICAN PARADIGMS (1938–56)

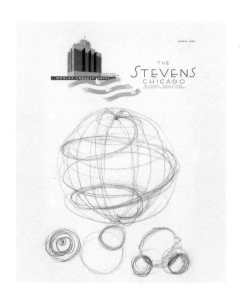

Mies and the Illinois Institute of Technology

In 1937 Frank Lloyd Wright received Mies van der Rohe with more warmth than he had received any other European who had come to pay him homage – except perhaps Erich Mendelsohn in 1924. Wright expressed his admiration for work in which he recognized that he himself had been an inspiration. In addition, Wright agreed to introduce Mies on 18 October 1938, during a ceremonial dinner celebrating the German architect's nomination to the directorship of the Armour Institute's School of Architecture. This was partly in order to lay claim to his paternity, as he said in his personal account of the soirée, which, incidentally, he left abruptly:[1]

"Ladies and gentlemen, I give you Mies van der Rohe. But for me there would have been no Mies – certainly none here tonight. I admire him as an architect and respect and love him as a man. Armour Institute, *I* give you my Mies van der Rohe. You treat him well and love him as I do. He will reward you."[2]

A month later, Mies wrote what was doubtless one of his last theoretical texts of any importance; in the American period his utterances became laconic and often repetitive in the

Opposite page:
Crown Hall,
Illinois Institute of
Technology, Chicago,
1950–56, view of the
entrance.

Above:
Study of spheres on
letterhead from the
Stevens Hotel,
note for teaching,
Chicago, 1940–41.

extreme, except when he let himself go by evoking his memories. In this text he insisted that alongside "practical objectives," the teaching of architecture should focus on the importance of values "anchored in the spiritual nature of man." He alluded to what could be learned from the study of "primitive" structures or works in brick. Concluding with the aphorism of Saint Augustine, "Beauty is the splendor of Truth," which was constantly on his lips thereafter, he assembled the fruits of his reading of Simmel, Dessauer, and Guardini into a definitive credo.

"We expect nothing from materials in themselves, but only from the right use of them. Even the new materials give us no superiority. Each material is only worth what we make of it.

In the same way that we learn about materials, we learn about our goals. We want to analyze them clearly. We want to know what they contain and what distinguishes a building for living in from other kinds of buildings.

We want to know what it can be, what it must be, and what it should be.

We want, therefore, to learn its essence.

We shall examine one by one every functions o a building, work out its character, and make it a basis for design.

Just as we acquainted ourselves with materials and just as we must understand the nature of goals, we must also learn about the spiritual position in which we stand.

No cultural activity is possible otherwise; for also in these matters we must know what is, because we are dependent on the spirit of our time.

Therefore we must come to understand the carrying and driving forces of our time. We must analyze their structure from the points of view of the material, the functional, and the spiritual.

We must make clear in what respects our epoch is similar to earlier ones and in what respects it differs."[3]

Thanks to his contacts in New York, Mies was familiar with the changing situation in American architecture schools, as is seen in the program that he presented to the president of the Armour Institute, Henry Townley Heald, on 10 December, 1937.[4] In his preamble, Mies referred to the goal of "training men who create organic architecture," revealing the effect produced on him by his meeting with Frank Lloyd Wright, whose work he had long known. The latter would show him, like a kind of "organic capitalism," his design for Broadacre City, extending an architectural term to the social project, which Mies had discovered in his prior reading on America.[5] His perception of the organic dimension of architecture was of a different order. It rested notably on his reading of Francé,[6] as well as on the comparisons between the plants photographed by Karl Blossfeldt and the skyscrapers published by

Werner Lindner in *Bauten der Technik*. But the Broadacre City project interested him all the more because it was receptive to the themes of deurbanization. Detlef Mertins remarked that Mies had brought from Germany a copy of Bruno Taut's *Dissolution of Cities* and Kropotkin's books on this theme.[7]

With the help of Rodgers and his colleagues from Dessau and Berlin – the urbanist Ludwig Hilberseimer and the photographer Walter Peterhans – Mies totally reconstructed the curriculum at the Armour Institute; for the first three years he taught the first semesters himself, placing the emphasis almost exclusively on construction and drawing:[8]

"First we taught them how to draw. That is the goal of the first year. And they learn how to draw. Then we taught them to build in stone, in brick, in wood, and made them learn something about engineering. We talked about concrete and steel. Then we taught them something about functions of buildings, and in the second year we tried to teach them a sense of proportion and a sense of space. And only in the last year did we come to a group of buildings... We don't teach them solutions, we teach them a way to solve problems."[9]

To encourage the consideration of the concrete issues of building, Mies suggested recruiting a carpenter and a mason and creating a laboratory for full-scale experimentation. Pro-

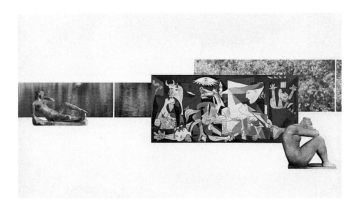

gressively integrating his former students into a closed school, whose principles they would export into other universities, he guided his American students (who seem to have grown very tired of drawing endless brick walls) more and more toward two fundamental building types: the courtyard house and the steel-framed tower.[10] Another frequent assignment was the design of a building that would have first a steel structure and then a wooden structure but would otherwise be identical.

For the first few months, Mies lived at the Blackstone Hotel, his Klee canvases stowed under his bed. On New Year's Eve in 1940 he met Lora Marx, who had been trained as a sculptor at Cranbrook Academy and who would help to bring him closer to the world of art.[11] His life became firmly rooted in the United States, and he obtained citizenship in 1944. With the outbreak and spread of the war, Mies turned his back on Germany. As the Allies unleashed a massive bombing campaign in Germany, he even accepted the idea that his country would be destroyed, if that was, as he said, the price for ridding the world of an "animal like Hitler."[12] His horizons were limited to Chicago, where culture and design were determined by a few dozen elite families, a situation that enabled him to reflect and act as never before. In 1939 Frank Lloyd Wright, who had suffered such hostility from a city that he nevertheless considered to be "the great-

est and most nearly beautiful city in our young nation,"[13] paid tribute to the willingness of its industrialists to accept new forms:
"To say that 'business' will someday know good architecture suited to its purpose, before art, science and education are able to recognize it, may be astonishing but, I believe, nevertheless, true… The manufacturer, world over, in this has been a leader. Perhaps this is because "culture," in quotation marks, had no place for it but in the final decisions of business – the mind of the superior businessman was more free than the pseudocultural academic to accept the change that is progress."[14]

The alliance between industrialists and businessmen had been at the origins of the First Chicago School. But Mies was not intimidated by the architecture of Louis Sullivan and the other members of the Chicago School. Later he rejected any suggestion that it had influenced him. "I really don't know the Chicago School," he declared, claiming that he had not really visited much of Chicago and had not been at all transformed by the experience of living in that city, whose affinities with Berlin were emphasized by a number of observers at the turn of the century.[15] Mies admitted no more than a vague interest in H. H. Richardson's Marshall Field wholesale store, demolished in 1935.

Two projects marked the turning point between Mies's concerns of the 1930s and his new American perspective. In 1942, at the request of *Architectural Forum* magazine and within the context of a remarkable series of issues preparing for the postwar period and devoted to the "new buildings of 194X," Mies developed theoretical designs for a Museum for a Small City.[16] Extending the work done with one of his students at the Illinois Institute of Technology, George Danforth, Mies returned to the play of horizontal and vertical planes within the rooms, and to the enclosure wall. His design is a kind of large box and, inside it, partitions that are not load-bearing receive the paintings. An auditorium plays with these planes. The columns virtually disappear under the floating roof, as do any references to the distant landscape (which was still an important feature of the Resor House). The interplay of partitions and isolated objects is illustrated by a collage, whose most striking feature is a reproduction of Picasso's *Guernica*, which alluded to the savagery of the Nazi war. (The painting had been shown in Chicago in 1939-40.[17]) In 1945 Philip Johnson suggested to Mies that he design a pavilion to present Picasso's painting in the garden of the Museum of Modern Art.[18]

The Concert Hall, designed at the same time, was also depicted in a collage, in which the horizontal and vertical planes are no longer

defined by low courtyard walls, or even by mountainous horizons. The photograph of a large metal envelope in which the walls of the room were arranged depicts the trusses of the frame of the assembly hall of the Glenn Martin Bomber factory, built in 1937 in Middle River, Maryland, by Albert Kahn, the architect of Ford and General Motors.[19] Along with the Museum for a Small City, this project inaugurated Mies's American building work and can also be interpreted as the conclusion of the relationship, begun twenty years earlier, with the industrial architecture of the United States.[20] At the same time, the image of the Galerie des Machines (Gallery of Machines) from the 1889 Paris exhibition, reproduced by Sigfried Giedion in 1928, seems to have haunted Mies.[21] This connection might be read as support for the American war effort. Rather, it shows the imprint of the great engineering works as disseminated in the publications of the Werkbund before 1914; Mies discovered their full range – real as much as metaphoric – as well as the potential for his own work.

Chicago was undoubtedly one place where the alliance between industrialists and architects, so fervently demanded by the Werkbund, stood out very clearly. After a brief moment of optimism that was embodied, in the midst of the Depression, by the 1933-34 exhibition "A Century of Progress," the influx of European émigrés was looked upon favorably by the president of the Container Corporation of America, Walter Paul Paepke, who supported the establishment in September 1937 of the New Bauhaus by László Moholy-Nagy.[22] Mies himself enjoyed the support both of Wright and of the profession at large, manifested in the person of Holabird, but it was at IIT that he discovered the industrial world. The Illinois Institute of Technology (IIT) was created in 1940 from the merger of the Armour Institute and Lewis College. Upon his arrival, which coincided with the reorganization of the Armour Institute's School of Architecture, Mies worked with Ludwig Hilberseimer on a site plan for its new campus.

After designing this first plan in 1939-40, Mies developed a second one in 1941. The new plan called for the clearance and redevelopment of six blocks (twenty-five hectares) in the insalubrious districts of the Near South Side, called the "Black Belt," where the brick building of the Armour Institute had stood since 1901, and from which the black population was to be expelled. A total of sixty square kilometers of slums were razed in this area under the Master Plan of Residential Land Use, developed in 1943 by the Chicago Plan Commission, which presided over the first large-scale American urban renovation on what was the biggest residential area deemed unhealthy.[23] The president of the institute, Henry T. Heald, who fully backed Mies, was enthralled by the idea of creating a real campus on a site where the expansion of the institution was planned well before his presidency.[24] Heald went as far as refusing a donation that stipulated the construction of a Gothic building. He defended Mies in the face of resistance from the architectural faculty, who were perpetually frus-

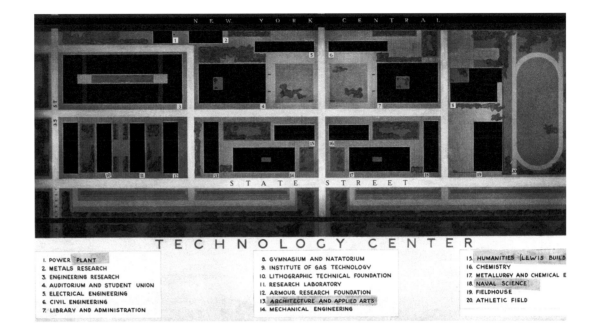

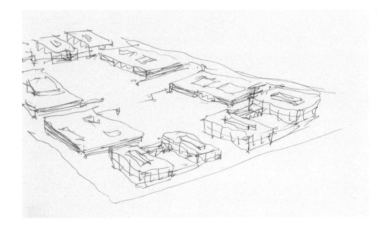

trated in an institution dominated by research centers financed by industry and the military.[25]

The initial plan abandoned the traditional composition developed in 1937 by Holabird and Root and called for the construction of twenty buildings on a rectangular area extending from Thirty-first to Thirty-fifth Streets and aligned with Thirty-third Street. The site was divided into a horizontal grid of twenty-four feet, set according to the common dimension of the classrooms, the drafting rooms, and the laboratories, with the vertical grid going from twelve to twenty-six feet.[26] The first version included a collection of linear buildings inserted in parallel on three superblocks, achieved by suppressing of one of the through streets. The individual elements, which are auditoriums, are autonomous compared with the orthogonal volumes of the main buildings, according to a principle proposed by Hilberseimer. The use of pilotis made it possible to see across the ground floors and unified the development in a promenade based on a cinematographic vision.[27]

In late 1940, the creation of the Illinois Institute of Technology led to a new program for a campus and its 2,500 students. Mies would later say that he found himself facing "the biggest decision that [he] ever had to make."[28] He simplified his project by returning the division into six blocks, on which he arranged three types of rectilinear buildings: large unitary volumes, classrooms on four levels, and multiuse buildings bringing together several program elements. The pilotis idea was abandoned. Only a portion of this plan, presented as a photo-

At right and left:
Fritz Schupp, Martin
Kremmer, Zeche Zollverein,
Essen, 1932, details of the
façade.

montage that imposed its prismatic order on the seemingly devastated background of the existing areas, would be built. Although difficult to perceive, Mies's sensitivity to this urban framework is nevertheless real, as noted by Rem Koolhaas, for whom "Mies without context is like a fish out of water."[29] Beyond taking into account the scales of neighboring buildings, the work undertaken at Mies's request by the landscape architect Alfred Caldwell, who liked to use native vegetation, helped to anchor the campus in the vision of a modernized regional landscape.

In all, Mies built twenty buildings on the east side of the campus, dedicated to teaching, research, housing, and facilities such as the power station and the chapel. He implemented a scheme that Joseph Rykwert described in 1949 as "slick, lucid," and "sickening." The critic condemned the "violent change of attitude" that had come over Mies since the 1930s.[30]

Before IIT abruptly ended his architectural assignment upon his retirement from the school in 1958, he worked mostly with Chicago architectural firms that dealt with technical design and problems of fluid engineering, which were particularly significant here. IIT managed to construct only two buildings before 1945; but after the war, having become extremely prosperous thanks to subsidized industrial and military research, it began work on others one by one. The photographs depict an ensemble of industrial buildings similar to those built by Erich Mendelsohn in the Weimar Republic and especially to those by Fritz Schupp and Martin Kremmer, who in 1932 built the Zeche Zollverein in Essen, few kilometers away from Krefeld. These buildings brought together a structure with welded steel porticos and steel-girdered walls surrounding partitions of brick and glass.[31] But, unlike the buildings in Chicago, these lacked rigor in the construction technique. Herbert Rimpl and Ernst Neufert, mod-

ern architects integrated into Nazi industrial and military policy, built similar structures after 1933. Mies inherited this culture, to which he was exposed during his time at Behrens's firm, but he moved away from it by strictly codifying the use of I or H beams produced by the local steel industry.

Combining brickwork and steel frames in varied configurations, Mies introduced the dimension of time into the whole enterprise, confident that the initial principles would not become obsolete:
"I was not afraid of that. The concept would not become outmoded for two reasons. It is radical and conservative at once. It is radical in accepting the scientific and technological driving and sustaining forces of our time. It has a scientific character, but it is not science. It uses technological means but it is not technology. It is conservative as it is not only concerned with a purpose but also with a

Above:
Metals and Minerals
Research Building, Illinois
Institute of Technology,
Chicago, 1942–43, east
façade.

Overleaf:
Metals and Minerals
Research Building, Illinois
Institute of Technology,
east façade.

meaning, as it is not only concerned with a function but also with an expression. It is conservative as it is based on the eternal laws of architecture: Order, Space, Proportion."[32]

Only nine laboratory and dormitory buildings rely on a concrete skeleton, with brick infill. Elsewhere, Mies propounded his interpretation of the Chicago experiments in steel-frame construction, developing a very precise grammar of steel sheets and profiles. The Metals and Minerals Research Building (1941-43), on the edge of the campus, was the first to be built. It is interesting to note that he had already departed from the newly created modular rule by subtracting a quarter of an inch from the twenty-four-foot grid in order to adjust it to the size of the bricks. Anchored on a high brick base and lit by small windows, the structure recycled used materials and tools,[33] which Mies arranged with a consummate elegance. Its exposed internal structure would be the most-discussed aspect.[34] Its side wall revealed the structure, which links I and H beams according to a principle that Mies's firm described as "Gothic" and compared to a "sausage," as Phyllis Lambert reports.[35]

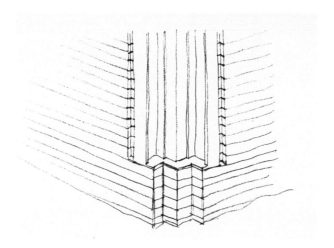

Project for the Library
and Administration
Building, Illinois Institute
of Technology, Chicago,
1944–45, sketch of the
corner (autograph, Mies
van der Rohe Archive,
Museum of Modern Art,
New York).

Alumni Memorial Hall,
Illinois Institute of
Technology, Chicago,
1945–46, view of the
corner.

Afterward, Mies designed highly repetitive buildings, in which the spatial organization hardly varies, and also unique buildings such as the library and administration block, a large rectilinear slab one hundred meters long, with glass panels that would have been the largest in America. This building, which was never built, would have signified on campus the symbolic and actual pre-eminence of reading and study.

Mies also began research on large containers, which would come to term at the Neue Nationalgalerie in Berlin. His building technique was modified with the imposition of fireproofing for certain structural elements, leading Mies to embark on endless questions about the possible variations, notably in the treatment of the angle where the posts and the vertical girders met at the end of the glass and brick panels. The detail developed for the angle of this building would inspire a rigorous series of solutions, this time of a more "classical" nature, for they reproduced the symmetry of the angles of Greek temples.[36]

The first postwar building at IIT was the Alumni Memorial Hall, dedicated to former students who had fallen in the war. For that design, Mies used glass panels opposite smaller, solid wall units. The staircases, tucked in between two brick walls and lit by golden light from the high windows, introduce an air of mystery into the building, where the spirit of Schinkel meets with echoes of the staircases in the Fagus Works by Gropius and Meyer. Moreover, the detailing of the recessed joint between the rolled steel profile that forms the corner of the building and the brickwork of the wall is strongly reminiscent of Schinkel's Altes Museum. It celebrates the external clarity of the metal skeleton; its sturdy base plate emphasizes its firm footing in the ground and the recessed joint expresses its separateness from the brick infill. In this complex array of buildings based on common structural principles, the boiler plant

Alumni Memorial Hall, Illinois Institute of Technology, one of the staircases.

(1949-50) and the chapel (1952) – a rectilinear box sliced into five bays and furnished in the most spartan way, its proportions recalling those of Schinkel's Neue Wache – stand out by their sheer mass and their distinctive treatment. Mies explained his position thus: "I chose an intensive rather than an extensive form to express my conception, simply and honestly, of what a sacred building should be."[37] On the east side of campus Mies also built a series of dormitories in reinforced concrete; these make use of solutions similar to those found in the Promontory Apartments, built in Chicago.[38]

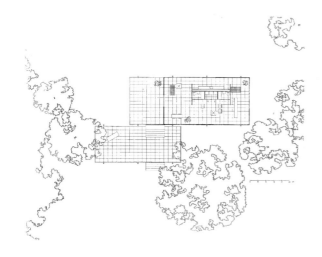

At left:
Edith Farnsworth House,
Plano, Illinois, 1945–50,
plan.

At right:
Edith Farnsworth House,
sketch of a plan with a
circular core.

The Farnsworth House

In 1947 the Museum of Modern Art, which had already contributed much to Mies's popularity in North America, dedicated its first one-man postwar show to him. Developed by the architect himself, the design of the exhibition, where models of his projects and furniture were framed by giant photographic prints, was an extension of his theoretical museum project dating from 1942. On this occasion, Philip Johnson published the first book devoted to Mies, making reference to several of his earliest works, which were not included in the show.[39] In the same context, the courtyard houses researched in the 1930s were, for the first time, presented by Johnson as a coherent sequence of studies.[40]

In 1945 Mies at last rediscovered the domestic scale, when, at a dinner among common friends, he met the kidney specialist Dr. Edith

Farnsworth. Reflecting on their encounter, she declared that she experienced the effect of "a storm, a flood, or other act of God."[41] The initial liking seems to have been mutual, and she visited the firm constantly and asked Mies to design a sort of country refuge on a site bordering the Fox River, eighty kilometers (50 miles) west of Chicago. In the middle of this large wooded plot, four hectares (twenty acres) in area, Mies built his first house after a fifteen-year hiatus from residential work. It is very different in principle from the courtyard houses of the 1930s and from his earlier houses. He was to admit that the "job" had been made "easier" for him because it involved a "single person"[42] and a site surrounded by private land, thus enabling him to adopt a solution very different from the one he would have used in an urban area.

The project was completed without haste, with the model of a first version exhibited at the Museum of Modern Art in 1947. Ground was broken in September 1949, and the work was completed in 1951, under the direct supervision of Mies. He himself executed wash drawings of the two versions, one on the ground and the other raised above it. The latter version was eventually chosen. There are echoes of past projects here: the raised main structure returned to the design of the Concrete Country House and, further back, to Schinkel's podium designs, while the glass walls recall the Tugendhat House and the Resor project. But the continuity stops here: the interpenetration of the internal and external spaces is not controlled or limited by walls, and the confluence of the forest glades takes place inside the glass volume. Never before had Mies placed

At right:
Mies on the site of the
Farnsworth House during
construction.

Overleaf:
Edith Farnsworth House,
exterior view.

the structural columns outside the main volume; this accentuates the impression of levitation.[43]

While eight I-shaped columns are present in the design from the outset (after the idea of four posts was abandoned), the box that they support underwent some variations. At first, the porch was enclosed, as seen in the 1947 model. Then the position of the central core changed. At first tucked to one side, then placed markedly off-center, taking the form of a cylindrical volume, then endowed with a flat partition and a curved partition,[44] it moved toward the axis of symmetry, without ever reaching it. The building's corners are open; all the services run through the core and under the floor. It is a glass box, twenty-eight by seventy-seven feet, with its south face parallel to the river.[45] There is a major transformation in the relationship between the walls and the vertical supports: the unity of the IIT buildings is dispelled, and the columns seem more forceful than the horizontal elements; the whole house seems to have been hoisted into place. However, any sense of effort is belied by the tactile surfaces, the factory polish applied to the steel before painting, and the finesse of the assembly of the floor slabs, carefully chosen by Mies to give the house a mechanically precise finish. Moreover, its relative compactness is a long way from the tentacular outreach of the 1920s designs.

A fragile shelter perched on posts and traversed by the spectacle of the river and the woods, the Farnsworth House has nothing of the solidity of a masonry house. In the face of floods and storms, it offers, as Richard Sennett has

remarked, a "modern expression of the sublime."[46] Indeed, its lightness makes it more like a tea pavilion, a temporary shelter, than a permanent building imposing its ascendancy on its site. Mies perfectly expressed the modesty of this house in its relationship with nature:

"Nature should also live its own life; we should not destroy it with the colors of our houses and interiors. But we should try to bring nature, houses, and human beings together in a higher unity. When you see nature through the glass walls of the Farnsworth House, it gets a deeper meaning than outside. More is asked from nature because it becomes part of a larger whole."[47]

The neutrality of the materials chosen – white enameled steel and Roman travertine defining a beige plane intersected by the diaphragm of the entrance wall – is presented as an expression of just this deference to nature, rather than, as has been suggested, the evocation of a sort of domestic temple, whether Shinto or Greek:

"The Farnsworth House has never been truly understood, I think. I myself have been in this house from morning until evening. Until then I had not known how colorful Nature can be. One must be careful to use neutral tones in interior spaces, for outside one has all sorts of colors. These colors are continually changing completely, and I would like to say that it's simply glorious."[48]

Mies's appreciation of nature was not reciprocated, however, and the building, which had no air conditioning, experienced severe environmental problems: the windows were covered in condensation in winter, and heat and insects became oppressive in summer, particularly as Mies would not allow any protec-

Above:
Edith Farnsworth House,
detail of the joinery of the
plate-glass wall.

Opposite page and at right:
Edith Farnsworth House,
glass façade.

tion around the porch. In the same way, the relationship between Mies and his client, which was cordial during construction, later deteriorated. Edith Farnsworth seemed, in Mies's own words, "to have thought that the architect came with the house." Disappointed with the building, she took a fierce dislike to its author, suing him for cost overruns in a legal proceeding that was much reported in the press. Mies won in 1953. As part of a campaign against the "Menace to the New America" represented by modernist architects in general and Mies in particular, the Hearst magazine *House Beautiful* gave Edith Farnsworth the last word.

Above:
Edith Farnsworth House,
view of the porch.

At left:
Edith Farnsworth House,
view from the porch
toward the river.

Opposite page:
Edith Farnsworth House,
interior view.

She confirmed that, far from being "free," Mies's space was "very fixed," to the point that she could not "put a clothes hanger in [here] without considering how it affects everything from the outside" and that "any arrangement of furniture becomes a major problem, because the house is transparent, like an X ray."[49] Subsequently a collector's piece, the house, according to its later owner, Peter Palumbo, who acquired it in 1972 and had to restore it at least twice following catastrophic floods, it "performs extremely well for a single person."[50]

Shortly afterward, Mies designed a theoretical project for a house fifty feet square – the 50 x 50 House – in cooperation with Myron Goldsmith, who assisted him in the firm on all structural questions. Again it was a simple box, but the core was thicker. The roof, of a rigid, braced construction, is supported by four columns, one in the middle of each side, instead of eight. But the American dream of the post-war family house had little in common with this transparent box, which was to remain Mies's last major project for a detached residence.

At left:
Project for the
50 x 50 House,
1950-52, perspectival
sketch and plan (autograph,
Mies van der Rohe Archive,
Museum of Modern Art,
New York).

At right:
Project for the
50 x 50 House,
plan.

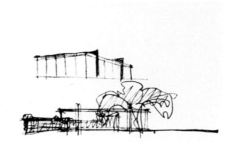

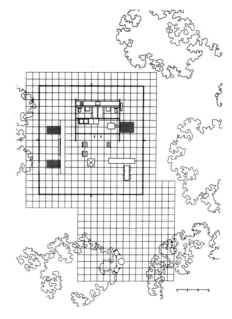

Crown Hall

For the Illinois Institute of Technology, Mies returned to the theme of the large building on a rectangular grid, which had been studied for the Library and Administration Building. He gave a first interpretation of it with the Commons Building, a symmetrical structure in which the kitchen was designed as a sort of box inside a box, and whose roof, thin as well as flat, did not suggest the vast volume below. With its twenty-four-by-thirty-two-foot grid, this building differed from all the others.[51] Shortly afterward, also at IIT, Mies built Crown Hall, for the schools of architecture and urban planning, which were expanded in 1950 with the annexation of the Institute of Design, initially created by Moholy-Nagy under the badge of the "New Bauhaus." Here he broke with the language that he had adopted for most of the other buildings, reformulating on a new scale the totally open configuration of the Farnsworth House, the 50 x 50 House and the Commons Building. He developed the principle of large girders outside the main volume, an idea he

had experimented with between 1945 and 1948 in an unbuilt project for the Cantor Drive-in Restaurant.

A single, uninterrupted space, 120 by 220 feet, with a height of eighteen feet, Crown Hall is roofed by a spectacular structure designed by Frank J. Kornacker, which essentially consists of four large girders of welded steel, under which the ceiling is suspended. The main floor is completely open and suitable for any combination of tables and teaching spaces. The more technical facilities and the classrooms are relegated to the basement, reflecting an education system centered on the studio work. The main entrance, facing the city and not the exterior of the campus, is approached by a steel stairway, covered in a skin of travertine, similar in its texture to that of the Farnsworth House. For Mies, this building was to remain "the clearest structure we have done, the best to express our philosophy."[52] But make no mistake: this reflects a new set of issues, not so

much because of the size of the space – Mies aspired to these vast spaces, as if they represented an ideal dwelling – but because the steel skeleton, which was exposed internally in the earlier buildings, is now invisible, as in the Farnsworth House.[53] Judged by Colin Rowe to be "too pure to be useful,"[54] Crown Hall is the first complete realization of Mies's idea of a big space where anything is possible; as early as the 1920s Mies compared this approach to Häring's strategies of adaptation to function:

"I said to him, 'For heaven's sake, why don't you plan the building big enough so that you can walk freely and not in only one predetermined direction? We don't know at all if the people will use it in the way we would like them to. First of all, the functions are not clear and, second, they are not constant – they change much faster than the building. Our building lasts for several hundred years. What will wear out are the elevators or heating systems, etc., but the structure will never wear out."[55]

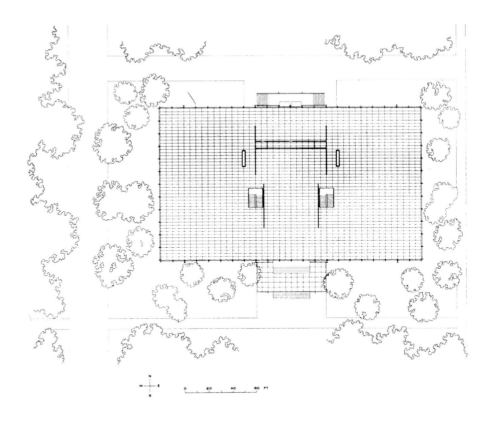

Top:
Crown Hall, Illinois Institute of Technology, Chicago, 1950–56, plan of the main floor.

Bottom:
Project for the Mannheim National Theater, 1952, view of the model.

Several weeks later, for the National Theater in Mannheim, Mies employed his first project designed on German soil since 1938, a structure with large girders, but returning to the framework device from the Cantor project. He participated in this prominent postwar competition in the company of Rudolf Schwarz, Richard Döcker, Hans Scharoun, and Otto Ernst Schweizer.[56] The rectilinear block, measuring 80 by 160 meters, is also the largest project that he had ever designed. Inserted in the Goethe-Platz, the rectangle of the plan is placed on the diagonal of the orthogonal grid of the plan for Mannheim. Unlike at Crown Hall, the volume envelopes not an open space but the elements of a "complicated spatial organism," bringing together two halls with 1,300 and 500 seats, respectively, placed at either end of the main floor. The lower level is for services. Mies would insist on this point in the presentation of the project, stressing the "clear separation of the functions and their spatial expression on separate planes," which had "the advantage

of great flexibility."[57] He sent a spectacular model to Mannheim, which made it possible for Schwarz to see in his project nothing but a "big glass box," at the time when he launched a memorable attack on the Bauhaus and its legacy.[58] Like Schwarz, whose project, despite several recommendations from experts, was once preferred by the local authorities, Mies

withdrew from the second round of the competition, and it was a mediocre copy of his project that was finally built by the Frankfurt-based architect Gerhard Weber.[59]

In 1952, ten years after the Concert Hall, Mies and a group of IIT students designed a Convention Hall for the South Side of Chicago. It

Preceding pages:
Crown Hall, Illinois Institute
of Technology, view of the
entrance side.

At left:
Crown Hall, Illinois Institute
of Technology, view of the
southwest corner.

Opposite page, top:
Crown Hall, Illinois Institute
of Technology, view of the
interior of the main floor.

Opposite page, bottom:
Project for the Convention
Hall, Chicago, 1952,
perspective of the interior,
photomontage (autograph,
Mies van der Rohe Archive,
Museum of Modern Art,
New York).

was a covered space almost as big as the factory he used in his collage. The exhibition and meeting hall, on a square plan with each side measuring 720 feet in length, would have been able to accommodate fifty thousand people. The two-dimensional steel truss framework was this time completely exposed and supported by peripheral columns, freeing the whole covered area. This program carried to its limits the theme of the great open space and won Mies the congratulations of his former employer, Bruno Paul, who hailed this "gigantic design."[60] It was intended as part of an urban project carrying out the intentions of Daniel Burnham's plan of 1909. It was eventually built after Mies's death, in a somewhat different form, by his former assistant Gene Summers within the C. F. Murphy firm.

CHICAGO AND AMERICAN PARADIGMS (1938–56)

Interior of the Art Club of
Chicago, 1948–51
(demolished).

Alongside these interpretations of the theme of the great covered space, Mies concerned himself with the elaboration and improvement of another building type that is characteristic of his American work: the skyscraper apartment block. These buildings were the first sign of a revival in the building industry, which Chicago had been waiting for since the Crash of 1929, through two decades of urban stag- nation scarcely ameliorated by the few build- ings produced by Roosevelt's Public Works Administration.[61] The phase of growth that began in the city after 1945 ushered in a vast urban redevelopment program. A massive influx of blacks from the South swelled the ghet- tos, while "Boss" Richard Daley, elected for the first of his three terms as mayor in 1955, built up his political machine.[62] In 1946 Mies met the young developer Herbert Greenwald, who had initially intended to employ Gropius; it was Greenwald who enabled Mies to add to his IIT work a range of new residential buildings. In total Mies constructed six high-rise build- ings for Greenwald, in addition to the four- teen others that he built in Chicago between 1948 and 1969.[63]

Lake Shore Drive: The Steel Towers

Between 1947 and 1949 Mies built for Green-wald the Promontory Apartments on the South Side, near the Museum of Natural History. The scarcity of steel in the immediate after-math of the war led Mies to defer his preoc-cupation with metal structures and build this twenty-one-story block with a skeleton of rein-forced concrete. Contrary to the impression given by all the photos published at the time and since, the two sides of the building are strongly differentiated. The façade overlook-ing the lake is flat, whereas the landward side has return wings that create a double T shape. A distinctive expression of the structure is the sequential decreasing of the thickness of the external piers every five stories, marked by a horizontal setback and giving the façade a kind of Gothic profile. Moreover, the joints and recessed lines that give the building tex-ture when seen close up are not obvious from a distance because of the uniform beige-gray color of the concrete frame and the brick infills.

Even before the Promontory Apartments were finished, Greenwald (in partnership with Robert Hall McCormick and Son) launched a second and more ambitious project in steel and glass, this time on the North Side. The twenty-six-story blocks at 860-880 Lake Shore Drive developed a steel-frame variation on the Promontory Apartments design. They are set at right angles, aligned with the urban grid of Chicago, with the irregular diagonal of the shore defining a trapezoidal external space. With their partially open ground floors, they form a filter between the Near Northside and the lake, motionless sentinels watching over the expanse of water.

The main steel skeleton forms three bays on the end wall and five on the main façade, with each bay filled by four aluminum window pan-els; and this five-by-three proportion becomes a recurrent feature in later projects by Mies. The initial purity of the structure was threat-ened by the local building code, which stipu-lated that the load-bearing elements should be coated with two inches of concrete. Mies obliged, then encased the coated beams and columns in a covering of steel to which non-load-bearing rolled steel I-beams were welded, thus creating a secondary framework joining the main uprights, stiffening the skin and visu-ally reinforcing the lines of force in a struc-ture that is both hidden and exposed. Mies jus-tified this transgression against the rationalist principles that he had always claimed to observe:

"It was very important to preserve and extend the rhythm which the mullions set up on the rest of the building. We looked at it on the model without the steel section attached to the corner column and it did not look right. Now, the other reason is that this steel section was needed to stiffen the plate which covers the corner column so this plate would not ripple, and also we needed it for strength when the sections were hoisted into place. Now, of course, that's a very good reason."[64]

The steel skeleton supports a secondary structure, into which the panels of the façade are inserted. The panels incorporate a thicker low rib and a recessed bar. Inside the apartments, the free plan that was originally proposed was replaced by rooms that were more closed, and the silver curtains that protected against the sun would, upon the completion of the towers, modestly hide the tenants' choices. The natural aluminum frame resonated with the dark linoleum and reflected from the ceiling and the white walls in a harmony that corresponded to the changing spectacle of the lake. These buildings suggest a collective form, as oblique views confirm. When the glass panels disappear into the relief of the façades, an overall form appears. It is scarcely modulated except by variations in detail. In this context, Mies explicitly challenged Sullivan's dictum "Form follows Function":

"We do the opposite. We reverse this, and make a practical and satisfying shape, and then fit the functions into it. Today this is the only practical way to build, because the functions of most buildings are continually changing, but economically the buildings cannot change."[65]

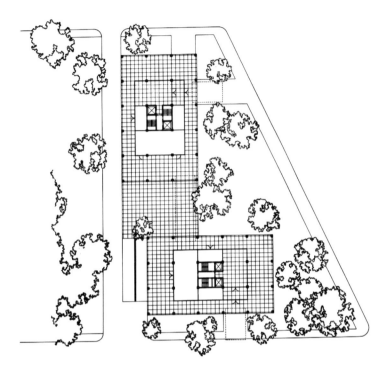

The pleasure Mies felt on the building site brings to mind the words he published in 1922 in *Früh-licht*, when he asserted, "Only skyscrapers under construction reveal the bold construc-tive thoughts, and then the impression of the high-reaching steel skeleton is overpowering."[66] Mies himself bought two small apartments in the complex, and he fitted them out, but took care not to live there, fearing, by his own admis-sion, that he might be constantly confronted by the complaints of the tenants. He remained in a more traditional Neo-Renaissance resi-dence on East Pearson Street with his collec-tion of paintings and etchings. When a visitor asked why he had not built a house for him-self – although he had designed one – Mies said that he would never have been able to hang his works by Klee – he owned twenty-three of them – and his collages by Schwitters on the glass walls of his own architecture.[67]

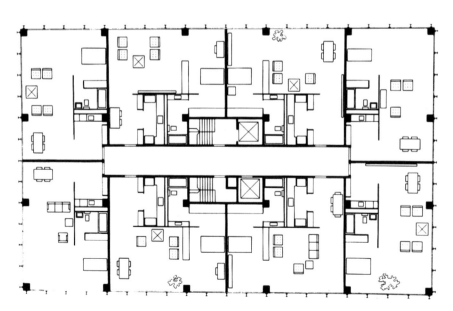

860-880 Lake Shore Drive, view of the site during the installation of the windows.

Fully exploiting the advantages conferred both by Mies's great reputation and by the financial and technical practices that enabled them to sell the apartments at 10 percent below market price, Greenwald and his associates undertook on numerous developments on an unusually ambitious scale. As a result, the structure of Mies's firm inevitably changed, since Greenwald expected it to generate all the working drawings. It also became more profitable, even though Greenwald, whose commissions accounted for 60 percent of the firm's profits, seems to have used every possible stratagem to delay the payment of Mies's fees.[68] Mies was hardheaded in all his financial relationships with clients, and when Erich Mendelsohn, toward the end of his life, was hoping for new commissions, Mies was able to give him the benefit of his experience in the management of contracts and remuneration.[69]

The apartments at 900-910 Lake Shore Drive (also known as 900 Esplanade) were built for Metropolitan Structures, the firm set up by Greenwald and Samuel Katzin. They differ from the two earlier tower blocks nearby in their height – they are two stories higher – and in their structure. Here the steel skeleton is entirely replaced by concrete, and the metal façade is no longer a visible expression of a concealed steel frame; its steel struts and panels of aluminum – now a relatively inexpensive material – lend an illusion of metal solidity to

a hidden mineral structure, thus undermining one of the basic principles of Miesian theory. Moreover, an air-conditioning system was installed, and its ducts passed between the frame and the façade, and a tinted glass that absorbed heat was used. The lobbies of the two towers are fronted by a glass wall set back from the plane of the façades, so that the buildings seem to float above a volume of air. Only a fine horizontal black line betrays the presence of the concrete floor slabs.

During the same period, Mies built for Greenwald, on exactly the same structural principles, the two high-rise blocks of the Commonwealth Promenade Apartments (there were originally to have been four). This time, the marked contrast between the main columns and the mullions of the windows was softened, as if Mies was prepared to admit that the whole of the exterior was simply a skin. These blocks transform the character of Lake Shore Drive, with their aluminum envelope contrasting with the obscurity of older blocks. Acting as a visual punctuation at the end of Lincoln Park, they stand out from the urban fabric of north Chicago. The space between them and a street intersection is occupied by a small swimming pool. The interplay of the large panels of turquoise glass and the aluminum offers a visual echo of the dominant colors of the lake, flooding the ground-level circulation area with color.

Top:
860-880 Lake Shore Drive, an entrance.

Bottom:
Mies van der Rohe at the window of an apartment at 860-880 Lake Shore Drive, between 1951 and 1953. Photo: Ferenc Berko.

Opposite page:
860-880 Lake Shore Drive, an entrance.

Overleaf:
900-910 Lake Shore Drive, Chicago, 1953–56, the lobby of 910 with a sculpture by Virginio Ferrari.

The last project designed for Greenwald was Lafayette Park (1955-63), a modern development applying the notion of *urbs in horto* (the Garden City) formulated by Ludwig Hilberseimer in his book *The New City*, for which Mies had written the introduction in 1944, underlining the importance of plans made for "life," but based on a clear "order."[70] Located on a thirty-one-hectare site 2.5 kilometers northeast of the center of Detroit, the Lafayette Park development is one of Mies's most successful large-scale projects – no doubt because of its relatively luxurious finish and site management. The commission came from the Citizens Redevelopment Committee, for which union leader Walter Reuther had worked since the early 1950s. The commission was originally given to Oscar Storonov, a friend of the unionist, as well as to Victor Gruen and to Minoru Yamasaki; funds from the 1949 Housing Act were tapped for the occasion. But only Greenwald was in a position to invest in the undertaking, leading his own team. Occupied by housing for black workers and nicknamed "Black Bottom," the sites of the Gratiot Redevelopment Area were razed between 1950 and 1954 and their eight thousand occupants were evicted.

After having been under the sway of Frank Lloyd Wright, the landscape architect Alfred Caldwell, who taught at IIT along with Mies and Hilberseimer, transposed the schematic dir-

ections of Ludwig Hilberseimer into an "integrated whole," implementing the "principle of order" claimed by Mies in a note on this project.[71] The origin of the plan went back to Hilberseimer's 1930 theoretical project for Berlin called *Mischbebauung*, or mixed development. Caldwell, initially adept in the Prairie style of landscaping, had become an advocate of Wrightian deurbanism. For his part, Mies had discovered the territorial ideas put forth by his friend Rudolf Schwarz in *Von der Bebauung der Erde*; Mies had annotated his copy of the book, which recommended that a hierarchical social organization be projected onto the ground.[72]

Opposite page, top:
Lafayette Park, Detroit,
1955-56, row houses.

Opposite page, bottom:
Lafayette Park, general
view.

At right:
Lafayette Park, row houses
and the tower.

On the urban grid erased by previous blocks,
the notion of the superblock, tested for IIT, was
implemented as on virgin territory. All non-
residential components were excluded from
this landscape, which brought to mind natural vegetation, a distant echo of Olmsted, the
pastoral dream without collective real life.[73]

These high-quality, generously planted external spaces separate the twenty-one-story
blocks, and the ground was remodeled, with
parking space 1.2 meters deep. The Pavilions
Apartments are similar to the Esplanade
Apartments in Chicago, whereas the Lafayette

At left:
2400 Lakeview, Chicago,
1962–63, lake façade.

Opposite page:
2400 Lakeview, view of the
corner.

Towers have a façade grid that is more narrow. There are two kinds of apartments on the lower levels – those on one floor with enclosed gardens and duplexes that are more complex than their exterior appearance suggests, with a rhythm of floor partitions that does not correspond to those of the bays. It is a rather rare case, and the quality of the housing itself, in particular the row houses and courtyard apartments, is a rare example of a successful collective development for middle-class residents who sought to enjoy a suburban quality of life within easy reach of the city center and whose lifestyle was dependent on the automobile.[74]

When Greenwald died in an airplane crash in 1959, Mies declared, "He was a man of our age who nonetheless had the values of every age."[75] Two years earlier, in a thank-you note (Greenwald had given him a ceramic bowl), Mies had confided in him how much he wished that someday the buildings they had constructed together "will be thought of as typically American as it is."[76]

After Greenwald's death, Bernard Weissbourd took over management of Metropolitan Structures. Although the company, largely financed by the insurance corporation Metropolitan Life,

expanded its business to other cities in the Northeast, Mies was forced to lay off half his office staff.[77] Nevertheless, from 1961 onward, Mies built the apartment block at 2400 Lakeview, on the edge of Lincoln Park in Chicago; its ground-floor lobby featured green marble walls. On a square plan, this building with its subtle silhouette marked the inauguration of Weissbourd's new policy of developing the smaller building lots in the north of Chicago. After 1960 Mies progressively lost interest in high-rise residential buildings, which he delegated to the members of his office.[78] From then on, he concentrated on developing the

finished form of the metal-clad tower, as he had devised it for these residential projects, into the big office blocks of which the Seagram Building was the prototype.

NEW MODERNISM

6. INDUSTRIAL CLASSICISM (1956–69)

Opposite page:
Seagram Building,
New York, 1954–58,
general view.

Above:
Westmount Square,
Montreal, 1965–69,
detail of a façade.

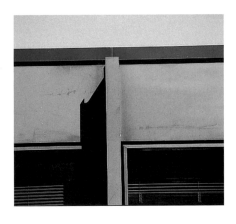

The Seagram Stele

In 1954, when he received the commission to design an office building in New York for the Canadian multinational corporation Joseph E. Seagram and Sons, Mies van der Rohe was sixty-eight. More than a quarter of a century after the first sketches of a Glass Skyscraper for Friedrichstrasse, here at last was his chance to translate his idea of a large office building into reality.[1] A fortuitous chain of events led him to this commission, which stood out both for its size and for its location. The president of the corporation, Samuel Bronfman,[2] had originally given the commission to the firm of Charles Luckman. In 1954, after Luckman's scheme was rejected, Bronfman's daughter, Phyllis Lambert, approached (among others) Philip Johnson, then curator of architecture and design at the Museum of Modern Art. Johnson steered her toward a group of distinguished modernist architects, from which, after a search lasting two months, she finally selected Mies. Lambert thereafter stayed in constant touch with Mies in her capacity as Director of Planning for the Seagram Building.[3] Grateful for Johnson's help in circulating his work at the Museum of Modern Art, Mies included him in the project.[4] Between December 1955 and February 1957, Johnson was the sole legal author of the project, for the New York Chapter of the American Institute of Architects refused Mies authorization to practice his profession on the pretext that he did not have a university diploma.[5]

As a piece of urban planning, Mies's design was radically new. Set on a granite platform on Park Avenue, the Seagram Building, completed in 1958, dominates its surroundings, commanding a particularly solemn approach sequence, which is flanked by a symmetrical pair of pools. The site occupies three-quarters of the block between Fifty-second and Fifty-third Streets, with its frontage on Park Avenue, formerly a residential thoroughfare that was beginning to fill up with offices. Instead of making the building rise straight from Park Avenue, Mies situated his tower, with its ground plan based on his favorite five-by-three proportion, in the dead center of the lot. This required a considerable financial sacrifice on the part of the client, who had to buy additional land; but Mies made symbolic amends by turning the Seagram Building, across Gordon Bunshaft's 1952 Lever House, into a major landmark, in both vertical and horizontal terms, on the landscape of Park Avenue. The firm would labor over the installation of a sculpture on the parvis, inaugurating a device so often repeated afterward. The curtain wall stops above the ground floor, whose ceiling extends to form an entrance canopy, so that the thirty-eight-story building appears to hover above the ground. Mies stressed that, for him, this was not only a response to a particular problem but the definition of a general solution:

"My concept and approach on the Seagram Building was no different from any other building that I might build. My idea, or better, "direction," in which I go is toward a clear structure and construction – this applies not to any one problem but to all architectural problems which I approach. I am, in fact, completely opposed to the idea that a specific building should have an individual character – rather, a universal character which has been determined by the total problem which architecture must strive to solve.

On the Seagram Building, since it was to be built in New York, and, since it was the first major office building which I was to build, I asked for two types of advice for the development of the plans. One, the best real estate advice as to the types of desirable rentable space and, two, professional advice regarding the New York City Building Code. With my direction established and, with these advisers, it was then only a matter of hard work."[6]

The mass of the building gives an impression of geometric unity, but the truth is more complex: it consists of two conjoined T-shaped configurations. On the four bottom floors, the main tower backs onto a rear block that occupies the full width of the site. On top of this block is a narrow central block of six floors, forming an inverted T. As at the Promontory Apartments, the main tower conceals a central return wing at the back of a single bay deep. The varying internal plans are unified by the fixed position of the vertical circulation shafts.[7] On the ground floor, the plaza leads without a change of level straight into the lobby, which is clad with travertine. Between the main tower and the rear block is a transverse galley parallel to Park Avenue, sheltered by two glass roofs designed by Philip Johnson, who also designed the restaurant, the Four Seasons, whose entrance terminates the axis of symmetry at the rear of the whole composition. The restaurant was built between 1957 and 1958 after various proposals for a museum or shop had been rejected.[8] The role of the New York architect, who was hired to fit out the rooms of the restaurant, with their steel chain draperies and suspended sculptures by Richard

Top:
Seagram Building, view of
the northwest corner.

Bottom:
Seagram Building, plan of
the ground floor and plan of
a typical floor.

Lippold, also extended to the overall interior. With the lighting consultant Richard Kelly, Johnson worked on the lighting of the foyer and the offices, in which luminous panels were used for the first time. He studied the layout of partitions and the wall coverings, from the marble panels of the lavatories, to the woven steel lining of the elevators.[9] Of necessity, the topmost floors of the tower house the mechanical equipment and are therefore opaque. The distinction between the base and the main block of the tower is strongly accentuated by the explicit presence of columns in the foyer and by the fact that above the foyer they are invisible except at the corners, whose treatment is very different from that in the residential apartment blocks in Chicago.

The frame of H-shaped mullions in bronze, a material that is both matte and ostentatious (its use was criticized by Reyner Banham[10]) stops flush with the corner columns, which are themselves sheathed in a layer of concrete and a skin of metal. The horizontals present in 860-880 Lake Shore Drive have disappeared. Belying any pretense of structural "honesty," the same façade formula continues on the

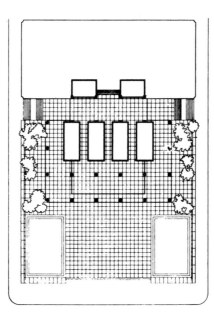

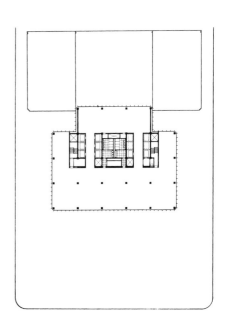

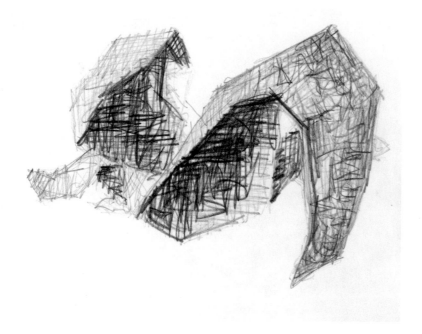

upper service level, with its concrete infill.[11] The bronze color of the whole building, which would have been difficult to produce in glass, seems to have been inspired by Samuel Bronfman, who was taken with the color of the old window frames of New York. The building thus offers the city a somber reflection of itself, subdivided by the uprights of the curtain wall, while the ground floor brings together lighter stone surfacing. Inside, the air conditioning is set back from the façade and so allows the floor depth as it appears on the elevation to be reduced to a minimum. A strict regulation of the Venetian blinds, which may be raised only in a limited number of positions, lends a visual order to the façade at all times, giving it a character more pictorial than architectonic.[12] The measure of the building's success is conveyed by the warmth with which Lewis Mumford, a champion of continuity and organic use of space, hailed the contrast that it created with

At right:
Seagram Building, aerial
view of the whole building
and the parvis.

the meanness of the New York buildings in general:

"Out of this stalled, rush-hour clutter of new
structures, brightly sordid, meretriciously up-
to-date, the Seagram building has emerged as
a Rolls-Royce accompanied by a motorcycle
escort that gives it space and speed. To an even
greater degree than its elegant neighbor, Lever
House, 375 has ambiance. From three sides,
it is wholly visible to the eye and approachable
by foot; instead of using up space, it creates
space. This act of detachment from the surrounding buildings was the most daring of all
the innovations its chief architectural designer,
Mies van der Rohe, made; by a heavy sacrifice of profitable floor area, he achieved for
this single structure an effect that usually is
created only when a group of buildings are
placed together on a plot even larger than a
city block, as in Rockefeller Center."[13]

The Skyscraper Variation

The public commissions received by Mies van der Rohe in Chicago from the late 1950s onward fundamentally transformed the image of the whole city, in which he explored the possibilities of the skyscraper theme first proposed in New York (although Seagram abandoned a proposal for a building in Chicago in 1959). Built in the Loop, on the site of several demolished buildings (including the Federal Building by Henry Ives Cobb, a classical structure dating to 1897), Mies's Federal Center (1959-64) constitutes his most powerful statement in the very center of the city.[14] Contrary to the original idea proposed by the authorities for a single building entirely filling the available lot, the Federal Center brings together the elements of the language forged for the Park Avenue site. Built on two esplanades of different sizes, its three rectangular prisms constitute a sort of autonomous citadel within the dense mass of surrounding office development. The lowest building along South Dearborn Street – the thirty-story courthouse – is reflected in the glass curtain wall of the forty-two-story tower, reinforcing the limits of the whole. In cross-section, the interior of the courthouse belies the image of tranquil repetitiveness conveyed by its curtain wall; the densely packed floors are relieved by the larger spaces of the twenty-one courtrooms.[15] As somber as Daniel Burnham's Monadnock Building, which forms a backdrop to Mies's complex and represents the swan song of load-bearing brick structures,

the Federal Center is lightened by the granite paving at ground level, which laps upward to line the entrance lobbies. The solemnity of the federal presence is relieved by the generosity of the urban space provided by the plaza, which runs along the sides of the buildings in open galleries created by recessing the glass walls of the ground floor.[16]

On the other side of the Chicago River, the fifty-eight-story IBM Building of 1967 is the highest structure Mies ever built. With its chilly, metallic presence, barely warmed by the granite floor and travertine walls of the entrance lobby, it rebukes the fantasy of the building next door, Marina City, designed by Mies's former Bauhaus student Bertrand Goldberg. Across from the Chicago Tribune by Hood and Howells, Mies also built the first stage of a massive program for roofing the Illinois Central Railway tracks; this was One Illinois Center (1967-70), overlooking the river in the form of a balcony with ingeniously managed accesses and transitions. But it was in Canada that Mies built two complexes that combine the theme of the tower with that of the horizontal service block.

The first of these developments was the Toronto Dominion Center, built in the center of the capital of Ontario between 1963 and 1969. The developer, Fairview Corporation, first gave the commission to Gordon Bunshaft, of SOM, whose project for a single tower was rejected.

The local firm John B. Parkin Associates then took up the project in cooperation with Mies. Like the Federal Center, the Toronto Dominion Center combined two office towers and a single-level banking pavilion above the pedestrian spaces and shops, located belowground.[17] Oriented with their large sides to the east-west, the Toronto Dominion Bank tower comprised fifty-six floors and the Royal Trust tower, whose plan was less elongated, forty-six. The rectangular grid was thirty by forty feet and not thirty by thirty, as before.

The base, containing a shopping center on the lower level, is wedged between King Street in the north and Wellington Street in the south. The difference in level between the two streets made it possible to create a car entrance at street level on Wellington. The composition of the empty spaces on a diagonal generates very rich visual relationships, which reinforce the transparency of the ground floor. Mies returned to certain picturesque features suggested by Camillo Sitte in the early twentieth century, but he enriched them precisely because the solids of the Sittean blocks are replaced by aerial volumes. The layout of the two plazas designed by Alfred Caldwell – one to the southeast planted with grass, which was unique for Mies, and one granite plaza in the northeast, across from the bank – reinforces the unity of the complex, which began as an autonomous entity in the city's business center.

Federal Center, Chicago, 1959–64, general view along West Adams Street, with the post office.

INDUSTRIAL CLASSICISM (1956–69)

Top:
Federal Center,
detail of the corner
with the post office.

Bottom:
Federal Center, view
of the larger tower
and the post office.

Opposite:
Federal Center, the
parvis and Alexander
Calder's stabile
sculpture *Flamingo*.

The mass of the bank – on a square plan with each side measuring 150 feet and subdivided into fifteen bays – continues the design undertaken at the Federal Center. The chromatic density of the interior, which cannot be gleaned from the exterior because it is blocked by dark windows, is striking. The green marble cladding of the columns, the blond wood of the furniture, and the beige granite of the floor create a warm universe under the light of 225 panels set in the covering grate. The orthogonal frame transposes the bulk of the static load: the wings of the I-beams get thicker between their extremities, resting on the columns of the façade and the center of the room, where there is maximum pressure. Moreover, their cast shadows make it rather difficult to perceive this arrangement.

The Westmount Square development in Montreal, which is more complex, was built between 1965 and 1968. It occupies the whole of a small block to the west of the city center, marking the point where denser building begins at the foot of a residential hill. Only three of the four planned towers were built: two of them are apartment blocks overlooking a two-story commercial wing that adjusts to the slope of the ground toward the south. Access to all the towers is via the large plinth, initially clad in travertine and later ill-advisedly refaced in granite. In Montreal, as in the other complexes in this series, the space between ground level and the ceiling of the entrance lobbies of the towers plays an essential role. It links the layer of stone for the floor, a layer of air, and the white soffit that illuminates and raises the build-

Top:
Toronto Dominion Center,
interior view of the lower
building.

Bottom:
Toronto Dominion Center,
view of a conference room.

ings. Connecting the towers to the urban space, the large stone paving slabs in all these complexes recall the tradition of stereotomy from which Mies came, especially in the work on the joints – smooth, attenuated, or effaced – in order to reconstitute the quarry bed when necessary.[18]

One of the few European projects in this series, which includes a building designed for the Commerzbank in Frankfurt, was to be set in London's City. Designed for the developer Peter Palumbo starting in 1967, the twenty-story tower proposed for Mansion House Square aroused passionate controversy: partisans and adversaries debated whether a Miesian skyscraper should be grafted onto a historic setting. The matter was not resolved

until more than fifteen years after Mies's death, when the project was abandoned and the Prince of Wales launched his crusade against modern architecture.[19] As a result, the corpus of Mies's great towers was never completed. The thirty-six towers built by Mies, of which only eight have a steel frame, might appear to be repetitive. With massive steles resting on transparent ground floors, supported by cushions of air, they are similar – in the strictly geometrical sense of the term – and yet subtly different, serving as foils to their urban settings, providing the standard for modern cities, and holding out a mirror to them. Unique in the wealth of contextual associations that they propose, they rarely disrupt the urbanity of urban life – unlike almost all of their imitators.

Top:
Westmount Square,
Montreal, view of
an entrance to the
shopping center.

Bottom:
Westmount Square,
Montreal,
view of a lobby.

Opposite page:
Westmount Square,
Montreal, view of the
ground floor.

From the late 1950s onward, Mies's office worked on a considerable number of residential and public buildings in Newark, Baltimore, and finally Montreal, where he built a luxury retreat for the bourgeoisie on the Ile des Sœurs, in the form of large slab blocks subtly placed above the banks of the St. Lawrence. On the same site, the Esso service station, also built by Mies, is touching in its simplicity and rationality. It recalls the scale of the designs for private houses of the preceding decades; all its technical systems are concealed under a long metal roof.[20]

Alongside his offices and residential towers, Mies rang in the changes on the second major building type in his postwar work: the horizontal box. The theme of Crown Hall was taken up in 1965 with a rectilinear block for the School of Social Service Administration at the University of Chicago – the only commission that institution ever gave to Mies – where it lays aside its solemnity by descending from its plinth. More horizontal than its predecessors, it uses window forms that contrast with the buttresses of the neo-Gothic buildings of the university. Its façades reveal the arrangement

Top:
School of Social Service
Administration, University
of Chicago, Chicago, 1965,
general view.

Bottom:
School of Social Service
Administration, University
of Chicago, view of the
lobby.

of its internal levels: while the entrance lobby and library occupy a volume corresponding to the entire height of the building, two staircases give lateral access to less spacious upper stories lit on the façade by windows occupying the upper two-thirds of the elevation, with the lower third serving to light a semi-basement.

The two successive extensions to the Houston Museum can be put in the same category. Concentric, they use a curved geometry, unusual for Mies, who normally took the view that steel profiles were produced by rolling-mills and were of necessity rectilinear. But above all, they allowed Mies to refine his experiments in exposing large volumes, giving a more concrete content to the museum theories of 1942.

In the end, the America in which Mies built showed itself to be very far from the imaginary one of his early days in Berlin. The urban reality of the South Side of Chicago, where he had built IIT, is in fact quite gloomy next to his pre-1930 idyllic visions of an America where economy and reason would coincide. If the construction of limited blocks of urban rationality, in Chicago or in Toronto, could help him

Top:
Brown Wing, Museum
of Fine Arts, Houston,
1966–69, interior view.

Bottom:
Brown Wing, Museum
of Fine Arts, Houston,
partial view of the façade.

get over this disappointment, the quasi mutism
of Mies van der Rohe with regard to the American metropolis contrasts with his former attention and clearly shows the distance separating
the far-removed expectation from the concrete
experience of an idealized urban setting.

Return to Berlin: The Neue Nationalgalerie

During this period, Mies also pursued the development of a third major type: that of large spaces free from internal supports, of which the Fifty by Fifty House is essentially a miniature version. The most important stage in this process was the design of an office building for Ron Bacardi in Santiago de Cuba, which was cut short by the Castro revolution. This project, commissioned by José M. Bosch, president of the company and an admirer of Crown Hall, was influenced by climatic conditions:

Mies abandoned the principle of the Crown Hall façade and recessed the glass wall under the shade of the overhanging roof. The structure of the Bacardi design – roof trusses carried by eight peripheral columns – was in reinforced concrete. The design called for a large glass volume with an asymmetrical plan where only one part of the activities would be located, with the rest housed in the base. But Mies then found the opportunity to transpose this principle into steel construction, thanks to the

project for a museum in Schweinfurt, intended to hold the collection of the industrialist Georg Schäfer, the father-in-law of Mies's grandson, Dirk Lohan. It was from this design, prepared in 1960-61, that he developed the Neue Nationalgalerie in Berlin, designed from 1962 on and built between 1965 and 1968. The commission went forward thanks partly to the petition, published in March 1961 by Ulrich Conrads, the editor in chief of the *Bauwelt* journal, on the occasion of Mies's seventy-fifth birthday, with the slogan "Mies should build in Berlin."[21]

The Berlin building, a fundamental component of the imagined Kulturforum facing east, next to Hans Scharoun's Philharmonic Hall, allowed Mies to weave together in an obvious way the threads of his German and his American work. Developed in successive touches within the firm, the great steel exhibition hall, which was in theory suitable for any and all uses, sits on a stone platform. Inside it, the permanent collections of the gallery are hidden away and deprived of natural light. However, the large glass volume on the upper level is suitable for any arrangement of contemporary art, as has been proven since,[22] and seems to herald the open platform of the Georges Pompidou Center in Paris, designed in 1971. The roof, developed after lengthy negotiations with the engineers, is a grille of constant thickness that is visible on the exterior and on the interior, where no false ceiling conceals it. Its panels

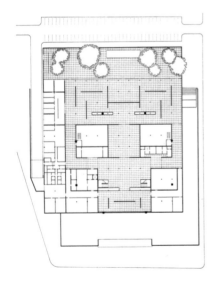

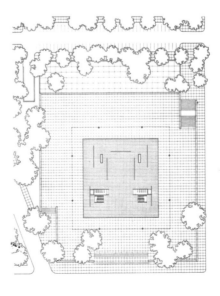

Opposite page, left
and right:
Neue Nationalgalerie,
Potsdamer Straße,
Berlin, 1962–68,
plans of the lower
and the upper level.

Above:
Neue Nationalgalerie,
general view from the
parvis.

cannot but be likened to those of the portico of Schinkel's Altes Museum, to which also belong the soaring position above the city and the transparency between the interior and the exterior.[23] The roof was made in sections of steel of a quality adapted to the level of pressure sustained by the various sections. The glass volume, fifty-four meters across, is reserved for temporary exhibitions, with the permanent collections housed in the base, whose envelope, opaque on the Postdamer Straße, is open on the west side. Though to some extent it absorbs the slope of the land toward the Landwehrkanal, the platform's relation to the site is comparatively dubious – and in essence just as unspecific as that of the

second Glass Skyscraper.[24] Thus Mies returned not only to the theme of the pavilion, which began with the Riehl House, but also to that of the acropolis, as redefined in Schinkel's plan for Orianda. Moreover, this project superimposes a pavilion in the shape of a temple opening onto the underground galleries, as in the building in Berlin.[25] In a letter to Werner Düttmann, the head of construction for the Berlin senate, Mies wrote: "I think the museum is a classic solution to the problem that was given to me."[26]

Having endeavored for twenty years to emphasize the importance of rolled steel profiles, even to the extent of masking the real struc-

ture of his towers, and having reduced the supports, in many of his European designs, to single vertical sections, Mies reverted with some serenity to the issue of the column.[27] He returned to the cruciform section used in Barcelona and in Brno and proposed for certain buildings at IIT. Six models would be made to perfect the columns, while one model of the overhang would make it possible to introduce a slight optical correction in order to avoid the impression of a spire, whose realization would prove arduous.[28] In passing, Mies took the opportunity to allude to Behrens's Turbinenhalle by taking up once more the theme of the ball-and-socket joint – this time connecting the columns not to the floor, but to the roof.

Top:
Neue Nationalgalerie,
interior view with an
installation by Ulrich
Rückriem.

Bottom:
Neue Nationalgalerie, view
from the Landwehrkanal.

Top:
Neue Nationalgalerie,
view of the interior.

Bottom:
Neue Nationalgalerie,
view of a coatroom and
a staircase.

INDUSTRIAL CLASSICISM (1956–69)

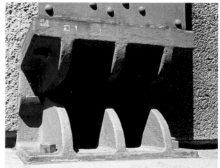

These exterior supports were a reference to Gothic flying buttresses, about which Mies had thought constantly since his days in Aachen and through his reading of Viollet-le-Duc, as is shown in his words and his "talking notes" from the 1950s to the IIT work.[29] In 1967 Mies would attend in person the installation, in a single day, of one thousand tons of the roof.

Such choices could only provoke the scepticism of historians of modern architecture such as Julius Posener, and the applause of those who, like Alison and Peter Smithson, saw the "big box Berlin" as "a big reliquary," accepting and making manifest the fact that art had identified itself with "show-business."[30] This was nonetheless the expression of an extra-ordinary effort on Mies's part to restore logical unity to his reflections on the meaning of the great open space and of structural clarity.[31] After this majestic return to Germany, where his arthritis had forced him to assign a large part of the on-site work to his grandson Dirk Lohan, he died on 17 August 1969.

The Poetics of Modernization

Adding to the multiple registers of his architecture between the wars, the mature work of Mies van der Rohe unfolded in a certain solitude. It was based on a rejection of invention as such and thus relied on a limited vocabulary of types and themes, some of which overlap.[32] Thus, the open floor of the skyscraper, with its vertical core, is akin to the designs of certain horizontal buildings, with their opaque central service area. The visible structure of the skyscraper designs was transposed onto low-rise buildings, which borrowed their vertical elements, despite the engineering problems involved. This self-limitation was especially important because the work of improving the detailing and refining the ultimate designs absorbed a considerable part of Mies's energy. He used to cite the German proverb "the Devil rests in the detail" (that is, the best of intentions can be thwarted by lack of care in carrying them out) and turn it on its head by saying that, on the contrary, God rests in the detail. Therein lies the key to this preoccupation. According to Hilberseimer, "Mies spends too much time with an issue; he just can't decide."[33] This attention

to detail was based on Mies's youthful experience, as shown in this comment recorded by Reginald Malcolmson: when Mies said to his father that details are hardly visible above the second floor, his father told him to go up to the top of the cathedral in Cologne, where he would see the same details as in the crypt.[34]

The mass of successive sketches of details of certain plans held at the Museum of Modern Art bears witness to his painstaking efforts, carried out in pencil in Apex notebooks and completed by experimentation with models.[35] Along with this meticulous work, not so much on the technical questions themselves as on their visual rationalization, another part of his energy was concentrated on the imposition of his typical grand forms on the landscape. Urban and sometimes suburban, this landscape was never a tabula rasa, but it was essentially a support for forms whose significance remained dissociable from their actual resting place. Mies's bases, front steps, and platforms define a space of negotiation between essentially universal types and specific locations.

The visual relationship of his buildings with these landscapes is, moreover, fundamentally different from that of Le Corbusier. Mies shared the latter's interest in framing but replaced the notion of piercing with that of total openness, filtered by the perspective effects of successive partitions. Thus exposed to the exterior, from which they could not be visually isolated except by curtains and blinds, the interior spaces of his American designs eliminate corridors and tend to minimize the limitations imposed by utilities, or even to deny them outright – Mies's antipathy to plumbing was notorious. According to architects in his office, he was wont to say that the true grandeur of the Gothic cathedrals was linked to the fact that they had no plumbing.[36] In this sense, Mies stands at the antipodes of New Brutalism, and in flat opposition to the ideas of Louis Kahn, for example, or to those of his friend Schwarz. When the latter asserted that architecture "is not simple function, but finds its roots in mystery and not in calculation," Mies asked him if he didn't think that all cathedrals were also "logic, construction, calculation."[37]

Totally aware of his place in the architecture of the twentieth century, Mies could not be accused of undue leniency in his verdicts on Le Corbusier. In 1965 he revealed, in Le Corbusier's funeral orations, that a "liberation" such as the one achieved by Le Corbusier ran the risk of leading to a "new Baroque."[38] He was no less critical of Gropius.[39] His remarks on the latter always showed a hint of condescension; with regard to Le Corbusier, he liked to say how out of place the rough concrete of the Unité d'habitation in Marseille would have been on Park Avenue, where everyone was so well dressed.[40] His veneration for Schinkel and Berlage aside, the architect he most respected was certainly Wright, in whose work he found more than an education, "a liberation," a body of work that would allow him to feel "much freer."[41] And this feeling was reciprocated, as has been seen.

But Mies never imitated Wright or Le Corbusier in their efforts to recruit clients. His painful relationship with politics – whether left wing, Nazi, or American – reveals both a certain lack of interest and, above all, a consistent refusal to compromise his work. Mies repeatedly and strenuously denied that he was a *Weltverbesserer* (reformer) or that he ever wanted to change the world except through his architecture. In the 1950s he said that he had "not wanted to change the world, but to express it,"[42] and he repeated this to Dirk Lohan at the end of his life: "I didn't intend to make the world a better place and I never said I did. I am an architect who is interested in construction [*Bauen*] and design [*Gestaltung*] in general, but one can also give to construction a wider meaning."[43]

When his daughter Georgia interviewed him in 1968, he railed against the idea of originality in architecture:
"I have spent my long life searching for what architecture was really about. And, more and more, I have come to the conclusion that architecture should be the expression of our civilization in its fundamental aspects and not its marginal aspirations. It is necessary to work on the essential, and that is where I see architecture properly speaking. The path was long and everything I did was meant to express this position, step by step. One cannot discover a new architecture every Monday morning. That would be naïve. Architecture has always been a very serious thing: it still makes it possible to describe the ages. And it will always be so!"[44]

Over six decades rich in political, cultural, and artistic change, Mies nevertheless created a personal oeuvre distinguished both by a constant effort to give rational form, intellectually and materially, to the designs of the elites who were committed to the transformation of society and by the refusal to appear as an original "author."[45] Using steel and glass, the materials of heavy industry, in configurations shaped by the aesthetic strategies of the avant-garde but nevertheless marked with the stamp of classicism, Mies produced categories of buildings as revealing of the world of capitalist production as the Florentine palaces were of the feudalism of the Quattrocento. In his early prototypes and in the variations upon them, Mies, more than any other modern architect, reveals himself as the one who gave form to modernization, definitively executing the program that Peter Behrens had sketched out for AEG at the beginning of the twentieth century. His work thus reflects that other Chicago School, the school of the modern social sciences, founded on the "crystal" that is the city with its populations and its ethnic and social groups, which provided an empirical basis for the creation of a model of conflict and arbitration that pretends to be universally applicable. Thanks to the possibilities opened up by IIT and by Greenwald's commissions, Mies himself was able to design such models, but their reproduction by other architects, who did not bind themselves with his rigor, proves that they were not reproducible. The mute presence of the bust of Mies by Hugo Weber, sheltered on the ground floor of the Crown Hall in Chicago, epitomizes his attitude toward the world. Molten in bronze, his massive face looks out with sovereign assurance at his century, his mouth caught between a rueful scowl at the "arbitrary and the sterile game" of the townscape around him and an eager appreciation of the quality of the stones and the metal that protect him from it.[46] He also seems caught in a silent reminiscence on his German childhood, which was so present in the great moments of his work. In fact, if the Palatine Chapel in Aachen seems to be at the origin of certain features of interior spaces imagined by Mies, the sovereign presence of the Gothic choir and of its stained glass above the little town do not fail to appear as the first source of skyscrapers with glass façades dreamed about in the early 1920s in Berlin and finally built in American cities in the 1950s.

Hugo Weber, bust of
Mies van der Rohe, 1961,
Crown Hall, Chicago.

NOTES

PREFACE

1 The four publications that marked the new historiographic climate addressed, respectively, the villas, the doctrine, the biography, and the conceptual work of Mies: Wolf Tegethoff, *Mies van der Rohe, Die Villen und Landhausprojekte* (Krefeld/Essen: Verlag Richard Bacht, 1981; published in English as *Mies van der Rohe: The Villas and Country Houses* [Cambridge, Mass.: MIT Press, 1985]); Franz Schulze, *Mies van der Rohe: A Critical Biography* (Chicago: University of Chicago Press, 1985); Arthur Drexler, ed., *The Mies van der Rohe Archive* (New York: Garland, 1986–93); Fritz Neumeyer, *Mies van der Rohe. Das kunstlose Wort: Gedanken zur Baukunst* (Berlin: Siedler Verlag, 1986; published in English as *The Artless Word: Mies van der Rohe on the Building Art* [Cambridge, Mass.: MIT Press, 1991]).

2 The Mies van der Rohe Archive essentially comprises two collections: (1) the general practice correspondence, housed at the Library of Congress in Washington, D.C., and consisting of approximately 22,000 documents, and (2) the drawings, correspondence, and manuscripts relating to Mies's plans, housed at the Museum of Modern Art in New York and consisting of approximately 20,000 items. In addition, there are the collections of the Bauhaus-Archiv in Berlin and other institutions.

3 The two catalogues are, respectively: Barry Bergdoll and Terence Riley, eds., *Mies in Berlin* (New York: Museum of Modern Art, 2001); Phyllis Lambert, ed., *Mies in America* (Montreal: Canadian Centre for Architecture; New York: Whitney Museum for American Art, 2001).

4 Sokratis Georgiadis, "'Mies' preussische Gefangenschaft," *Archplus* 161 (June 2002): p. 84–87.

5 Juan Jose Lahuerta, "Su alcune fotografie di Mies (frammenti)," *Casabella* 64, nos. 684–685 (December 2000–January 2001): p. 38–43; and most important: Claire Zimmerman, "Modernism, Media, Abstraction: Mies van der Rohe's Photographic Architecture in Barcelona and Brno (1927–31)" (Ph.D. diss., Graduate Center, City University of New York, 2005).

6 Werner Oechslin, "Mies's Steady Resistance to Formalism and Determinism: A Plea for Value-Criteria in Architecture," in Phyllis Lambert, ed., *Mies in America*, p. 82.

7 It is only in later editions of *Space, Time and Architecture* that Mies makes a real appearance. See Fritz Neumeyer, "Giedion en Mies van der Rohe: een paradox in de historiografie van het Moderne," *Archis* (April 1992): p.47–51.

8 Elaine S. Hochman, *Architects of Fortune: Mies van der Rohe and the Third Reich* (New York: Weidenfeld & Nicolson, 1989), p. 24. A far more solid and nuanced view of Mies's relationship to German politics is given by Richard Pommer, "Mies van der Rohe and the Political Ideology of the Modern Movement in Architecture," in Franz Schulze, ed., *Mies van der Rohe: Critical Essays* (New York: Museum of Modern Art; Cambridge, Mass.: MIT Press, 1990), p. 96–145.

9 Maurice Culot and Léon Krier, "A European Perspective on the Mies van der Rohe Centennial," in *The Chicago Architecture Annual* (Chicago: Metropolitan Press Publications, 1986), p. 13–14.

10 The literature dealing with these aspects of Mies's outlook can be found in Juan Pablo Bonta, "The Analysis of Mies: A New Language or Old Clichés?" *Design Book Review* 10 (Autumn 1986), p. 20–29; Bonta, "Mies as Text," *Design Book Review* 13 (Autumn 1987), p. 20–25; Winfried Nerdinger, "Nachlese zum 100. Geburtstag; neue Literatur zu Mies van der Rohe," *Kunstchronik* 41, no. 8 (August 1988): p. 419–429.

11 Philip Johnson, in John W. Cook and Heinrich Klotz, *Conversations with Architects* (New York: Praeger, 1973), p. 73.

12 Elaine S. Hochman, *Architects of Fortune*, p. 24.

13 Francesco Dal Co has reproduced and explained these notes: "Il centenario di Mies," *Domus* 668 (January 1986): p. 8–11.

14 "Ludwig Mies van der Rohe: An Address of Appreciation," *Architectural Association Journal* 75, no. 834 (July–August 1959), p. 29. The remarks were made by Mies on 27 May 1959 at the Architectural Association.

15 Mies van der Rohe, interview by Peter Carter, *20th Century*, Spring 1964, p. 139.

16 Mies van der Rohe, interview by Peter Blake, "Four Great Makers of Modern Architecture" (typed transcription of a symposium held at Columbia University, New York, March–May 1961), p. 93–104.

17 Mies van der Rohe, "Baukunst und Zeitwille!" *Der Querschnitt* 4 (1924): p. 31.

18 Mies van der Rohe, "Bauen," *G* 2 (September 1923): p. 1.

19 Massimo Cacciari, "Mies's Classics," *Res* 16 (Autumn 1988): p. 9–16.

20 Mies van der Rohe, "Gegen Willkür und Spielerei," interview by Anna Teut, *Die Welt*, 10 October 1964.

21 This is particularly the view of Elaine S. Hochman in *Architects of Fortune*, p. 56–57.

22 "Ludwig Mies van der Rohe: An Address of Appreciation," p. 29.

23 Mies van der Rohe, "6 Students Talk with Mies," in *Student Publications of the School of Design, Raleigh* 2, no. 3 (Spring 1952): p. 25.

24 Barry Bergdoll. "Fifteen Years of Publication on Mies van der Rohe (2000–2015)," Architectura, vol. 44, no. 2 (2014): p. 177–182.

25 Johannes Cramer, Dorothée Sack, and Barry Bergdoll. "Neues zu Mies van der Rohe," Architectura, vol. 44, no. 2 (2014): p. 97–100.

26 Lutz Robbers, "Filmkämpfer Mies," In Mies van der Rohe im Diskurs. Innovationen - Haltungen - Werke. Aktuelle Positionen. Ed. by Kerstin Plüm (Bielefeld: transcript, 2013): p. 63–96. Dietrich Neumann. "'Eislandschaften Zeigende Tapeten ...': Mies van der Rohes Patente zur Wandgestaltung und Drucktechnik von 1937–1950," In Mies van der Rohe und das Neue Wohnen. Ed. by Helmut Reuter and Birgit Schulte (Ostfildern: Hatje Cantz, 2008): p. 265–279.

1. CHILDHOOD IN THE RHINELAND AND EARLY DAYS IN BERLIN (1886–1914)

1 Maria Ludwig Michael was born on 27 March 1886. Both of his parents were of very old Catholic descent: see the memo concerning the Aryan credentials of the Mies family from the Berlin police headquarters, 28 November 1938, personal documents, file 1, Museum of Modern Art.

2 Georgia van der Rohe, *La Donna è mobile; Mein bedingungsloses Leben* (Berlin: Aufbau Verlag, 2001), p. 16.

3 Mies van der Rohe, comments collected by Peter Carter in "Mies van der Rohe. An Appreciation on the Occasion, This Month, of His 75th Birthday," *Architectural Design* 31, no. 3 (March 1961): p. 97.

4 Certificate of 18 January 1956, Aachen, personal documents, file 3, Museum of Modern Art.

5 Mies van der Rohe, interview by Dirk Lohan, Chicago, Summer 1968, p. 11. The typed transcript of the interview (in German) is at the Museum of Modern Art.

6 Mies van der Rohe, interview by Dirk Lohan.

7 Josef Strzygowski, *Der Dom zu Aachen und seine Entstehung, ein kunstwissenschaftlicher Protest* (Leipzig: J. C. Hinrichs'sche Buchhandlung, 1904), p. 80–92. See also Ernst Günther Grimme, *Der Dom zu Aachen, Architektur und Ausstattung* (Aachen: Einhard-Verlag, 1994), p. 341–343.

8 Proof kept in the Mies Archive (box 62), Library of Congress, Washington, D.C. Goebbels's first name remains unknown to this day.

9 Of Nietzschean inspiration, *Die Zukunft* published (1892–1922) texts on the architecture of Kurt Scheffler, Henry van de Velde, and August Endell, but also articles by the sociologists Werner Sombart and Georg Simmel and the writers Heinrich Mann and August Strindberg.

10 Franz Schulze, *Mies van der Rohe: A Critical Biography*, p. 17–19; Wolf Tegethoff, "Catching the Spirit: Mies' Early Work and the Impact of the 'Prussian Style,'" in Bergdoll and Riley, eds., *Mies in Berlin*, p. 135.

11 Hochschule für bildende Künste, certificate of 7 February 1956, box 62, Library of Congress, Washington, D.C.

12 On Bruno Paul, see Joseph Popp, *Bruno Paul* (Munich: F. Bruckmann, 1916); A. Ziffer, ed., *Bruno Paul, Deutsche Raumkunst und Architektur zwischen Jugendstil und Moderne* (Munich: Klinkhardt & Biermann, 1992).

13 Mies van der Rohe, interview by Dirk Lohan, p. 26.

14 The date of 1910 is proposed in a convincing manner by Jörg Limberg, "Haus Riehl, Neubabelsberg. Sanierung und denkmalpflegerische Begleitung," in Johannes Cramer and Dorothée Sack, eds., *Mies van der Rohe. Frühe Bauten: Probleme der Erhaltung – Probleme der Bewertung* (Petersberg: Michael Imhof Verlag, 2004), p. 37.

15 Fritz Neumeyer, *Mies van der Rohe. The Artless Word: Mies van der Rohe on the Building Art*, p. 45–46.

16 The impact of English models on this house is, in my opinion, overestimated by Schink. See Arnold Schink, *Mies van der Rohe: Beiträge zur ästhetischen Entwicklung der Wohnarchitektur* (Stuttgart: Karl Krämer, 1990), p. 42.

17 Paul Mebes, *Um 1800, Architektur und Handwerk im letzten Jahrhundert ihrer Entwicklung* (Munich: F. Bruckmann, 1908), p. 81.

18 Anton Jaumann, "Vom künstlerischen Nachwuchs, Haus Riehl," *Innendekoration* 21 (July 1910): p. 266–273, and "Architekt L. Mies, Villa des Prof. Dr. Riehl in Neubabelsberg," *Moderne Bauformen* 9 (1910): p. 42–48.

19 Hermann Muthesius, *Landhaus und Garten* (Munich: F. Bruckmann, 1910), p. I, plates 50 and following.

20 Barry Bergdoll, "The Nature of Mies's Space," in Bergdoll and Riley, eds., *Mies in Berlin*, p. 69–71.

21 Karl Foerster, *Winterharte Blütenstauden und Sträucher der Neuzeit* (Leipzig: J. J. Weber, 1924).

22 Fritz Neumeyer, "Mies's First Project: Revisiting the Atmosphere at Klösterli," in Bergdoll and Riley, eds., *Mies in Berlin*, p. 309–317.

23 Fritz Neumeyer, *Mies van der Rohe. The Artless Word: Mies van der Rohe on the Building Art*, p. 55–61.

24 Mies van der Rohe, interview by Dirk Lohan, p. 29.

25 Fritz Hoeber, *Peter Behrens* (Munich: Georg Müller & Eugen Rentsch, 1913); Stanford O. Anderson, *Peter Behrens and the New Architecture of Germany, 1900–1917* (Cambridge, Mass.: MIT Press, 2000).

26 Mechthild Heuser, "Die Fenster zum Hof, Die Turbinenhalle, Behrens und Mies van der Rohe," in Hans Georg Pfeifer, ed., *Peter Behrens, Wer aber will sagen, was Schönheit sei? Grafik, Produktgestaltung, Architektur* (Düsseldorf: Beton-Verlag, 1990), p. 108–121.

27 Tilmann Buddensieg and Hennig Rogge, *Industriekultur, Peter Behrens und die AEG, 1907–14* (Berlin: Gebr. Mann, 1979).

28 Mies van der Rohe, interview by Dirk Lohan, p. 27.

29 On the sources of Mies's architecture, see, among others: Sandra Honey, "Who and What Inspired Mies van der Rohe in Germany," *Architectural Design* 49, no. 3–4 (1979): p. 99–102.

30 Paul Westheim, "Mies van der Rohe. Entwicklung eines Architekten," *Das Kunstblatt* 2 (February 1927): p. 55–62.

31 Hartmut Frank, "Monument und Moderne," in Romana Schneider and Wilfried Wang, eds., *Moderne Architektur in Deutschland 1900 bis 2000, Macht und Monument* (Stuttgart: Gerd Hatje, 1998), p. 230–232.

32 Moreover, the Orianda designs would haunt Mies for a long time: Wolf Tegethoff, "Orianda-Berlin, Das Vorbild Schinkels im Werk Mies van der Rohes," *Zeitschrift des Deutschen Vereins für Kunstwissenschaft* 25, nos. 1–4 (1985): p. 174–184.

33 Andres Lepik, "Mies and Photomontage, 1910–38," in Bergdoll and Riley, eds., *Mies in Berlin*, p. 324–129.

34 Max Schmidt, *Das Bismarck-Nationaldenkmal auf der Elisenhöhe bei Bingerbrück (Hundert Entwürfe aus dem Wettbewerb)* (Düsseldorf: Düsseldorfer Verlags-Anstalt, 1911).

35 Jan Maruhn, "Building for Art: Mies van der Rohe as the Architect for Art Collectors," in Bergdoll and Riley, eds., *Mies in Berlin*, p. 318–323.

36 Dietrich von Beulwitz, "The Perls House by Mies van der Rohe," *Architectural Design* 53, nos. 10–11 (1983): p. 63–71.

37 Wolfram Hoepfner and Fritz Neumeyer, *Das Haus Wiegand von Peter Behrens in Berlin-Dahlem: Baugeschichte und Kunstgegenstände eines herrschaftlichen Wohnhauses* (Mainz: Philipp von Zabern, 1979).

38 Peter Behrens, *Zur Erinnerung an die Einweihung des Verwaltungsgebäudes der Mannesmannröhren-Werke in Düsseldorf, 10. Dezember 1912* (Düsseldorf: Mannesmann, 1913).

39 See Fritz Hoeber, *Peter Behrens*, p. 172.

40 Mies's contribution is revealed only by a note from Stanford Anderson, who gives this information on the basis of a letter of 1962 from Henry-Russell Hitchcock, who said he heard it from Paul Schneider-Esleben. See Schneider-Esleben, *Peter Behrens*, p. 312.

41 Karl Schaefer, "Gebäude der Kaiserlich-Deutschen Botschaft in St. Petersburg," *Der Profanbau* 12 (1914): p. 309–348.

42 On the experiences of Mies in St. Petersburg, see Sergius Ruegenberg, "Der Skelettbau ist keine Teigware," *Bauwelt* 77, no. 11 (14 March 1986): p. 346.

43 "Mies Speaks," *The Architectural Review* 144, no. 362 (December 1968): p. 451. (This is the transcript of an interview given to the Berlin RIAS). Fritz Neumeyer notes that the concept of "grand form" was developed by Wölfflin, whom Mies met at the Riehls: "Mies's First Project," p. 311.

44 Sergio Polano, "Rose-shaped, Like an Open Hand, Helene Kröller-Müller's House, the Kröller-Müllers," *Architectures for a Collection, Rassegna* 15, no. 56, (December 1993): p. 23–27.

45 Mies van der Rohe, *Print* 11, no. 1 (1957): p. 39.

46 "Mies Speaks," p. 451.

47 Julius Meier-Graefe to Mies van der Rohe, Paris, 18 November 1912, early plans, file 1, Museum of Modern Art; Franz Schulze, *Mies van der Rohe, Critical Essays*, p. 58–64.

48 His daughter gave evidence of his adventures: "Er war ein Casanova. Interview mit Georgia van der Rohe," *Der Spiegel* 20 (14 May 2001): p. 218.

49 Christiane Kruse, "Haus Werner – ein ungeliebtes Frühwerk Mies van der Rohes," *Zeitschrift für Kunstgeschichte* 56, no. 4 (1993): p. 554–563.

50 Markus Jager, "Das Haus Warnholtz von Ludwig Mies van der Rohe (1914/15)," *Zeitschrift für Kunstgeschichte* 65, no. 1 (2002): p. 123–136.

51 Edgar Wedepohl, "Form und Raum; Gespräch im Berliner Grunewald," *Wasmuths Monatshefte für Baukunst* 10, no. 9 (1926): p. 394.

52 This would enable the critic Werner Hegemann to use this house in his polemics against the roof terrace, when Mies became more radical: Werner Hegemann, "Schräges oder flaches Dach," *Wasmuths Monatshefte für Baukunst* 11, no. 5 (1927): p. 120–127.

53 They are noted by Wolf Tegethoff, "Catching the Spirit," in Bergdoll and Riley, eds., *Mies in Berlin*, p. 148.

54 This austerity aroused the criticism of the local administration; see Renate Petras, "Drei Arbeiten Mies van der Rohes in Potsdam-Babelsberg," *Architektur der DDR* 23, no. 2 (1974): p. 120. See also Martin Gaier and Claudia Mohn, "Haus Mosler, Neubabelsberg. Dokumentation einer Zerstörung. Planungs-, Ausführungs- und Veränderungsgeschichte des Hauses," in Cramer and Sack, eds., *Mies van der Rohe. Frühe Bauten*, p. 71–86.

2. THEORETICAL PROJECTS FOR THE METROPOLIS (1918–24)

1 Paul Westheim, "Mies van der Rohe. Entwicklung eines Architekten," p. 55–62.

2 Mies van der Rohe to Walter Gropius, Berlin, 11 February 1919, Bauhaus-Archiv, Berlin.

3 Alfred Dambitsch, ed., *Berlins dritte Dimension* (Berlin: Ullstein, 1912).

4 Walther Rathenau; see Alfred Dambitsch, ed., *Berlins dritte Dimension*, p. 20.

5 Bruno Möhring; see Alfred Dambitsch, ed., *Berlins dritte Dimension*, p. 12. For more on this architect, who was extremely important in the debate on the urbanism of Berlin, see Ines Wagemann, *Der Architekt Bruno Möhring 1863–1929* (Witterschlick: M. Wehle, 1992).

6 Peter Behrens, *Berlins dritte Dimension*, p. 10–11. See also his article "Einfluss von Zeit- und Raumnutzung auf moderne Formentwicklung," in *Jahrbuch des Deutschen Werkbundes 1914* (Jena: Eugen Diederichs, 1914), p. 8.

7 In any case, Fritz Neumeyer makes note of it in *Mies van der Rohe. The Artless Word*, p. 182–183.

8 August Endell, *Die Schönheit der großen Stadt* (Stuttgart: Strecker & Schroeder, 1908). Endell's texts were republished by Helge David: August Endell, *Vom Sehen, Texte 1896–1925* (Basel/Berlin/Boston: Birkhäuser, 1995).

9 Karl Scheffler, *Die Architektur der Großstadt* (Berlin: Bruno Cassirer, 1913); see Fritz Neumeyer, "Architektur als mythisches Bild: Anmerkungen zur imaginären Realität des gläsernen Hochhauses am Bahnhof-Friedrichstraße," in Fritz Neumeyer, *Ludwig Mies van der Rohe: Hochhaus am Bahnhof Friedrichstraße, Dokumentation des Mies-van-der-Rohe-Symposiums in der Neuen Nationalgalerie* (Berlin: Ernst Wasmuth, 1993), p. 9–29.

10 On the German responses to the skyscraper program, see: Florian Zimmermann, ed., *Der Schrei nach dem Turmhaus. Der Ideenwettbewerb Hochhaus am Bahnhof Friedrichstraße Berlin 1921/1922* (Berlin: Argon-Verlag, 1988); Rainer Stommer, *Hochhaus, der Beginn in Deutschland* (Marburg: Jonas, 1990); Dietrich Neumann,

"Die Wolkenkratzer kommen!" *Deutsche Hochhäuser der zwanziger Jahre, Debatten, Projekte, Bauten* (Brunswick, Wiesbaden: Vieweg, 1990).

11 On this subject, see the subtle remarks by Juan Antonio Ramírez, *The Beehive Metaphor from Gaudí to Le Corbusier* (London: Reaction Books, 2000), p. 92–97.

12 Martin Mächler, "Zum Problem des Wolkenkratzers," *Wasmuths Monatshefte für Baukunst* 5 (1920–21): p. 191–205 and 260–273.

13 Siegfried Kracauer, "Über Turmhäuser," *Frankfurter Zeitung*, 2 March 1921, reproduced in Dietrich Neumann, "Die Wolkenkratzer kommen!" p. 11.

14 Detlef Mertins, "Architecture of Becoming: Mies van der Rohe and the Avant-Garde," in Bergdoll and Riley, eds., *Mies in Berlin*, p. 113. Dietrich Neumann. "Mies – Dada – Montage: Notes on a Reception History" in: Mies van der Rohe: Montage. Collage. Ed. by Andreas Beitin, Wolf Eiermann & Brigitte Franzen. (London: Koenig Books, 2017): p. 56–69.

15 Ludwig Hilberseimer and Udo Rukser, "Amerikanische Architektur," *Kunst und Künstler* 18 (1920): p. 541–42. The building by Graham was well known in Germany: "Der neue Equitable-Bau in New York: Das größte Gebäude der Welt," *Bauwelt* 4, no. 17 (1914): p. 27–28.

16 Mies van der Rohe, "Hochhäuser," *Frühlicht* 1, no. 4 (1922): p. 124. Translation in Fritz Neumeyer, *Mies van der Rohe. The Artless Word*, p. 240.

17 Paul Scheerbart, *Glasarchitektur* (Berlin: Verlag Der Sturm, 1914).

18 Rosemarie Haag Bletter, "Mies and Dark Transparency," in Bergdoll and Riley, eds., *Mies in Berlin*, p. 330–357.

19 Francesco Dal Co and Manfredo Tafuri, *Architettura contemporanea* (Milan: Electa, 1992), p. 129.

20 Arthur Korn, *Glas im Bau und als Gebrauchsgegenstand* (Berlin: Ernst Pollak Verlag, 1929), p. 18–21.

21 *The International Competition for a New Administration Building for the Chicago Tribune* (Chicago: Tribune Co., 1923).

22 See the responses of Martin Wagner, Werner Hegemann, and Heinrich Mendelssohn on the question "Soll Berlin Wolkenkratzer bauen?" *Wasmuths Monatshefte für Baukunst* 12 (June 1928): p. 286–289.

23 Carl Gottfried, "Hochhäuser," *Qualität* 3, nos. 5–12 (August 1922–March 1923): p. 63–66.

24 "Mies Speaks," p. 451.

25 Mies van der Rohe, "Hochhäuser." Werner Graeff pointed out that Mies was afraid that the huge section of glass would blind passersby and horses on the Friedrichstraße: Werner Graeff to Ludwig Gläser, 6 July 1968, Museum of Modern Art, quoted by Wolf Tegethoff, "From Obscurity to Maturity: Mies van der Rohe's Breakthrough to Modernism," in Franz Schulze, *Mies van der Rohe: Critical Essays*, p. 42.

26 Spyros Papapetros, "Malicious Houses: Animation, Animism, Animosity in German Architecture and Film – From Mies to Murnau," *Grey Room* 20 (Summer 2005): p. 6–37.

27 Walther Rathenau, in Alfred Dambitsch, ed., *Berlins dritte Dimension*, p. 20–21.

28 Karl Scheffler, *Moderne Baukunst* (Berlin: Julius Bard, 1907), p. 15; quoted in Fritz Neumeyer, *Mies van der Rohe. The Artless Word*, p. 115.

29 William Stanley Parker, "Skyscrapers Anywhere," *Journal of the American Institute of Architects* 11, no. 9

(September 1923): p. 372, and Walter Curt Behrendt, "Skyscrapers in Germany," *Journal of the American Institute of Architects*, p. 366.

30 Mies van der Rohe to Werner Jakstein, 13 September 1923, box 1, Library of Congress, Washington, D.C. A translation of this letter appears in Fritz Neumeyer, *The Artless Word*, p. 359, note 14 and p. 109.

31 Published in *De Stijl* 4 (1922); see also *KI – Konstruktivistische Internationale schöpferische Arbeitsgemeinschaft 1922–1927, Utopien für eine europäische Kultur* (Stuttgart: Hatje, 1992).

32 The write-up of the review appeared in July 1923, with the publication of issue no. 1, by Werner Graeff, El Lissitzky, and Hans Richter. Mies van der Rohe, who would finance the publication out of his own pocket, joined from issue no. 2 in September 1923, and Friedrich Kiesler from issue no. 3 in June 1924. Two other issues followed, until April 1926. See the reissue of all editions, published in 1986 in Munich by Der Kern.

33 Hans Richter, *Köpfe und Hinterköpfe* (Zurich: Die Arche, 1967), p. 69.

34 *G* 3, p. 13.

35 The exhibition was mounted at the Léonce Rosenberg Gallery from 15 October to 15 November 1923: Yve-Alain Bois, Jean-Paul Rayon, Bruno Reichlin, *De Stijl et l'architecture en France* (Paris: Institut français d'architecture; Liège: Pierre Mardaga, 1985). It was doubtless on this occasion that Charles de Noailles had the idea of asking Mies van der Rohe to design his house at Hyères, which was finally built by Mallet-Stevens.

36 Ludwig Glaeser, *Ludwig Mies van der Rohe: Drawings in the Collection of the Museum of Modern Art* (New York: Museum of Modern Art, 1969).

37 Wolf Tegethoff mentions a sunbreaker effect; see "From Obscurity to Maturity; Mies van der Rohe's Breakthrough to Modernism," p. 50.

38 Mies van der Rohe, "Bürohaus," *G* 1 (July 1923): p. 3.

39 It was at this time that the work of Le Corbusier was published in Germany: Paul Westheim, "Architektur in Frankreich, Le Corbusier-Saugnier," *Wasmuths Monatshefte für Baukunst* 7, nos. 3-4 (1923): p. 69–82. Dietrich Neumann credits Wilhelm Deffke, a former draftsman of Behrens, who was working for Mies, of having offered a precedent and an inspiration with a building he had designed for the Reemstma tobacco company in Erfurt: Dietrich Neumann. "Neue Überlegungen zu Mies van der Rohes Bürohausentwurf von 1925." *Architectura*, vol. 44, no. 2 (2014): p. 163–176.

40 Mies van der Rohe, "Bürohaus," undated manuscript, box 3, Museum of Modern Art. The translation of Mies's manifesto appears in Fritz Neumeyer, *The Artless Word*, p. 241.

41 The newspaper received it too late for publication: manuscripts, file 3, Museum of Modern Art.

42 Karl Scheffler, *Moderne Baukunst* (Berlin: Julius Bard, 1907). Hermann Sörgel, *Architektur-Ästhetik* (Munich: Piloty & Loehle, 1923), vol. 1, p. 256.

43 Peter Behrens, in Alfred Dambitsch, ed., *Berlins dritte Dimension*, p. 10–11.

44 Mies van der Rohe, "Bürohaus." An English translation of Mies's article appears in Fritz Neumeyer, *The Artless Word*, p. 241.

45 Mies van der Rohe, "Bauen." An English translation appears in Fritz Neumeyer, *Mies van der Rohe. The Artless Word*, p. 242–243.

46 Wolf Tegethoff, "From Obscurity to Maturity: Mies van der Rohe's Breakthrough to Modernism," p. 52–53. On the precise date of this project, see Andreas Marx and Paul Weber, "Zur Neudatierung von Mies van der Rohes Landhaus in Eisenbeton," *Architectura,* vol. 38, no. 2 (2008): p. 127–166.

47 This exhibition was organized by André Lurçat with the help of Van Doesburg: Jean-Louis Cohen, *André Lurçat (1894–1970): L'autocritique d'un moderne* (Paris: IFA; Liège: Pierre Mardaga, 1995), p. 73–75.

48 Mies van der Rohe, manuscript dated 19 June 1924 for an undated conference, box 61, Library of Congress, Washington, D.C.; in Fritz Neumeyer, *Mies van der Rohe. The Artless Word*, p. 250.

49 Mies van der Rohe, "Bauen," in Fritz Neumeyer, *Mies van der Rohe. The Artless Word*, p. 242.

50 Werner Oechslin, "Mies's Steady Resistance to Formalism and Determinism: A Plea for Value-Criteria in Architecture," in Lambert, ed., *Mies in America*, p. 33.

51 Peter Eisenman, "Mies Reading ..." in John Zukowsky, ed., *Mies Reconsidered: His Career, Legacy and Disciples* (Chicago: Art Institute of Chicago; New York: Rizzoli, 1986), p. 41.

52 Wolf Tegethoff, who submitted the most rigorous analysis of these plans, alluded to the correspondence between Gropius and Mies; see *Mies van der Rohe, The Villas and Country Houses,* p. 32.

53 Wolf Tegethoff, *Mies van der Rohe, The Villas and Country Houses,* p. 39. Mies denied this interpretation, stating that he had only wanted to spare the public from having to read through prints of the plans: "Ludwig Mies van der Rohe: An Address of Appreciation," p. 30.

54 Mies van der Rohe, manuscript of 19 June 1924 for an undated conference, box 61, Library of Congress, Washington, D.C. An English translation of the manuscript appears in Fritz Neumeyer, *The Artless Word*, p. 250.

55 Wolf Tegethoff, *Mies van der Rohe: The Villas and Country Houses* (New York: Museum of Modern Art; Cambridge, Mass.: MIT Press, 1985), p. 16.

56 Hans Berger to Mies van der Rohe, Spittal, 14 January 1926, general correspondence, file 2, Museum of Modern Art.

57 Mies rejected this parallel, which was first made in 1936: Alfred H. Barr, *Cubism and Abstract Art* (New York: Museum of Modern Art, 1936), p. 156–157.

58 Hans Richter, "Filmmomente," *De Stijl* 6, no. 5 (1923). This parallel is presented in a convincing way by Bruno Reichlin in "Mies' Raumgestaltung: Vermutungen zu einer Genealogie und Inspirationsquelle," in Adolph Stiller, ed., *Das Haus Tugendhat: Ludwig Mies van der Rohe* (Salzburg: Anton Pustet, 1999), p. 53–61.

59 Hans Richter, *Köpfe und Hinterköpfe*, p. 70.

60 These convergences were mentioned by Hilberseimer: Ludwig Hilberseimer, *Mies van der Rohe* (Chicago: P. Theobald, 1956), p. 42.

61 Mies van der Rohe, "A Tribute to Frank Lloyd Wright," *College Art Journal* 6, no. 1 (Autumn 1946): p. 41–42. This text, written in 1940, was intended for a Museum of Modern Art catalogue dedicated to Wright, which was not published. Fritz Neumeyer, *The Artless Word*, p. 321.

62 Mies van der Rohe, "Gelöste Aufgaben. Eine Forderung an unser Bauwesen," *Bauwelt* 52 (1923): p. 7–19.

63 Leo Frobenius, *Das unbekannte Afrika, Aufhellung der Schicksale eines Erdteils* (Munich: Beck, 1923). The echo of Semper's analyses is also evident: Gottfried Semper,

Der Stil in den technischen und tektonischen Künsten oder Praktische Ästhetik (Frankfurt a. M.: Verlag für Kunst und Wissenschaft, 1860–63).

64 Mies van der Rohe, "Industrielles Bauen," *G* 3 (June 1924): p. 11–13. Mies paid homage to Ford in his lecture of 19 June 1924, box 61, Library of Congress, Washington, D.C. Translation in Fritz Neumeyer, *Mies van der Rohe. The Artless Word*, p. 251.

65 Fritz Hoeber, *Peter Behrens*, endpapers.

66 Ludwig Hilberseimer, *Berliner Architektur der 20er Jahre* (Mainz and Berlin: Florian Kupferberg, 1967), p. 61.

67 Fritz Neumeyer, *Mies van der Rohe. The Artless Word*, p.102–106. On Francé, the author of some one hundred works on the marvels of the plant world and biomorphism, see Oliver Botar, "Prolegomena to the Study of Biomorphic Modernism: Biocentrism, László Moholy-Nagy's 'New Vision' and Ernö Kállai's 'Bioromantik'" (Ph. D. diss., University of Toronto, 1998).

68 Mies van der Rohe, "Baukunst und Zeitwille!" p. 31–32. The illustrations provided by Mies for this text came from Werner Lindner, *Die Ingenieurbauten in ihrer guten Gestaltung* (Ernst Wasmuth, 1923). An English translation of Mies's text appears in Fritz Neumeyer, *The Artless Word*, p. 245.

69 Otto Wagner, *Moderne Architektur. Seinen Schülern ein Führer auf diesem Kunstgebiete* (Vienna: A. Schroll, 1896).

70 Hans Richter, "Der neue Baumeister," *Qualität* 4, nos. 1–2 (January–February 1925): p. 3–9. Here Richter fundamentally opposes the *Baumeister* and the *Architekt*.

3. FOUNDATIONS OF A NEW DOMESTIC SPACE (1925–30)

1 The signatures on the manifesto were those of Jürgen Bachmann, Otto Bartning, Peter Behrens, Otto Firle, Hugo Häring, Erich Mendelsohn, Mies, Hans Poelzig, Otto-Rudolf Salvisberg, Emil Schaudt, Walther Schildbach, and Bruno Taut: bulletin of 26 April 1926, file 2, Museum of Modern Art. On Mies office during the Berlin years, see Andreas Marx and Paul Weber. "Von Ludwig Mies zu Mies van der Rohe: Wohnung und Atelier 'Am Karlsbad 24' (1915–1939)," In *Mies van der Rohe und das Neue Wohnen*. Ed. by Helmut Reuter and Birgit Schulte (Ostfildern: Hatje Cantz, 2008), p. 24–39.

2 See the correspondence with the client: small plans, file 2, Museum of Modern Art.

3 Paul Westheim, "Mies van der Rohe. Entwicklung eines Architekten," p. 59.

4 A view of the dining room is reproduced in Bergdoll and Riley, eds., *Mies in Berlin*, p. 321.

5 Barry Bergdoll, "The Nature of Mies's Space," p. 87.

6 Paul Westheim, "Das Haus eines Sammlers," *Das Kunstblatt* 3 (March 1926): p. 106–113. Mies had built his first monument for Laura Perls, mother of his second client: Tobias Arera-Rütenik. "Mies van der Rohes Aufbruch in die Moderne: das Grabmal Laura Perls von 1919." Architectura, vol. 44, no. 2 (2014): p. 107–116.

7 The masterpiece by Fuchs (1870–1940), which gave rise to the nickname *Sittenfuchs* (Fox of Manners), remains: *Illustrierte Sittengeschichte; vom Mittelalter bis zur Gegenwart* (Munich: A. Langen, 1909–12). See also Ulrich Weitz, *Salonkultur und Proletariat: Eduard Fuchs, Sammler, Sittengeschichtler* (Stuttgart: Stoeffler & Schnetz, 1991).

8 Hugo Perls, *Warum ist Kamilla schön? Von Kunst, Künstlern u. Kunsthandel* (Munich: Paul List, 1962). See Franz Schulze, *Mies van der Rohe: A Critical Biography*, p. 127.

9 Mies van der Rohe to Donald Drew Egbert, 6 February 1951, quoted by Donald Drew Egbert, *Social Radicalism and the Arts: A Cultural History from the French Revolution to 1962* (New York: Knopf, 1972), p. 661–662.

10 Sergius Ruegenberg, "Der Skelettbau ist keine Teigware," p. 350.

11 Marco De Michelis gave the best anaylsis of this episode in "Sul monumento a Rosa Luxemburg e Karl Liebknecht di Ludwig Mies van der Rohe," in Jeffrey T. Schnapp, ed., *In Cima, Giuseppe Terragni per Margherita Sarfatti, architetture della memoria nel' 900* (Venice: Marsilio, 2004), p. 45–51.

12 The sculpture, made in 1909 by Moreau-Vauthier, is located not in the cemetery but in the Samuel de Champlain square, on the avenue Gambetta side.

13 Mies van der Rohe, interview by Lisa Dechêne, *Deutsche Volkszeitung*, 5 September 1969, quoted by Rolf-Peter Baacke and Michael Nungesser, "Ich bin, ich war, ich werde sein!" in *Wem gehört die Welt – Kunst und Gesellschaft in der Weimarer Republik* (Berlin [West]: NGBK, 1977), p. 287.

14 The Society had sent him some documents concerning his activities since 1923; box 2, Library of Congress, Washington, D.C.

15 Richard Pommer, "Mies van der Rohe and the Political Ideology of the Modern Movement in Architecture," in Franz Schulze, ed., *Mies van der Rohe: Critical Essays*, p.96–145.

16 Romano Guardini, *Briefe vom Comer See* (Mainz: Matthias-Grünewald-Verlag, 1927). These texts had already been published in 1923 and 1925 in *Die Schildgenossen*, a Quickborn magazine.

17 Lecture dated 17 March 1926, Dirk Lohan's archive, Chicago published by Fritz Neumeyer, *Mies van der Rohe. The Artless Word*, p. 256.

18 Friedrich Dessauer, *Philosophie der Technik* (Bonn: F. Cohen 1927). Mies van der Rohe, unpaginated notebook, 17 March 1928, manuscripts, file 1, Museum of Modern Art.

19 Rudolf Schwarz, *Wegweisung der Technik* (Potsdam: Müller & Kiepenheuer, 1928). On Schwarz, see Wolfgang Pehnt and Hilda Strohl, *Bewohnte Bilder: Rudolf Schwarz 1897–1961, Architekt einer anderen Moderne* (Ostfildern: Hatje Cantz, 1997).

20 In 1934, Mies refused to hand over the documentation concerning this complex for a RIBA exhibition. Mies van der Rohe to RIBA, Berlin, 6 October 1934, Library of Congress, Washington, D.C.

21 Le Corbusier, *Vers une architecture* (Paris: G. Crès & Co, 1924), p. 198–199; Fritz Neumeyer, "Schinkel im Zeilenbau. Mies van der Rohes Siedlung an der Afrikanischen Straße in Berlin-Wedding," in Andreas Beyer, Vittorio Magnago Lampugnani, and Günter Schweikhart, eds., *Hülle und Fülle: Festschrift für Tilmann Buddensieg* (Alfter: VDG – Verlag und Datenbank für Geisteswissenschaften, 1993), p. 415–431.

22 Fritz Neumeyer, "Neues Bauen in Wedding," in *Der Wedding im Wandel der Zeit* (Berlin: Koll, 1985), p. 26–34.

23 Mies van der Rohe, preface to *Bau und Wohnung* (Stuttgart: Julius Hoffmann, 1927), p. 7. Translation in Fritz Neumeyer, *Mies van der Rohe. The Artless Word*, p. 259.

24 Rudolf Schwarz, "Großstadt als Tatsache und Aufgabe," *Die Schildgenossen* 8, no. 4 (1927): p. 301–307.

25 On the preparation, construction, and echo of the estate, see Karin Kirsch, *Die Weißenhofsiedlung: Werkbund-*

Ausstellung "Die Wohnung," Stuttgart 1927 (Stuttgart: Deutsche Verlags-Anstalt, 1987), and Christian Otto and Richard Pommer, *Weißenhof 1927 and the Modern Movement in Architecture* (Chicago: University of Chicago Press, 1991).

26 The critic Walter Curt Behrendt, editor of *Die Form*, acted as the intermediary between some of these architects and Mies, notably facilitating a difficult mediation between Mies and Häring: Werner Oechslin, "Mies's Steady Resistance to Formalism and Determinism: A Plea for Value-Criteria in Architecture," p. 59–65.

27 Mark Stankard, "Re-covering Mies van der Rohe's Weissenhof: The Ultimate Surface," *Journal of Architectural Education* 55, no. 4 (May 2002): p. 247–256.

28 Mies van der Rohe, "Zu meinem Block," in *Bau und Wohnung* (Stuttgart: Julius Hoffmann, 1927), p. 77 (Deutscher Werkbund publication).

29 *Deutsche Bauhütte* 36, no. 9 (1932): p. 110.

30 Henri Bergson, *L'Évolution créatrice* (Paris: Presses Universitaires de France, 1941), p. 129; published in English as: Creative Evolution (New York: H. Holt & Co., 1911). See Detlef Mertins, "Architecture of Becoming: Mies van der Rohe and the Avant-Garde," in Bergdoll and Riley, eds., *Mies in Berlin*, p. 133.

31 Mies van der Rohe, "Über die Form in der Architektur," *Die Form* 2, no. 2 (1927): p. 59; preface to *Bau und Wohnung*, manuscripts, file 6, Museum of Modern Art.

32 Mies van der Rohe to Le Corbusier, Berlin, 1 February 1929, Library of Congress, Washington, D.C.

33 Le Corbusier to Mies van der Rohe, 10 April 1928, Fondation Le Corbusier, D2(1)106.

34 The Lilly Reich archives (Berlin, 1885–1947) are kept at the Museum of Modern Art. See Sonja Guenther, *Lilly Reich: Innenarchitektin, Designerin, Ausstellungsgestalterin* (Stuttgart: Deutsche Verlags-Anstalt, 1988); Matilda McQuaid, *Lilly Reich, Designer and Architect* (New York: Museum of Modern Art, 1996). The memories of Mies's daughter reveal her sufferings on this point: Georgia van der Rohe, *La Donna è mobile*, p. 55.

35 Walter Cohen, "Haus Lange in Krefeld," *Museum der Gegenwart* 1, no. 4 (first quarter, 1931): p. 160–168. The two houses became subsidiaries of the museum in Krefeld in 1955 (Lange) and 1981 (Esters) and were the setting for many artistic experiments, on the basis of which Kleinman and Van Duzer analyzed their layouts. Kent Kleinman and Leslie Van Duzer, *Mies van der Rohe: The Krefeld Villas* (New York: Princeton Architectural Press, 2005).

36 "Ludwig Mies van der Rohe: An Address of Appreciation," p. 31.

37 Justus Bier, "Mies van der Rohes Reichspavillon in Barcelona," *Die Form* 4, no. 16 (15 August 1929): p. 423.

38 Claire Zimmerman, "Modernism, Media, Abstraction," p. 140–149. On Mies's relationship to the photographers before 1933, see Helmut Reuter, Rolf Sachsse, and Wolf Tegethoff, "Mies and the Photographers I," In Helmut Reuter and Birgit Schulte, eds., *Mies and Modern Living: Interiors, Furniture, Photography*, (Ostfildern: Hatje Cantz, 2008), p. 253–263. And Rolf Sachsse. "Mies and the Photographers II." Ibid., p. 253–263.

39 Juan Pablo Bonta, *Anatomia de la interpretación en arquitectura* (Barcelona: Gili, 1984).

40 On the reconstruction, already envisaged during the 1950s, as is shown in the letters of Oriol Bohigas to Mies (box 20, Library of Congress, Washington, D.C.), see *El pavello alemany de Barcelona de Mies van der Rohe, 1929-1986* (Barcelona: Fundacio publica del pavello, 1987).

41 "Mies Speaks," p. 451.

42 Mies van der Rohe, comments collected by Peter Carter, "Mies van der Rohe: An Appreciation on the Occasion, This Month, of His 75th Birthday," *Architectural Design* 31, no. 3 (March 1961): p. 100.

43 Arthur Drexler, ed., *The Mies van der Rohe Archive*, vol. 2, 1st section, drawing 14.22.

44 Sergius Ruegenberg, in Barry Bergdoll, "The Nature of Mies's Space," p. 92.

45 Josep Quetglas, "Fear of Glass," in Beatriz Colomina and K. Michael Hays, eds., *Architecture Production* (New York: Princeton Architectural Press/Revisions 2, 1988), p. 122–151; Josep Quetglas, *Der gläserne Schrecken, Imágenes del Pabellón de Alemania* (Montreal: Section b, 1991).

46 Caroline Constant, "The Barcelona Pavilion as Landscape Garden: Modernity and the Picturesque," *AA Files 20* (Autumn 1990): p. 46–54.

47 Robin Evans, "Mies van der Rohe's Paradoxical Symmetries," *AA Files* 19 (Spring 1990): p. 56–58.

48 Quoted by Juan Pablo Bonta, *Architecture and its interpretation*, (London: Lund Humphries Publishers, 1979), p. 155.

49 Sergius Ruegenberg, "Der Skelettbau ist keine Teigware," p. 347. Frobenius paid a visit to the Riehls: Fritz Neumeyer, "Mies's First Project...," p. 315.

50 The "Five Points of a New Architecture," published in German in the Stuttgart exhibition catalogue of 1927, had not escaped Mies's attention.

51 Frank Lloyd Wright to Philip Johnson, 26 February 1932, Museum of Modern Art.

52 Philip Johnson to J. J. P. Oud, 2 September 1930, NAI, Oud Archive, Rotterdam.

53 On Brno: Vladimír Šlapeta, *Die Brünner Funktionalisten, Moderne Architektur in Brno* (Innsbruck: Technische Fakultät der Universität Innsbruck, 1985). On the Tugendhat family, see Karel Menšík and Jaroslav Vodička, *Vila Tugendhat Brno* (Brno: Odbor vnitrich veci Narodniho vyboru, 1986).

54 Julius Bier, "Kann man im Haus Tugendhat wohnen?" *Die Form* 6, no. 10 (1931): p. 392–393.

55 For more on the villa, see Jan Šapak, "Vila Tugendhat," *Umění* 1 (1987): p. 167–179, and especially Adolph Stiller, ed., *Das Haus Tugendhat: Ludwig Mies van der Rohe.*

56 Julius Posener, "Eine Reise nach Brünn," *Bauwelt* 60, no. 36 (1969): p. 1244–1245.

57 Grete Tugendhat, "Zum Bau des Hauses Tugendhat," *Bauwelt* 60, no. 36 (1969): p. 1246–1247.

58 Walter Curt Behrendt, *Der Sieg des neuen Baustils* (Stuttgart: F. Wedekind, 1927), p. 52.

59 Bruno Reichlin, "Mies' Raumgestaltung: Vermutungen zu einer Genealogie und Inspirationsquelle," in Adolph Stiller, ed., *Das Haus Tugendhat: Ludwig Mies van der Rohe*, p. 56.

60 Paul Westheim, "Mies van der Rohe. Die Entwicklung eines Architekten," p. 57–58.

61 Fritz Tugendhat, "Die Bewohner des Hauses Tugendhat äussern sich," *Die Form* 6, no. 11 (1931): p. 438. On the garden, see Kamila Krejčiřková and Lucie Valdhansová, "Markéta Müllerová, Author of the Garden Design at Villa Tugendhat, and Women in Czech Landscape Architecture," in Iveta Černa and Lucie Valdhansova, eds., *Villa Tugend- hat: Zahrada/the Garden*. Ed. (Brno: Muzeum města Brna, 2017), p. 114–119. Jana Tichá. "The Space Beyond the Glass." Ibid., p. 18–31.

62 On the living conditions in the house, see Jan Šapák, "Das Alltagsleben in der Villa Tugendhat," *Werk, Bauen + Wohnen* 12 (1983): p. 15–23.

63 Roger Ginsburger and Walter Riezler, "Zweckhaftigkeit und geistige Haltung," *Die Form* 6, no. 11 (1931): p. 431–437.

64 Wilhelm Lotz, "Wettbewerb für ein Bürohaus am Hindenburgplatz in Stuttgart," *Die Form* 4, no. 6 (1929): p. 151–153. Curt Gravekamp, "Mies van der Rohe: Glashaus in Berlin," *Das Kunstblatt* 4 (1930): p. 111–112.

65 Ludwig Hilberseimer, "Eine Würdigung des Projektes Mies van der Rohes für die Umbauung des Alexanderplatzes," *Das neue Berlin* (February 1929): p. 39–41. See also Paul Westheim, "Umgestaltung des Alexanderplatzes," *Bauwelt* 20, no. 13 (1929): p. 312–313.

66 Mies van der Rohe, conference on 17 March 1926, in Fritz Neumeyer, *Mies van der Rohe. The Artless Word*, p. 254.

67 Mies van der Rohe, "Die Voraussetzungen des baukünstlerischen Schaffens," February 1928, in Fritz Neumeyer, *Mies van der Rohe. The Artless Word*, p. 300.

68 The observations come from architects such as Peter Behrens, Bruno Möhring, and August Endell, and from intellectuals such as Georg Simmel, Werner Sombart, and Karl Scheffler. See the texts collected by Francesco Dal Co in *Teorie del moderno: architettura, Germania, 1880-1920* (Rome: Laterza, 1982).

69 Karl Scheffler, *Die Architektur der Großstadt* (Berlin: Bruno Cassirer Verlag, 1913), p. 13, 17.

70 Mies owned two essential books on America that were published in Germany: Lewis Mumford, *Vom Blockhaus zum Wolkenkratzer. Eine Studie über amerikanische Architektur und Zivilisation* (Berlin: Bruno Cassirer Verlag, 1925, a translation of *Sticks and Stones*, published in 1924); Martin Wagner, *Städtebauliche Probleme in amerikanischen Städten und ihre Rückwirkung auf den deutschen Städtebau* (Berlin: Deutsche Bauzeitung, 1929).

71 Mies van der Rohe, conference on 17 March 1926, in Fritz Neumeyer, *Mies van der Rohe. The Artless Word*, p. 369. Mies had a copy of the German translation of *Urbanism: Le Corbusier, Städtebau* (Berlin and Leipzig: Deutsche Verlags-Anstalt, 1929).

72 On this question, the Munich-based architect and theoretician Herman Sörgel wrote: "America has no culture, but we have no civilization": "Amerika," *Baukunst* 1, no. 12 (1925): p. 323.

73 Mies van der Rohe, conference, 17 March 1926, in Fritz Neumeyer, *Mies van der Rohe. The Artless Word*, p. 255–256. The Siedlungsverband Ruhrkohlengebiet, created by Robert Schmidt after World War I, is the setting for the first European experiment in regional planning.

74 Mies van der Rohe, conference, 19 June 1924, in Fritz Neumeyer, *Mies van der Rohe. The Artless Word*, p. 250.

75 Mies van der Rohe, conference, 17 March 1926, in Fritz Neumeyer, *Mies van der Rohe. The Artless Word*, p. 256.

4. FROM THE BAUHAUS TO THE THIRD REICH (1930–38)

1 Sybil Moholy-Nagy, "Modern Architecture Symposium," *Journal of the Society of Architectural Historians* 24 (March 1965): p. 83.

2 Franz Schulze, *Mies van der Rohe: A Critical Biography*, p. 98.

3 Claude Schnaidt, *Hannes Meyer: Bauten, Projekte und Schriften* (Teufen: A. Niggli, 1965); Matthias Schirren, ed., *Hannes Meyer, 1889-1954: Architekt, Urbanist, Lehrer* (Berlin: Ernst und Sohn, 1989).

4 Mies van der Rohe, "The End of the Bauhaus," *Student Publications of the School of Design*, Raleigh 3, no. 3 (Spring 1953): p. 16.

5 On Hilberseimer, see Marco De Michelis, ed., "Ludwig Hilberseimer, 1885–1967," *Rassegna* 27 (1979); Richard Pommer, ed., *In the Shadow of Mies: Ludwig Hilberseimer Architect, Educator and Urban Planner* (Chicago: The Art Institute; New York: Rizzoli, 1988).

6 Sandra Honey, "Mies at the Bauhaus," *Architectural Association Quarterly* 10, no. 1 (1978): p. 51–59.

7 Howard Dearstyne, *Inside the Bauhaus* (New York: Rizzoli, 1986), p. 226.

8 Georgia van der Rohe, *La Donna è mobile*, p. 236.

9 Philip Johnson, interview by Jean-Louis Cohen, New York, 10 April 1991.

10 Franz Schulze appeared sceptical as to his personal commitment in the project: Arthur Drexler, ed., *The Mies van der Rohe Archive*, vol. 3, p. 52.

11 Wallis Miller, "Tangible Ideas: Architecture and the Public at the 1931 German Building Exhibition in Berlin" (Ph.D. diss., Princeton University, 1999); Wallis Miller, "Mies and Exhibitions," in Bergdoll and Riley, eds., *Mies in Berlin*, p.338–349.

12 Wilhelm Lotz, "Die Halle II auf der Bauausstellung," *Die Form* 6, no. 7 (1931): p. 341–349. "Deutsche Bauausstellung Berlin 1931," *Der Baumeister* 29, no. 7 (July 1931): p. 261–268.

13 Henry-Russell Hitchcock Jr., "Architecture Chronicle: Berlin; Paris; 1931," *The Hound and Horn* 5, no. 1 (October–December 1931): p. 96.

14 Set in the heart of an area of East Berlin long reserved for the Stasi, it became accessible in 1989. Volker Velter, "Landhaus Lemke in Berlin Hohenschönhausen," *Bauwelt* 12 (1991): p. 536. See Heribert Sutter, "Haus Lemke, Berlin-Hohenschönhausen, Baugeschichte, Voruntersuchung und Instandsetzungskonzept," in Cramer and Sack, eds., *Mies van der Rohe. Frühe Bauten*, p. 115–28. Mies also worked in the following years on a small house in Berlin: Carsten Krohn. "Haus Bueren: ein Unbekannter Bau von Mies van der Rohe in Berlin." Architectura, vol. 44, no. 2 (2014): p. 101–104.

15 Karl Otto Lüfkens, "Die Verseidag-Bauten von Mies van der Rohe (1933 bis 1937), ein Dokument der Architektur des XX. Jahrhunderts," *Die Heimat, Zeitschrift für niederrheinische Kultur- und Heimatpflege* 48 (December 1977): p. 57–61. Wolf Tegethoff, "Industriearchitektur und Neues Bauen: Mies van der Rohes Verseidag-Fabrik in Krefeld," *Archithese* 13 (May–June 1983): p. 33–38.

16 Hans-Peter Schwanke, "Haus Heusgen in Krefeld – ein bislang unbeachteter Bau Ludwig Mies van der Rohes," *Denkmalpflege im Rheinland* 20, no. 4 (2003): p. 177–80; Michael Kasiske, "Haus Heusgen," *Bauwelt* 39 (2002): p. 4.

17 On this confrontation, see Mies van der Rohe, "The End of the Bauhaus," p. 16.

18 Peter Hahn, ed., *Bauhaus Berlin, Weingarten, Kunstverein Weingarten* (Berlin: Bauhaus-Archiv, 1985).

19 Comments reported by Bertrand Goldberg, "Kindergarten Plauderei," *Inland Architect* (March–April 1986): p. 28.

20 Howard Dearstyne, *Inside the Bauhaus*, p. 243.

21 Georgia van der Rohe, *La Donna è mobile*, p. 56.

22 Adolf Hitler, *Die deutsche Kunst als stolzeste Verteidigung des deutschen Volkes* (Munich: Eher, 1934).

23 Philip Johnson, "Architecture in the Third Reich," *Hound and Horn* 7, no. 1 (October–December 1933): p. 138.

24 Albert Speer, confidence shared with Elaine S. Hochman on 29 July 1974; see *Architects of Fortune: Mies van der Rohe and the Third Reich*, p. 213.

25 Their names were published in the *Völkischer Beobachter* on 18 August 1934. The names of Wilhelm Furtwängler, Georg Kolbe, Emil Nolde, and Richard Strauss are also found there.

26 Ivano Panaggi to Walter Gropius, 25 August 1934, Peter Hahn (ed.), *Bauhaus Berlin*, Berlin 1985, p. 225.

27 Walter Gropius to Eugen Hönig, 27 March 1934, quoted by Barbara Miller-Lane, *Architecture and Politics in Germany, 1918–1945* (Cambridge, Mass.: Harvard University Press, 1968), p. 181.

28 George Nelson, "Architecture of Europe Today: 7 – Van der Rohe [sic], Germany," *Pencil Points* 16, no. 9 (September 1935): p. 453–460.

29 Friedrich Paulsen, "Der Reichsbank Wettbewerb," *Monatshefte für Baukunst und Städtebau* 17 (1933): p. 337–44. "Der Wettbewerb der Reichsbank," *Deutsche Bauzeitung* 67, no. 607 (14 August 1933): p. 607–614.

30 Claire Zimmerman, "German Pavilion, International Exposition, Brussels, 1934," in Bergdoll and Riley, *Mies in Berlin*, p. 284.

31 Richard Pommer, "Mies van der Rohe and the Political Ideology of the Modern Movement in Architecture," p. 126–228.

32 Marco De Michelis, "Sul monumento a Rosa Luxemburg e Karl Liebknecht di Ludwig Mies van der Rohe," p. 45.

33 Mies van der Rohe, "Autobahnen als künstlerisches Problem," *Die Autobahn* 5, no. 10 (1932): p. 1; in Fritz Neumeyer, *Mies van der Rohe. The Artless Word*, p. 313. On the history of the German highway program, see Rainer Stommer, ed., *Reichsautobahn: Pyramiden des Dritten Reiches. Analysen zur Ästhetik eines unbewältigten Mythos* (Marburg: Jonas, 1982); Martin Kornrumpf, *HaFraBa e.V. Deutsche Autobahnplanung 1926–1934* (Bonn-Bad Godesberg: Kirschbaum Verlag, 1990).

34 Georgia van der Rohe, *La Donna è mobile*, p. 56.

35 Some of these drawings, which occupy half of the fourth volume of *The Mies van der Rohe Archive*, are analyzed in Kurt W. Forster, "Four Unpublished Drawings by Mies van der Rohe: A Commentary," *Res* 16 (Autumn 1988): p. 5–8.

36 Bauhaus, letters to Philip Johnson, Dessau, 16 April 1931, 19 February and 1 September 1932, file 1, Museum of Modern Art.

37 Henry-Russell Hitchcock and Philip Johnson, *The International Style, Architecture Since 1922* (New York: W. W. Norton, 1932). On the story of the exhibition and this book, about which Mies wrote to Johnson that it had given "a good representation of the development of modern architecture in Europe," see Terence Riley, *The International Style, Exhibition 15 and the Museum of Modern Art* (New York: Rizzoli, 1992).

38 Mies van der Rohe to Philip Johnson, Berlin, 23 January 1934, file 1, Museum of Modern Art.

39 John A. Holabird to Mies van der Rohe, 20 March 1936; Mies van der Rohe to John A. Holabird, 20 May 1936, Library of Congress, Washington, D.C. Mies finally refused on 20 June 1936: Mies van der Rohe to President Willard Hotchkiss, Library of Congress, Washington, D.C.

40 Alfred H. Barr to Mies van der Rohe, 20 June 1936, Library of Congress, Washington, D.C. On the emigration of the Germans, see Kathleen James, "Changing the Agenda: From German Bauhaus to US Internationalism. Ludwig Mies van der Rohe, Walter Gropius, Marcel Breuer," in *Exiles and Emigres: The Flight of European Artists from Hitler* (Los Angeles Museum of Art, 1997), p. 235–252.

41 Cammie McAtee, "Alien #5 044 325: Mies's First Trip to America," in Phyllis Lambert, ed., *Mies in America*, p. 132–145.

42 General correspondence, file 6, Museum of Modern Art.

43 Cammie McAtee, "Alien #5 044 325," p. 153–155.

44 Franz Schulze, *Mies van der Rohe: A Critical Biography*, p. 210–211.

45 The adventurer and writer Karl May (1842–1912) published the first account of the adventures of the Indian Winnetou in 1878, and the volumes of the Winnetou Trilogy in 1893. In 1910 a fourth volume would trace his belated trip to America of 1908.

46 On the development of this collage, see Neil Levine, "'The Significance of Facts': Mies's Collages Up Close and Personal," *Assemblage* 37 (1998): p. 77–81.

47 Today the Klee painting is in the collection of the Neue Galerie in New York. On Mies's collection, see Vivian Endicott Barnett, "The Architect as Art Collector," in Phyllis Lambert, *Mies in America*, p. 91–131.

48 Cammie McAtee, "Alien #5 044 325," p. 176.

49 Georgia van der Rohe, *La Donna è mobile*, p. 81.

50 Franz Schulze, "How Chicago Got Mies – and Harvard Didn't," *Inland Architect* 21, no. 5 (May 1978): p. 23–24.

51 Lilly Reich would go to Chicago in the summer of 1939, but she would return to Germany shortly before war broke out.

5. CHICAGO AND AMERICAN PARADIGMS (1938–56)

1 On the sequence of events at this surprising gala dinner, see Kevin Harrington, "Table Talk: Ludwig Mies van der Rohe," *Chicago Architectural Journal* 9 (2000): p. 84–89.

2 Frank Lloyd Wright, *An Autobiography* (New York: Duell, Sloan and Pearce, 1943), p. 429. Mies repaid Wright when, in 1943, he signed his petition to the United States government to organize the start of Broadacre City over the whole Union territory.

3 Mies van der Rohe, inaugural speech as director of the ITT, 20 November 1938, manuscript, Library of Congress, Washington, D.C., published in Fritz Neumeyer, *The Artless Word*, p. 317. The translation was modified by the author.

4 Mies van der Rohe to Henry Heald, 10 December 1937, Library of Congress, Washington, D.C.

5 Frank Lloyd Wright, "M. Wright Talks on Broadacre City to Ludwig Mies van der Rohe," *Taliesin* 1 (October 1940): p. 10–18.

6 On Mies's organicism, see Detlef Mertins, "Living in a Jungle: Mies, Organic Architecture, and the Art of City Building," in Phyllis Lambert, ed., *Mies in America*, p. 591–641.

7 Detlef Mertins, "Living in a Jungle," p. 623.

8 Stanley Tigerman, "Mies van der Rohe, a Moral Modernist Model," *Perspecta* 22 (1986): p. 112–35; Werner Blaser, *Mies van der Rohe, Lehre und Schule* (Basel/Berlin/Boston: Birkhäuser Verlag, 1981); Rolf Achilles, Kevin Harrington, and Charlotte Myrhum, eds., *Mies van der Rohe: Architect as Educator* (Chicago: University of Chicago Press, 1986); Cammie McAtee, "Mies van der Rohe and Architectural Education: The Curriculum at the Illinois Institute of Technology, Students Projects and Built Works" (Ph.D. diss., Queen's University, Kingston, 1996).

9 Mies van der Rohe, interview by Peter Blake, "Four Great Makers of Modern Architecture," p. 103.

10 Edward Duckett and Joseph Fujikawa, in William S. Shell, *Impressions of Mies. An Interview with Mies van der Rohe. His Early Chicago Years 1938–1948* (Chicago, 1988).

11 Georgia denounced the hold that Marx had over the life of her father: Georgia van der Rohe, *La Donna è mobile*, p. 238–262.

12 Comments reported by Joseph Fujikawa, in William S. Shell, *Impressions of Mies: An Interview with Mies van der Rohe. His Early Chicago Years 1938–1948*, p. 29.

13 Frank Lloyd Wright, *The Future of Architecture* (New York: Horizon Press, 1953), p. 260. The text is based on a talk given in London in 1939.

14 Frank Lloyd Wright, *The Living City* (New York: Horizon Press, 1958), p. 164, quoted by Hugh Dalziel Duncan, *Culture and Democracy: The Struggle for Form in Society and Architecture in Chicago and the Middle West During the Life and Times of Louis H. Sullivan* (Totowa, N.J.: Bedminster Press, 1965).

15 Comments reported by Katharine Kuh, "Mies van der Rohe: Modern Classicist," *Saturday Review of Literature*, 23 January 1965, p. 61.

16 On this program, see Andrew M. Shanken, "From Total War to Total Living: American Architecture and the Culture of Planning, 1939–194X" (Ph.D. diss., Princeton University, 1999).

17 Vivian Endicott Barnett, "The Architect as Art Collector," in Phyllis Lambert, ed., *Mies in America*, p. 109.

18 Philip Johnson to Mies van der Rohe, 16 October 1945, Library of Congress, Washington, D.C.

19 On the work of Kahn, see George Nelson, *Industrial Architecture of Albert Kahn, Inc.* (New York: Architectural Book Publishing Co., 1939); Grant Hildebrand, *Designing for Industry: The Architecture of Albert Kahn* (Cambridge, Mass.: MIT Press, 1974); Federico Bucci, *Albert Kahn, Architect of Ford* (New York: Princeton Architectural Press, 1993); Myron Goldsmith told Jordy of Mies's interest in Kahn: William H. Jordy, *American Buildings and Their Architects*, vol. 4 (Garden City, N.Y.: Anchor Press, 1976), p. 224.

20 On this collage, see the precise anaylsis of Neil Levine, "'The Significance of Facts': Mies's Collages Up Close and Personal," p. 84–87.

21 Phyllis Lambert, "Space and Structure," in Phyllis Lambert, ed., *Mies in America*, p. 424.

22 Later, with Robert H. Hutchins and Mortimer J. Adler, Paepke set up the Aspen Institute for Humanistic Studies: James Sloane Allen, *The Romance of Commerce and Culture: Capitalism, Modernism and the Chicago-Aspen Crusade for Cultural Reform* (Chicago: University of Chicago Press, 1969, 1983).

23 Harold M. Mayer and Richard C. Wade, *Chicago: Growth of a Metropolis* (Chicago: University of Chicago Press, 1969), p. 375. On the insertion of Mies's project in the renovation of the Near South Side, see Sarah Whiting, "Bas-Relief Urbanism: Chicago's Figured Field," in Phyllis Lambert, ed., *Mies in America*, p. 643–691.

24 "Ludwig Mies van der Rohe: An Address of Appreciation," p. 35.

25 Henry T. Heald, in *Four Great Makers of Modern Architecture*, p. 105–108. An engineer, Henry Townley Heald (1904–75) was president of IIT from 1940 to 1952.

26 Thomas Hall Beeby, "Vitruvius Americanus: Mies' Ornament," *Inland Architect* 21, no. 5 (May 1978): p. 12–15.

27 Phyllis Lambert, "Learning a Language," in Phyllis Lambert, ed., *Mies in America*, p. 253. This analysis is especially useful for all the accounts of Mies's collaborators, which support the precise analysis of the project solutions.

28 Mies van der Rohe, quoted in "Mies van der Rohe," *Architectural Forum* 97, no. 5 (November 1952): p. 104.

29 Rem Koolhaas, "Miestakes," in Phyllis Lambert, ed., *Mies in America*, p. 721.

30 Joseph Rykwert, "Mies van der Rohe," *Burlington* 91 (September 1949): p. 269.

31 Wilhelm Kästner, *Fritz Schupp, Martin Kremmer* (Berlin, Leipzig, and Vienna: Friedrich Ernst Hübsch Verlag, 1930); Ernst Völter, ed., *Architekt gegen oder und Ingenieur: Fritz Schupp, Martin Kremmer* (Berlin: W. und S. Loewenthal, 1929).

32 Mies van der Rohe, comments collected by Peter Carter in "Mies van der Rohe: An Appreciation on the Occasion, This Month, of His 75th Birthday," *Architectural Design* 31, no. 3 (March 1961): p. 106.

33 Mies van der Rohe, interview by Peter Blake, p. 101–102.

34 "Metals and Minerals Research Building, Illinois Institute of Technology," *Architectural Form* 79, no. 5 (November 1943): p. 88–90.

35 Phyllis Lambert, "Learning a Language," p. 291.

36 Colin Rowe, "Chicago Frame: Chicago's Place in the Modern Movement," *Architectural Review* 120, no. 718 (November 1956): p. 285.

37 "A Chapel by Mies van der Rohe," *Arts and Architecture* 70, no. 1 (January 1953): p. 19.

38 Werner Blaser, *Mies van der Rohe: IIT Campus* (Basel/Berlin/Boston: Birkhäuser, 2002).

39 Terence Riley, "Making History: Mies van der Rohe and the Museum of Modern Art," in Bergdoll and Riley, eds., *Mies in Berlin*, p. 11–23.

40 Terence Riley, "From Bauhaus to Court-House," in Bergdoll and Riley, eds., *Mies in Berlin*, p. 330–337.

41 Edith Farnsworth, unpublished memoirs, Farnsworth Collection, Newberry Library, Chicago, quoted in the excellent analysis by Alice T. Friedman, *Women and the Making of the Modern House: A Social and Architectural History* (New York: Abrams, 1998), p. 131.

42 Mies van der Rohe, interview for the BBC, May 1959, quoted by Wolf Tegethoff, *Mies van der Rohe, The Villas and Country Houses*, p. 131.

43 In connection with these columns Tegethoff mentions the precedent of the H. G. Chamberlain House by Walter Gropius and Marcel Breuer in Wayland, Massachusetts (1940): Wolf Tegethoff, *Mies van der Rohe, The Villas and Country Houses*, p. 131.

44 See the sketch kept at the Canadian Centre for Architecture, Montreal, DR 1990:0029:035.

45 See the details reproduced in Maritz Vandenberg, *Farnsworth House: Ludwig Mies van der Rohe* (London: Phaidon, 2003).

46 Richard Sennett, *The Conscience of the Eye* (New York: A. Knopf, 1991), p. 144.

47 Mies van der Rohe, comments collected by Christian Norberg-Schulz, *L'Architecture d'aujourd'hui* 79 (September 1958): p. 100.

48 Mies van der Rohe, interview for the BBC, May 1959, quoted by Wolf Tegethoff, p. 131.

49 Quotation published in Joseph A. Barry, "Report on the American Battle Between Good and Bad Modern Houses,"

House Beautiful 95 (May 1953): p. 270. See also Elisabeth Gordon, "The Threat to the Next America," *House Beautiful* 95 (May 1953): p. 126–130 and 250–251.

50 Peter Palumbo, "Farnsworth Impressions," *Inland Architect* (March–April 1986): p. 43 and 46.

51 Thomas H. Beeby, "Toward a Technological Architecture? Case Study of the Illinois Institute of Technology Commons Building," *Perspecta* 31 (2000): p. 10–21 and 45.

52 "Mies' Enormous Room," *Architectural Forum* 105 (August 1956): p. 105.

53 See Frampton's remarks: Kenneth Frampton, *Studies in Tectonic Culture, the Poetics of Construction in Nineteenth and Twentieth Century Architecture* (Cambridge, Mass.: MIT Press, 1995), p. 159–207.

54 Colin Rowe, "Neo-Classicism and Modern Architecture II," in *The Mathematics of the Ideal Villa and Other Essays* (Cambridge, Mass.: MIT Press, 1976), p. 151.

55 "Mies Speaks," p. 452.

56 Hans Curjel, "Die Mannheimer Theaterprojekte," *Das Werk* 40, no. 10 (October 1953): p. 312–15. See also the projects in *Die neue Stadt* 7, no. 4 (April 1953): p. 149–168.

57 "Mies van der Rohe, a Proposed National Theatre for the City of Mannheim," *Arts and Architecture* 70, no. 10 (October 1953): p. 19.

58 Rudolf Schwarz, "Bilde Künstler, rede nicht," *Baukunst und Werkform* 6 (January 1953): p. 9–17.

59 Drawing on numerous accounts, a detailed analysis of the competition and its context is given in Thilo Hilpert, ed., *Mies van der Rohe im Nachkriegsdeutschland. Das Theaterprojekt Mannheim 1953* (Leipzig: E. A. Seemann Verlag, 2001).

60 Bruno Paul to Mies van der Rohe, Düsseldorf, 20 January 1956, file 3, personal documents, Museum of Modern Art.

61 Carl W. Condit, *Chicago 1930–1970: Building, Planning and Urban Technology* (Chicago: University of Chicago Press, 1974).

62 On the ethnic form of the city during this phase, see Arnold R. Hirsch, *Making the Second Ghetto: Race and Housing in Chicago, 1940–1960* (Cambridge: Cambridge University Press, 1983). On municipal management of the city, see Mike Royko, *Boss: Richard J. Daley of Chicago* (New York: Dutton, 1971).

63 John W Stamper, "Patronage and the City Grid: The High-Rise Architecture of Mies van der Rohe in Chicago," *Inland Architect* 30, no. 2 (March–April 1986): p. 34–41.

64 Mies van der Rohe, quoted in "Mies van der Rohe," *Architectural Forum* 97 (November 1952): p. 99.

65 Ibid., p. 94.

66 Mies van der Rohe, "Hochhäuser," p. 124, published in Fritz Neumeyer, *Mies van der Rohe. The Artless Word*, p. 240.

67 Vivian Endicott Barnett, "The Architect as Art Collector," p. 90–131.

68 Joseph Fujikawa, in William S. Shell, *Impressions of Mies*, p. 15–16 and 24.

69 See the correspondence exchanged between the two architects in 1953, box 40, Library of Congress, Washington, D.C.

70 Ludwig Mies van der Rohe, introduction to Ludwig Hilberseimer, *The New City, Principles of Planning* (Chicago: Paul Theobald, 1944), p. XV.

71 Mies van der Rohe, manuscript for a talk on urbanism, box 61, Library of Congress, Washington, D.C., quoted in

Detlef Mertins, "Lafayette Park: Collaboration in Order," in Charles Waldheim, ed., *Case: Hilberseimer/Mies van der Rohe, Lafayette Park Detroit* (Munich: Prestel; Cambridge, Mass.: Harvard University, Graduate School of Design, 2004), p. 13.

72 Rudolf Schwarz, *Von der Bebauung der Erde* (Heidelberg: Verlag L. Schneider, 1949). See Detlef Mertins, "Living in a Jungle," p. 627–631.

73 Caroline Constant, "Hilberseimer and Caldwell: Merging Ideologies in the Lafayette Park Landscape," in Charles Waldheim, ed., *Case: Hilberseimer/Mies van der Rohe*, p. 95–111.

74 "Siedlung Lafayette Park in Detroit," *Bauen und Wohnen* 15, no. 11 (1960): p. 392–399; Lise Newman, "Lafayette Park Detroit, Michigan: Mies van der Rohe and Ludwig Hilberseimer," *Modernist Visions and the Contemporary American City Center* 5 (1989): p. 124–127.

75 Mies van der Rohe, elegy for Herbert S. Greenwald, 12 February 1959, box 61, Library of Congress, Washington, D.C.

76 Mies van der Rohe to Herbert S. Greenwald, 2 January 1957, box 30, Library of Congress, Washington, D.C.

77 Joseph Fujikawa would implement the main part of these plans for Mies's practice.

78 Joseph Fujikawa, in William S. Shell, *Impressions of Mies. An Interview on Mies van der Rohe; his Early Chicago Years 1938–1948*, p. 20. Phyllis Lambert retraced the itinerary of the main members of the team: "Mies and His Colleagues," in Phyllis Lambert, ed., *Mies in America*, p. 565–589.

6. INDUSTRIAL CLASSICISM (1956–69)

1 Kurt W. Forster, "The Seagram Building Reconsidered," *Skyline*, February 1982, p. 28–29.

2 Samuel Bronfman (1891–1971) founded one of the largest North American multinationals.

3 Phyllis Bronfman Lambert, "How a Building Gets Built," *Vassar Alumnae Magazine* 44 (February 1959): p. 14.

4 Johnson mentions - perceptively - the idea of "returning a favor": Philip Johnson, interview by Jean-Louis Cohen, New York, 10 April 1991.

5 Phyllis Lambert, "Stimmung at Seagram: Philip Johnson Counters Mies van der Rohe," *Grey Room* 20 (Summer 2005): p. 38–59.

6 Mies van der Rohe, in Peter Carter, "Mies van der Rohe, an Appreciation on the Occasion, This Month, of His 75th Birthday," *Architectural Design* 31, no. 3 (March 1961): p. 115. See also Mies's remarks in an undated interview at the Architectural League in New York, box 62, p. 4–7, Library of Congress, Washington, D.C.

7 See Jordy's analyses: William H. Jordy, *American Buildings and Their Architects*, p. 251–277; "Seagram Building, New York, USA," *Architectural Design* 29 (February 1959): 72–77; see also Hubert Damisch, *Modern' Signe, Recherches sur le travail du signe dans l'architecture moderne* (Paris: Corda/Cehta, 1977), p. 40.

8 Notice for the registration of the Four Seasons restaurant, Landmarks Preservation Commission, New York, 1989.

9 Phyllis Lambert, "Stimmung at Seagram."

10 Banham considered it a kind of gimmick light-years away from the "industrial vernacular" of the Chicago buildings: Reyner Banham, "Mies van der Rohe on Trial: Almost Nothing Is Too Much," *Architectural Review* 132, no. 786 (August 1962): 125–128.

11 Philip Johnson, in John W. Cook and Heinrich Klotz, *Conversations with Architects*, p. 19.

12 K. Michael Hays, "Abstraction's Appearance (Seagram Building)," in Robert Somol, ed., *Autonomy and Ideology: Positioning an Avant-Garde in America* (New York: Monacelli Press, 1997), p. 277–291; see also Mechthild Heuser, "Mies van der Rohes Rückkehr zum Textil," *Der Architekt* 5 (May 1998): p. 271–274.

13 Lewis Mumford, "The Lesson of the Master," *The New Yorker*, 13 September 1958, p. 141–158.

14 This work was designed by a group called Chicago Federal Center Architects, comprising Mies, Schmidt, Garden and Erickson, C. F. Murphy Associates, and A. Epstein & Sons.

15 Carl Condit, *Chicago 1930–1970: Buiding, Planning and Urban Technology*, p. 129–134.

16 Werner Blaser, *Mies van der Rohe: Federal Center Chicago* (Basel/Berlin/Boston: Birkhäuser, 2004).

17 Phyllis Lambert, "Punching Through the Clouds: Notes on the Place of the Toronto-Dominion Centre in the North-American Œuvre of Mies," in Detlef Mertins, ed., *The Presence of Mies* (New York: Princeton Architectural Press, 1994), p. 33–47.

18 France Vanlaethem, "Le Westmount Square," *Architecture Québec* 71 (February 1993): p. 16.

19 On these revealing polemics, see "Mansion House Square," *International Architect* 3 (1984): p. 19–38; "Mansion House Square Debate," *Architects' Journal* 37 (1934): nos. 28, 34, 36, 37; Joseph Rykwert and Martin Filler, "A Posthumous Mies: Two Views," *Art in America* 74, no. 4 (April 1986): p. 152–156.

20 Anne Cormier, "L'Ile des Sœurs" and Jean-François Bédard, "La Station-Service de l'Ile des Sœurs," *Architecture Québec* 71 (February 1993): p. 18–21.

21 Ulrich Conrads, "'Einfälle sind keine Ideen': Zurückgedacht an Mies' Fünfundsiebzigsten," *Bauwelt* 92, no. 47 (December 2001): p. 36–39.

22 Detlef Mertins, "Mies' Event Space," *Grey Room* 20 (Summer 2005): p. 60–73.

23 Jean-Pierre Cêtre, "Neue Nationalgalerie recto verso," *Faces* 47 (Winter 1999–2000): p. 35.

24 Mark Jarzombek, "Mies van der Rohe's New National Gallery and the Problem of Context," *Assemblage* 2 (February 1987): p. 33–43.

25 See the analysis of Wolf Tegethoff, "Die Neue Nationalgalerie im Werk Mies van der Rohes und im Kontext der Berliner Museumsarchitektur," in Christoph Hölz, Ulrike Steiner, and Zentralinstitut für Kunstgeschichte München, eds., *Berlins Museen: Geschichte und Zukunft* (Munich: Deutscher Kunstverlag, 1994), p. 281–292.

26 Mies van der Rohe to Werner Düttmann, 26 February 1963, Library of Congress, Washington, D.C., quoted by Wolf Tegethoff, "Die Neue Nationalgalerie im Werk Mies van der Rohes und im Kontext der Berliner Museumsarchitektur," p. 288.

27 Didier Laroque, "Le secret," *L'Architecture d'aujourd'hui* 245 (June 1986): p. v-xi.

28 Jean-Pierre Cêtre, "Neue Nationalgalerie recto verso," p. 39.

29 "Mies on Viollet le Duc," comments collected by Christian Norberg-Schulz, *L'Architecture d'aujourd'hui* 79 (September 1958): p. 41; and "Talking Notes," in Phyllis Lambert, ed., *Mies in America*, p. 216.

30 Julius Posener, "Absolute Architektur," *Neue Rundschau* 84, no. 1 (1973): p. 79–95; Alison and Peter Smithson, "Mies van der Rohe," *Architectural Design* 39, no. 7 (July 1969): p. 363–366.

31 Among the numerous interpretations of this building, see Peter Serenyi, "Mies' New National Gallery: An Essay in Architectural Content," *Harvard Architecture Review* 1 (Spring 1980): p. 181–189.

32 On Mies's solitude, see Massimo Cacciari, "Res aedificatoria; il 'classico' di Mies van der Rohe," *Casabella* 629 (December 1995): p. 3–7.

33 Joseph Fujikawa, in William S. Shell, *Impressions of Mies*, p. 33.

34 Reginald Malcolmson, "A Paradox of Humility and Super-star," *Inland Architect* 21, no. 5 (May 1978): p. 17–18.

35 Phyllis Lambert, "Mies Immersion: Introduction," in Phyllis Lambert, ed., *Mies in America*, p. 211–217.

36 Joseph Fujikawa, in William S. Shell, *Impressions of Mies*, p. 20.

37 Remarks recorded by Alfons Leitl, "Anmerkungen zur Zeit. Mies van der Rohe in Deutschland," *Baukunst und Werkform* 6 (June 1953).

38 Mies van der Rohe, Eulogy to Le Corbusier, 1965, in Fritz Neumeyer, *Mies van der Rohe. The Artless Word*, p. 334.

39 Regarding relations between Mies and Gropius, see Sigfried Giedion, *Walter Gropius, Work and Teamwork* (New York: Reinhold, 1954), p. 17–18.

40 Mies van der Rohe, interview by Peter Blake, p. 98.

41 Mies van der Rohe, *Print* 11, no. 1 (1957): p. 39.

42 Mies van der Rohe, interview by the Architectural League, p. 98.

43 Mies van der Rohe, interview by Dirk Lohan, p. 32.

44 Georgia van der Rohe, *La donna è mobile*, p. 247.

45 Vittorio Gregotti, "Res aedificatoria: dialogo con Massimo Cacciari," *Casabella* 59, no. 629 (December 1995): p. 2–3.

46 Mies van der Rohe, "Gegen Willkür und Spielerei."

BIOGRAPHY

1886

Maria Ludwig Michael Mies is born on 27 March in Aachen. His house, at 29 Steinkaulstraße, is east of the center of the old city. He is the son of Michael Mies (Aachen, 29 March 1851–31 December 1927), a maker of headstones and monumental masonry, and Amalie Rohe, a native of Belgium (Montjoie [today called Monschau], 14 April 1843 – Aachen, 31 May 1928). He is the youngest of five children, the eldest being Ewald, born 13 October 1877.

1896

He attends the Domschule in Aachen, where he will remain until 1899.

1899

He is a student at the Gewerbeschule, a vocational school in Aachen, where he will remain until 1901.

1901

While helping in his father's business, he also works for Max Fischer, an Aachen-based producer of plaster and stucco molding, and for the architects Goebbels and Albert Schneider.

1905

He moves to Berlin. Working for the municipal department of Rixdorf, in the suburbs of the capital, he designs the interior of the council chamber of the town hall. He spends several months in the Kaiser's army before being discharged following a case of pneumonia. He becomes a draftsman for Paul Thiersch in Bruno Paul's Berlin office, where he will remain until 1907.

1906

He receives the commission for his first house, a residence for Professor Alois Riehl, in Neubabelsberg. The Riehls give him financial support to make an excursion to Italy with Joseph Popp; he spends several weeks there.

1908

In October, he is hired as a draftsman in the Neubabelsberg office of Peters Behrens, who is working on an overall program to design the architecture, products, and media materials for the Allgemeine Elektrizitäts-Gesellschaft (AEG). Under Behrens's influence, he discovers the architecture of Karl Friedrich Schinkel, to which he would remain devoted throughout his life.

1910

Ludwig enters the competition for a monument to Bismarck at Bingen, on the Rhine, with his brother Ewald. Taking a leave of absence of several months from Behrens's office in an attempt to set up a firm in Aachen, Mies designs the Perl House, in Zehlendorf.

1911

He works for Behrens on the project for the Kröller-Müller House at The Hague.

1912

The Kröller-Müllers abandon Behrens and entrust the design of their house to Mies, who spends the summer in The Hague, where he discovers the architecture of Hendrik Petrus Berlage. He travels to Paris.

1913

He sets up his own agency in Lichterfelde in collaboration with Ferries Goebbels and W. von Waldhausen. He completes the Werner House, in Zehlendorf. On 10 April, he marries Ada Bruhn, born in Lübeck in 1885. He first met her at the Riehls and often visited her in Hellerau, where she was studying with the composer Émile Jacques-Dalcroze. They have three daughters: Dorothea, born in 1914, who, as a dancer and actress, changed her name to Georgia; Marianne, born in 1915; and Waltraut, born in 1917.

1914

He designs a house for his family on a plot of land purchased in Werder, near Potsdam, where the couple often live.

1915

He and Ada move to an apartment at 24 Am Karlsbad, in Berlin's Tiergarten neighborhood, where he would set up his office in the 1920s and where he would live until 1938. He breaks ground on the Urbig House, in Neubabelsberg, and meets the sculptor Wilhelm Lehmbruck.

1915–18

He is drafted into the imperial corps of engineers in Frankfurt, Berlin, and Romania. A son is born from his Transylvanian liaisons.

1919

He moves back to Berlin. At the Der Sturm gallery he buys his first painting, *Winter II*, by Wassily Kandinsky.

1920

He becomes close to members of the Dada group in Berlin and spends time with Hans Richter, Johannes Baader, Raoul Hausmann, Kurt Schwitters, and Hannah Höch.

1921

He participates in the competition for the design of a skyscraper office tower on the Friedrichstraße, in Berlin-Mitte. He and Ada separate; she leaves the apartment on Am Karlsbad with their daughters. He remains in the building, where he works and lives alone with a butler.

1922

He joins the Novembergruppe and the following year becomes head of the architecture section. He adds "van der Rohe" to his family name, changing its pronunciation and spelling it Miës. He publishes his first article in Bruno Taut's journal, *Frühlicht*. He pursues the construction of traditional houses, such as the Eichstädt House in Berlin-Nikolassee and the Feldmann House in Berlin-Wilmersdorf.

1923

He presents his Glass Skyscraper and his project for a Concrete Country House at the Große Berliner Kunst-ausstellung. He participates in the International Architecture Exhibition organized by the Bauhaus in Weimar, and in October his projects are part of the Paris exhibition of architects belonging to De Stijl. He becomes a member of the Association of German Architects and of the Deutscher Werkbund.

1923–25

Together with Hans Richter and Werner Graeff, he contributes to the journal *G, Material für elementare Gestaltung*.

1924

He is one of the founders of the Der Ring architects' association. The Brick Country House project is presented at the Große Berliner Kunstausstellung. He builds the Mosler House in Neubabelsberg, the last of these traditional structures.

1925

Hans Prinzhorn asks him to write a book entitled *Baukunst*, but this project does not go forward. Sergius Ruegenberg joins the firm, where he will stay until 1934. Mies begins a relationship with the interior decorator Lilly Reich (1885–1947), who lives close to Am Karlsbad. Their affair will last until his departure for America in 1938.

1926

He becomes vice president of the Deutscher Werkbund. His work is shown at the exhibition of the Nancy-Paris committee, organized by André Lurçat. In the Berlin-Friedrichsfelde cemetery, he builds the monument to Karl Liebknecht and Rosa Luxemburg; it echoes the brickwork of the Wolf House, which he completes at the same time in Guben. He joins the Friends of the New Russia Society.

1927

In Berlin-Wedding, he builds a social housing development on the Afrikanische Straße, his first big commission. He coordinates a national housing exhibition that the Werkbund has organized in Stuttgart. For that exhibit, he designs the site plan as well as an apartment building with a metal frame and the Glasraum. He is also involved in the design of furniture with steel tube frames. With Lilly Reich, he builds the Velvet and Silk Café for a fashion exhibition in Berlin.

1928

He builds houses for the Krefeld industrialists Hermann Lange and Josef Esters, and he designs the Adam department store building in Berlin as well as a bank in Stuttgart.

1929

He is the architect representing Germany at the Barcelona International Exhibition. The highlight is the reception pavilion, for which he designed the furniture. He stays at the Hotel Colón, opposite the Barcelona cathedral. Back in Berlin, he competes for the redevelopment of the Alexanderplatz and designs a house for the painter Emil Nolde. He becomes a member of the International Congresses for Modern Architecture.

1930

In August he becomes the third director of the Bauhaus, after the dismissal of Hannes Meyer. He builds the Tugendhat House in Brno. He meets Philip Johnson, who hires him to work on his apartment in New York.

1931

He coordinates the housing sector of the Deutsche Bauausstellung in Berlin and, there, builds the House for a Childless Couple. He is elected to the Prussian Akademie der Künste. The mass production of his furniture begins.

1932

Starting in October, Mies installs the Bauhaus in a factory in Berlin-Steglitz, following its expulsion from Dessau. He builds the Lemke House in Berlin-Hohenschönhausen and designs the Gericke House. Philip Johnson and Henry-Russell Hitchcock show his work at the Museum of Modern Art in New York in their exhibit on modern architecture.

1933

He participates in the competition for the Reichsbank headquarters in Berlin. The Nazis shut down the Bauhaus in April and, in July, his teachers reject the conditions set for its reopening. Mies becomes affiliated with the Reichskulturkammer. He begins to work on studies for courtyard houses.

1934

He designs the German Pavilion at the 1935 Brussels Exhibition. In April, he designs the mining industry section of the exhibition "Deutsches Volk – Deutsche Arbeit" in Berlin. In August, he signs a motion supporting Hitler. The former Bauhaus member Herbert Hirche becomes his collaborator and remains in that capacity until 1938.

1935

In January, the Nazis destroy the monument to Rosa Luxemburg and Karl Liebknecht. Mies designs a house for Margarete Hubbe in Magdeburg and one for Ulrich Lange in Krefeld. He receives his first invitation to teach in the United States.

1936

His designs for the German Textile Exhibition in Berlin do not go forward, and he loses his last hope of a public commission. He receives invitations from several American universities. For his fiftieth birthday, his friends give him Max Beckmann's painting *Alfi mit Maske*.

1937

In July, he is forced to resign from the Akademie der Künste. Between 20 August 1937 and 5 April 1938, he travels in the United States to work on a house for Helen and Stanley Resor; he will continue working on these designs until 1940. He visits New York, where he stays at the University Club; Chicago; and Taliesin, Wisconsin, where he meets Frank Lloyd Wright.

1938

He designs an administrative building for the Verseidag factories in Krefeld. In August, he emigrates to the United States permanently. In October, he assumes leadership of the Armour Institute's School of Architecture in Chicago, where he lives first at the Stevens Hotel, then at the Blackstone Hotel. He begins to collect paintings, especially works by Paul Klee.

1939

He sets up his office in the Railway Exchange Building, in collaboration with his former Bauhaus student John Rodgers. George Danforth becomes his first American draftsman, remaining with the firm until 1943. Mies works on the plan for the Armour Institute campus on the South Side of Chicago. He vacations with Lilly Reich in Pike Lake, Wisconsin.

1940

After its merger with Lewis College, the Armour Institute becomes the Illinois Institute of Technology. Mies meets Lora Marx, with whom he will share his life until 1969.

1941

He moves into an apartment at 200 East Pearson Street, on the Near North Side of Chicago. Taking up his prior designs, he develops the plan for the Illinois Institute of Technology.

1942

At the request of *Architectural Forum*, he develops designs for a Museum for a Small City as well as a Concert Hall. He builds his first work on the IIT campus, the Metals and Minerals Research Building, and during the war, develops the Library and Administration Building, which are never realized.

1944

On 14 December, he becomes an American citizen. Edward Duckett joins the firm, where he will remain until 1965, introducing models as the preferred mode of representation.

1945

Mies moves his office to 37 South Wabash Avenue in Chicago's Loop. Joseph Fujikawa joins the firm and ensures its posterity after Mies's death. According to his daughter Georgia, Mies stopped by every afternoon.

1946

At IIT he builds Alumni Memorial Hall. He meets the Chicago developer Herbert Greenwald, who would become the primary client for his apartment buildings. In Berlin, the communists build an ephemeral reconstruction of the monument to Rosa Luxemburg and Karl Liebknecht. Myron Goldsmith joins the firm and, until 1953, contributes to the thinking on large-scale structures.

1947

Philip Johnson organizes a retrospective exhibit of Mies's work at the Museum of Modern Art in New York, and Mies designs the exhibition. He also designs the show on Theo Van Doesburg at the University of Chicago.

1949

He builds the Promontory Apartments in Chicago and begins to design Edith Farnsworth's weekend house in Plano, Illinois, which he finishes in 1951. The latter would lead to painful legal disputes.

1950

He designs the 50 x 50 House, so named because the square house was to be fifty feet on each side. Gene Summers joins the firm and works there until 1965.

1951

Mies builds two apartment towers at 860-880 Lake Shore Drive in Chicago and for a time considers living there himself. Ada Bruhn dies on 3 November.

1952

He moves his office to 230 East Ohio Street in Chicago, and in the end he occupies an entire floor there. Gene Summers becomes the main figure on the team.

1953

He participates in the competition for the Mannheim National Theater, the first German project designed in fifteen years. He returns to Germany for a three-week visit and is received as an honorary member of the Akademie der Künste in Düsseldorf. He develops a design for the Convention Center in Chicago.

1954

He builds the expansion of the Museum of Fine Arts in Houston and, together with Philip Johnson, receives the commission for his first high-rise office tower, the Seagram Building in New York. During his visits to New York, he stays at the Barclay Hotel.

1956

He builds Crown Hall for the School of Architecture at IIT. He builds a second housing development on Lake Shore Drive, called 900 Esplanade. He becomes a member of the American Academy of Arts and Sciences.

1957

He becomes a member of the Akademie der Künste in Berlin (West) and receives Germany's Pour le Mérite Cross, designed by Schinkel.

1958

He completes the Seagram Building and builds the first phase of row houses at Lafayette Park, in Detroit, according to a plan by Ludwig Hilberseimer and the landscape architect Alfred Caldwell. He retires from the Illinois Institute of Technology and, at the same time, loses the commissions from that institution, which are entrusted to Skidmore, Owings & Merrill. Peter Carter joins the firm, where he will stay until after the death of Mies.

1959

Mies receives the Gold Medal of the Royal Institute of British Architects and is admitted to the Académie d'architecture in Paris. On that occasion, accompanied by Lora Marx, he makes his second postwar voyage to Europe, visiting Greece and returning to Aachen. He begins to design the Federal Center of Chicago, which he will complete in 1964. He sits on the jury of the São Paulo Biennale and meets Lucio Costa in Rio.

1960

He designs an unrealized project for the Schäfer Museum in Schweinfurt.

1961

He builds the Bacardi headquarters in Mexico, after designing an initial version of the building for a site in Santiago de Cuba.

1962

His grandson Dirk Lohan joins the firm, and he will help to keep it going after the death of his grandfather. Arthritis keeps Mies in bed for months on end.

1963

He begins to design the Toronto Dominion Center in Toronto, which he will finish in 1969. On 6 December, Lyndon Johnson gives him the Medal of Freedom, which had been conferred on him by John F. Kennedy. After many years of negotiation, the East German authorities permit the shipment to Chicago of the archive boxes containing Mies's drawings and correspondence prior to 1938.

1964

Mies travels to Berlin for the design of the Neue Nationalgalerie.

1965

He begins to design the Westmount Center in Montreal, which will be completed in 1968. Gene Summers leaves the firm.

1966

He begins the IBM Regional Office Building project in Chicago. Suffering from cancer of the esophagus, he spends the summer in a Swiss resort called Montana.

1967

He develops a project for Mansion House Square in London.

1968

He completes construction work on the Neue Nationalgalerie in Berlin, having traveled there to see the installation of the first stone and the roof. He bequeaths to the Museum of Modern Art in New York a collection of approximately twenty thousand drawings and other documents.

1969

Ludwig Mies van der Rohe dies on 17 August in Chicago. He is buried in the Graceland cemetery. A ceremony is organized on 25 October at IIT's Crown Hall. His office will continue to function until 1975.

PRINCIPAL PROJECTS

This list is based on information put together by Pierre Adler for the Mies van der Rohe Archive, Museum of Modern Art, New York. Projects that were not built are in italics. As far as possible, the addresses of the buildings have been given.

1907–1910
Alois Riehl House, Bergstraße 3, Neubabelsberg (today Potsdam-Babelsberg).

1910
Competition project for a monument to Bismarck, Elisenhöhe, Bingen.

1911
Hugo Perls House, Hermannstraße 14–16, Berlin-Zehlendorf.

1912
Project for the Anthony George Kröller and Helene Müller house, Wassenaar, The Hague.

1912–13
Ernst Werner House, Quermatenweg 2–4, Berlin-Zehlendorf.

1914
Project for a house for the architect, Werder.

1915
Johann Warnholtz House, Heerstraße, Berlin-Charlottenburg (destroyed in 1959).

1917
Franz Urbig House, Luisenstraße 9, Neubabelsberg.

1919
Tomb for Laura Perls, Weissensee Cemetery, Berlin.

1921
Project for the Petermann House, Neubabelsberg.

1921
Competition project for an Office Skyscraper, Friedrichstraße, Berlin.

1921
Maximilian Kempner House, Sophienstraße 5–7, Berlin-Charlottenburg (destroyed).

1922
Project for a Glass Skyscraper, Friedrichstraße Berlin.

1922
Kuno Feldmann House, Erdenerstraße 10–12, Berlin-Wilmersdorf.

1922
Project for the Georg Eichstädt House, Dreilindenstraße 22, Berlin-Nikolassee.

1922
Project for a Concrete Office Building, Berlin.

1922
Project for a Concrete Country House, Berlin or Nauen.

1922
Project for the Lessing House, Neubabelsberg.

1923
Project for a Brick Country House, Neubabelsberg.

1923
Ryder House, Wiesbaden.

1924
Mosler House, Kaiserstraße 28–29, Neubabelsberg.

1924
Butte school extension, Helene-Lange-Straße, Potsdam.

1924–26
Urban house extension, Ulmenallee 32, Berlin-Charlottenburg.

1925
Project for a traffic tower, Berlin.

1925
Project for the Walter Dexel House, Jena.

1925
Project for the Ernst Eliat house, Nedlitz, Potsdam.

1925–27
Erich Wolf house, Teichhornstraße, Guben (destroyed).

1926
Monument to Alois Riehl, Klein-Glienicke cemetery, plot 122, Neubabelsberg.

1926
Monument to Karl Liebknecht and Rosa Luxemburg, Friedrichsfelde cemetery, Berlin (destroyed).

1926–27
Social Housing Scheme, Afrikanische Straße, Berlin-Wedding.

1927
Site plans for the model housing estate and residential building for the Deutscher Werkbund, Weißenhofsiedlung, Stuttgart (destroyed).

1927
'Glass room,' Deutscher Werkbund Exhibition, Weißenhofsiedlung, Stuttgart.

1927
Velvet and Silk Café, Fashion exhibition, Berlin (with Lilly Reich; destroyed).

1928
Extension to the Fuchs House (formerly Perls house), Berlin-Zehlendorf.

1928
Project for the David Saul Adam Building, corner of Friedrichstraße and Leipziger Straße, Berlin.

1928
Building project for the Württembergische Landesbank, Hindenburgplatz, Stuttgart.

1928
Competition project for the redevelopment of the Alexanderplatz, Berlin.

1929
Building project for offices and a hotel, Friedrichstraße, Berlin.

1929
Josef Esters House, Wilhelmshofallee 97, Krefeld.

1929
Hermann Lange House, Wilhelmshofallee 91, Krefeld.

1929
German Pavilion at the International Exhibition, Barcelona (destroyed, rebuilt in 1986).

1929
Exhibition stands for German industry, Barcelona (with Lilly Reich).

1929
Project for Emil Nolde House, Am Erlenbusch, Berlin-Zehlendorf.

1929–30
Fritz and Grete Tugendhat House, Cernopolní 45, Brno.

1930
Competition project for a golf club, Krefeld.

1930
Competition project for a monument to the dead inside Schinkel's Neue Wache, Berlin.

1930
Apartment for Philip Johnson, 424 East 52nd Street, New York.

1931
Mini-canteen at the Bauhaus, Dessau.

1931
House for a Childless Couple and Apartment for a Bachelor at the Berlin Building Exposition, Berlin (destroyed).

1931–35
Vereinigte Seidenwebereien AG factory, Krefeld.

1931–38
Projects for courtyard houses.

1932
Project for the Herbert Gericke House, Berlin-Wannsee.

1932
Refitting of a factory for the Bauhaus, Berlin-Steglitz.

1932
Karl Lemke House, Oberseestrasse 56–57, Berlin-Hohenschönhausen.

1932
Heusgen House, Hülser Talring 153, Krefeld (partly realized)

1933
Competition project for the headquarters of the Reichsbank, Berlin.

1934
Mining industries stand, "Deutsches Volk – Deutsche Arbeit" exhibition, Berlin.

1934
Project for a house for the architect, Tyrol, Austria.

1934
Competition project for the German Pavilion at the International Exhibition of 1935, Brussels.

1934
Project for a service station.

1934
Addition to and remodeling of the Bueren house, Berlin.

1935
Project for the Margarete Hubbe House, Magdeburg.

1935
Project for the Ulrich Lange House, Krefeld.

1937
Project for an office block for the Vereinigte Seidenwebereien AG, Krefeld.

1937–38
Project for the Stanley Resor House, Jackson Hole, Wyoming.

1939
Preliminary designs for the campus plan, Illinois Institute of Technology, Chicago.

1940–41
Design for the plan of the campus, Illinois Institute of Technology Chicago.

1941–43
Metals and Minerals Research Building, Illinois Institute of Technology, Chicago (associate architects Holabird and Root).

1942
Project for a Museum for a Small City.

1942
Project for a Concert Hall.

1944–45
Project for the Library and Administration Building, Illinois Institute of Technology, Chicago.

1945
Mooringsport and Meredosia electric power stations, Louisiana.

1945
Project for a gymnasium and swimming pool, Illinois Institute of Technology, Chicago.

1945–46
Alumni Memorial Hall, Illinois Institute of Technology, Chicago (associate architects Holabird and Root).

1945–46
Perlstein Hall, Center for Metallurgic and Chemical Research, Illinois Institute of Technology, Chicago (associate architects Holabird and Root).

1945–46
Wishnick Hall, Chemistry Building, Illinois Institute of Technology, Chicago (associate architects Friedman, Altschuler and Sincere).

1945–50
Project for the drive-in Cantor restaurant, 38th Street, Indianapolis.

1945–50
Boiler Plant, Illinois Institute of Technology, Chicago.

1945–50
Edith Farnsworth House, Fox River, Plano, Illinois.

1945–47
Project for Cantor House, Indianapolis.

1946–49
Promontory Apartments residential block, 5530 South Shore Drive, Chicago (associate architects Pace Associates and Holsman, Holsman, Klekamp and Taylor).

1947
Electricity Station, Illinois Institute of Technology, Chicago.

1947
Project for a theater.

1947–55
Institute of Gas Technology, Illinois Institute of Technology, Chicago (associate architects Friedman, Altschuler and Sincere).

1948
Project for a building for the Student Union, Illinois Institute of Technology, Chicago.

1948
Plans for the Algonquin Apartments residential complex, Cornell Avenue, Chicago (associate architects Pace Associates).

1948–51
Residential complex, 860-880 Lake Shore Drive, Chicago (associate architects Pace Associates and Holsman, Holsman, Klekamp and Taylor).

1948–51
Interiors for the Art Club of Chicago, 109 East Ontario, Chicago (destroyed).

1948–53
Mechanical Engineering Building for the American Association of Railroads, Illinois Institute of Technology, Chicago (associate architects Friedman, Altschuler and Sincere).

1948–56
American Association of Railroads building, Illinois Institute of Technology, Chicago (associate architects Friedman, Altschuler and Sincere).

1949–50
Cantor commercial center office block, Illinois and Ohio Street, Indianapolis.

1949–52
St. Saviour Chapel, Illinois Institute of Technology, Chicago.

1950
Project for the Leon J. Caine House, Winnetka, Illinois.

1950–51
Project for prefabricated row houses with steel framework.

1950–52
Project for the 50 x 50 House.

1950–52
Mechanical Engineering Building for the Research Institute, Illinois Institute of Technology, Chicago (associate architects Friedman, Altschuler and Sincere).

1950–52
Harry Berke office blocks, Michigan and Meridian Streets, Indianapolis.

1950–56
Crown Hall, Illinois Institute of Technology, Chicago (associate architects Pace Associates).

1951–52
Robert McCormick House, 299 Prospect Avenue, Elmhurst, Illinois.

1951–52
Fraternity House Pi Lambda Phi, Bloomington, Indiana.

1951–55
Carman Hall, Bailey Hall and Cunningham Hall residential blocks, Illinois Institute of Technology, Chicago (Pace Associates, architects).

1952–53
Commons Building, Illinois Institute of Technology, Research Institute, Chicago (associate architects Friedman, Altschuler and Sincere).

1952–53
Project for the National Theater, Mannheim.

1952–54
Project for a Convention Center, Cermak Road, Chicago.

1953–56
Esplanade residential complex, 900-910 Lake Shore Drive, Chicago (associate architects Friedman, Altschuler and Sincere).

1953–56
Commonwealth Promenade residential complex, North Sheridan Road, Chicago.

1954
General plan for the Museum of Fine Arts, Houston.

1954
Cullinan Hall, Museum of Fine Arts, Houston (associate architects Straub, Rather and Howze).

1954–58
Joseph E. Seagram Building, 375 Park Avenue, New York (in cooperation with Philip Johnson, Kahn and Jacobs, associate architects).

1954–55
Physics-Electronics Research Building, Illinois Institute of Technology, Chicago.

1955
Project for the Lubin residential hotel, New York.

1955–56
General plan for the residential complex at Lafayette Park, Detroit.

1955–57
American Association of Railroads laboratory, Illinois Institute of Technology, Chicago (associate architects Friedman, Altschuler and Sincere).

1956–58
Extension of the Metals Research Building, Illinois Institute of Technology, Chicago (associate architects Holabird and Root).

1957
Project for a commercial building for the Pratt Institute, Brooklyn, New York.

1957
Project for the Kayser office blocks, 845 North Michigan Avenue, Chicago.

1957–58
Project for a residential complex, Battery Park, New York.

1957–59
Project for the Quadrangle Apartments residential complex Brooklyn, New York.

1957–60
Project for the Bacardi office block, Santiago de Cuba, Cuba.

1957–60
Project for the Seagram office block, Michigan Avenue, Chicago.

1957–62
Project for the American Consulate, Avenida Paulista, São Paulo.

1958
Complex of individual houses, Lafayette Park, Detroit.

1958–60
Complex of individual and collective houses, Colonnade Park, Newark.

1958–61
Bacardi office block, Del Cedro, Mexico (associate architects Saenz Cancio, Martin, Guttierez).

1959–63
Home Federal Savings and Loans Association, Des Moines, Iowa (associate architects Smith, Vorhees and Jensen).

1959–64
Federal Center, federal and post court, Chicago (in collaboration with Schmidt, Garden & Erickson, C. F. Murphy Associates and A. Epstein and Son).

1960
Town houses, Lafayette Park, Detroit.

1960–61
Museum project for Georg Schäfer, Schweinfurt.

1960–63
One Charles Center office complex, Baltimore.

1960–63
Project for the Friedrich Krupp administrative building, Hügelpark, Essen.

1961
Urban plan, Place de la Montagne, Montreal.

1962–63
Residential block, 2400 Lakeview Avenue, Chicago (associate architects Greenberg and Finfer).

1962–65
School of Social Service and Administration Building, University of Chicago, Chicago.

1962–65
Highfield House apartment block, Baltimore.

1962–65
Meredith Memorial Hall, Drake University, Des Moines.

1962–68
Neue Nationalgalerie, Potsdamer Straße, West Berlin.

1962–68
Sciences Center, Duquesne University, Pittsburgh.

1963
Lafayette Towers, Lafayette Park, Detroit.

1963–69
Toronto-Dominion Center, Toronto (architects John B. Parkin Associates and Bregman and Hamann, consultant architect Mies van der Rohe).

1966
Project for the K-4 school, Church Street South, New Haven, Connecticut.

1966
Project for an apartment block, Foster City, San Mateo, California.

1966
Martin Luther King Jr. Library, G Street / 10 and 11 Streets, Washington, D.C.

1966–69
Brown Wing, Museum of Fine Arts, Houston.

1966–69
IBM Regional Office Building, Chicago (in association with C. F. Murphy Associates).

1967
Project for an office block for Lloyds Bank, Mansion House Square, London (in association with William Holford and Partners).

1967–69
Project for an office block for the Commerzbank A.G., Frankfurt-am-Main.

1967–69
Residential building No. 1, Ile des Sœurs, Montreal (working architect Philippe Bobrow).

1967–69
Project for Radio King Studio, Seattle, Washington.

1967–69
Esso service station, Ile des Sœurs, Montreal (working architect Paul La Pointe).

1967–70
Office blocks on the plots of Illinois Central, 111 East Wacker Drive, Chicago.

1968
Westmount Square, Montreal (working architects Greespon, Freedlander, Plachta & Kryton).

1968–69
Residential buildings Nos. 2 and 3, Ile des Sœurs, Montreal (working architect Edgar Tornay).

1968–69
Project for the Northwest Plaza, Chicago.

1968–69
Project for Dominion Square, Montreal.

BIBLIOGRAPHY

Bibliographic references are in chronological order.

Ludwig Mies van der Rohe's writings

"Hochhäuser," *Frühlicht*, vol. 1, no. 4, 1922, p. 122–124.

"Gelöste Aufgaben: Eine Forderung an unser Bauwesen," *Bauwelt*, vol. 52, 1923, p. 719.

"Bürohaus," *G*, no. 1, July 1923, p. 3.

"Bauen," *G*, no. 2, September 1923, p. 1.

"Baukunst und Zeitwille!," *Der Querschnitt*, no. 4, 1924, p. 31–32.

"Industrielles Bauen," *G*, no. 3, June 1924, p. 8–13.

"Brief an die Form," *Die Form*, vol. 1, no. 7, 1926, p. 127.

"Vorwort," *Bau und Wohnung,* Stuttgart, Julius Hoffmann, 1927, p. 7.

"Zu meinem Block," *Bau und Wohnung*, Stuttgart, Julius Hoffmann, 1927, p. 77.

"Über die Form in der Architektur," *Die Form*, vol. 2, no. 2, 1927, p. 59.

"Wir stehen in der Wende der Zeit. Baukunst als Ausdruck geistiger Entscheidung," *Innendekoration*, vol. 39, no. 6, 1928, p. 262.

"Zum Thema: Ausstellungen," *Die Form*, vol. 3, no. 4, 1928, p. 121.

"Schön und praktisch bauen! Schluss mit der kalten Zweckmäßigkeit," *Duisburger Generalanzeiger*, vol. 49, 26 January 1930, p. 2.

"Geschäftshaus Adam," *Das Kunstblatt*, vol. 14, no. 6, 1930, p. 111–113.

"Über Sinn und Aufgabe der Kritik," *Das Kunstblatt*, vol. 14, no. 3, 1930, p. 178.

"Die neue Zeit," *Die Form*, vol. 5, no. 15, 1931, p. 406.

"Programm zur Berliner Bauausstellung," *Die Form*, vol. 6, no. 7, 1931, p. 241.

"Autobahnen als baukünstlerisches Problem," *Die Autobahn*, vol. 5, no. 10, 1932, p. 1.

"Haus H., Magdeburg," *Die Schildgenossen*, vol. 14, no. 6, 1935, p. 514–515.

"Museum for a Small City," *Architectural Forum*, vol. 78, no. 5, 1943, p. 84–85.

Introduction to Ludwig Hilberseimer, *The New City, Principles of Planning*, Chicago, Paul Theobald, 1944.

"A Tribute to Frank Lloyd Wright," *College Art Journal*, vol. 6, no. 1, Autumn 1946, p. 41–42.

"Architecture and Technology," *Arts and Architecture*, vol. 67, no. 10, October 1950, p. 30.

"The End of the Bauhaus," *Student Publications of the School of Design*, Raleigh, vol. 3, no. 3, Spring 1953, p. 16.

"A Chapel. Illinois Institute of Technology," *Arts and Architecture*, vol. 70, January 1953, p. 18–19.

"Walter Gropius," in Sigfried Giedion, *Walter Gropius, Work and Teamwork*, New York, Reinhold, 1954, p. 17–18.

Foreword to Rudolf Schwarz, *The Church Incarnate: The Sacred Function of Christian Architecture*, Chicago, H. Regnery & Co., 1958.

"Wohin gehen wir nun?," *Bauen und Wohnen*, vol. 15, no. 11, 1960, p. 391.

"Eulogy for Le Corbusier," 1969, English typescript, Library of Congress.

"Baukunst unserer Zeit (meine berufliche Laufbahn)," foreword to Blaser, Werner, *Mies van der Rohe. Die Kunst der Struktur, – l'Art de la Structure,* Zurich, Verlag für Architektur Artemis, 1965, p. 5–6. Reprinted as *Mies van der Rohe: The Art of Structure – Die Kunst der Struktur,* Basel, Birkhäuser Verlag, 1993.

"Leitgedanken zur Erziehung in der Baukunst," in Blaser, Werner, *Mies van der Rohe: Die Kunst der Struktur – l'Art de la Structure,* Zurich, Verlag für Architektur Artemis, 1965, p. 50–51.

"Walter Gropius 1883–1969," *Deutsche Bauzeitung*, vol. 103, no. 12, 1969, p. 597.

"Peterhans' Seminar für visuelles Training der Architektur-abteilung des IIT," n. d., in Blaser, Werner, *Mies van der Rohe, Lehre und Schule*, Basel, Birkhäuser Verlag, 1977, p. 34–35.

Interviews with Ludwig Mies van der Rohe

"6 Students Talk with Mies," in *Student Publications of the School of Design*, Raleigh, vol. 2, no. 3, Spring 1952, p. 21–28.

Mies van der Rohe, *Print*, vol. 2, no. 1, 1957, p. 39 (transcription of recorded *Conversations Regarding the Future of Architecture*, Louisville, Reynolds Metals Co., 1956).

Norberg-Schulz, Christian, "Rencontre avec Mies van der Rohe," *L'Architecture d'aujourd'hui*, no. 79, September 1958, p. 40–41.

"Ludwig Mies van der Rohe: An Address of Appreciation," *Architectural Association Journal*, vol. 75, no. 834, July-August 1959, p. 26–46.

"Mies van der Rohe, An Appreciation on the Occasion, This Month, of His 75th Birthday," comments collected by Peter Carter, *Architectural Design*, vol. 31, no. 3, March 1961, p. 95–121.

Interview by Peter Blake, in *Four Great Makers of Modern Architecture: The Verbatim Record of a Symposium Held at the School of Architecture from March to May 1961*, New York, Trustees of Columbia University, 1963, p. 93–104.

"Gegen Willkür und Spielerei," interview by Anna Teut, *Die Welt*, 10 October 1964.

Interview by Peter Carter, *20th Century*, Spring 1964, p.138–143.

Interview by Dirk Lohan, Chicago, Summer 1968, typed German text, New York, Museum of Modern Art, Mies van der Rohe Archive.

"Mies Speaks," *The Architectural Review*, vol. 144, no. 362, December 1968, p. 451–452 (This is the transcript of an interview given to the Berlin RIAS).

Interview by Lisa Dechêne, *Deutsche Volkszeitung*, 5 September 1969.

"Ludwig Mies van der Rohe in Conversation with H. T. Cadbury-Brown," *AA Files,* no. 66, 2013, p. 68–80.

Writings about Mies van der Rohe

Book publications, exhibition catalogues and academic papers

Johnson, Philip, *Mies van der Rohe*, New York, Museum of Modern Art, 1947.

Bill, Max, *Ludwig Mies van der Rohe*, Milan, Il Balcone, 1955.

Hilberseimer, Ludwig, *Mies van der Rohe*, Chicago, P. Theobald, 1956.

Blake, Peter, *Mies van der Rohe. Architecture and Structure*, Harmondsworth, Penguin Books, 1960.

Drexler, Arthur, *Mies van der Rohe*, New York, George Braziller, 1960.

Blaser, Werner, *Mies van der Rohe: Die Kunst der Struktur – l'Art de la Structure*, Zurich, Verlag für Architektur Artemis, 1965. Reprinted as *Mies van der Rohe: The Art of Structure – Die Kunst der Struktur,* Basel, Birkhäuser Verlag, 1993.

Pawley, Martin, *Mies van der Rohe*, London, Thames & Hudson, 1970, photographs by Yukio Futagawa.

Carter, Peter, *Mies van der Rohe at Work*, New York, Praeger, 1974.

Bonta, Juan Pablo, *Anatomia de la interpretación en arquitectura: resena semiotica de la critica del Pabellon de Barcelona de Mies van der Rohe*, Barcelona, Gili, 1975.

Papi, Lorenzo, *Mies van der Rohe*, Florence, Sansoni, 1975.

Glaeser, Ludwig, *Ludwig Mies van der Rohe: Furniture and Furniture Drawings from the Design Collection and the Mies van der Rohe Archive*, New York, Museum of Modern Art, 1977.

Spaeth, David A., *Ludwig Mies van der Rohe, An Annotated Bibliography and Chronology*, New York, Garland, 1979.

Blaser, Werner, *Mies van der Rohe, Lehre und Schule*, Basel, Birkhäuser Verlag, 1981.

Schulze, Franz, *Mies van der Rohe: Interior Spaces*, Chicago, Arts Club of Chicago, 1982.

Blaser, Werner, *Il design di Mies van der Rohe*, Milan, Electa, 1982.

Bonta, János, *Ludwig Mies van der Rohe*, Berlin, Henschel Verlag, Kunst und Gesellschaft, Budapest, Akádemiai Kiadó, 1983.

Norberg-Schulz, Christian, *Casa Tugendhat Brno*, Rome, Officina Edizioni, 1984.

Spaeth, David A., *Mies van der Rohe*, New York, Rizzoli, 1985 (preface by Kenneth Frampton).

Schulze, Franz, *Mies van der Rohe: A Critical Biography*, Chicago, University of Chicago Press, 1985 (published in association with the Mies van der Rohe Archive, Museum of Modern Art). New and revised edition, Chicago, University of Chicago Press, 2012.

Tegethoff, Wolf, *Mies van der Rohe: The Villas and Country Houses,* New York, Museum of Modern Art, Cambridge, Mass., MIT Press, 1985.

Neumeyer, Fritz, *Mies van der Rohe, das kunstlose Wort: Gedanken zur Baukunst*, Berlin, Siedler Verlag, 1986; published in English as *The Artless Word: Mies van der Rohe on the Building Art*, Cambridge, Mass., MIT Press, 1991.

Drexler, Arthur (ed.), *The Mies van der Rohe Archive*, New York, Garland, 1986–1993 (14 vols., introduction and notes by Franz Schulze).

Mies van der Rohe, *European Works*, London, Academy Editions, New York, St. Martin's Press, 1986.

Blaser, Werner, *Mies van der Rohe: Less is More*, Zurich, Waser, 1986.

Achilles, Rolf, Harrington, Kevin, and Myhrum, Charlotte (eds.), *Mies van der Rohe: Architect as Educator*, Chicago, The University of Chicago Press, 1986.

Zukowsky, John (ed.), *Mies Reconsidered: His Career, Legacy and Disciples*, Chicago, Art Institute of Chicago, New York, Rizzoli, 1986.

El Pavelló Alemany de Barcelona de Mies van der Rohe, 1929–1986, Barcelona, Ajuntament de Barcelona, 1987.

Shell, William S., *Impressions of Mies. An Interview on Mies van der Rohe: His Early Chicago Years 1938–1948*, Chicago, n. n., 1988.

Hochman, Elaine S., *Architects of Fortune: Mies van der Rohe and the Third Reich*, New York, Weidenfeld and Nicolson, 1989.

Schink, Arnold, *Mies van der Rohe: Beiträge zur ästhetischen Entwicklung der Wohnarchitektur*, Stuttgart, Karl Krämer, 1990.

Schulze, Franz (ed.), *Mies van der Rohe: Critical Essays*, New York, Museum of Modern Art, Cambridge, Mass., MIT Press, 1990.

Neumeyer, Fritz (ed.), *Ludwig Mies van der Rohe: Hochhaus am Bahnhof Friedrichstraße. Dokumentation des Mies van der Rohe-Symposiums in der neuen Nationalgalerie*, Berlin, Ernst Wasmuth, 1993.

Quetglas, Josep, *Der gläserne Schrecken: Imágenes del Pabellón de Alemania*, Montréal, Section b, 1991.

Cohen, Jean-Louis, *Mies van der Rohe*, London, Spon Press, 1994.

McAtee, Cammie, *Mies van der Rohe and Architectural Education: The Curriculum at the Illinois Institute of Technology, Students Projects and Built Works*, Ph.D. diss., Kingston, Queen's University, 1996.

Mertins, Detlef (ed.), *The Presence of Mies*, New York, Princeton Architectural Press, 1994.

Erfurth, Helmut and Tharandt, Elisabeth (eds.), *Ludwig Mies van der Rohe, die Trinkhalle, sein einziger Bau in Dessau*, Dessau, Anhaltische Verlagsgesellschaft mbH, 1995.

Schulze, Franz, *The Farnsworth House*, Chicago, Lohan Associates, 1997.

Blaser, Werner, *Mies van der Rohe: Farnsworth House*, Basel, Birkhäuser Verlag, 1999.

Hammer-Tugendhat, Daniela and Tegethoff, Wolf, *Ludwig Mies van der Rohe: Das Haus Tugendhat*, Vienna, New York, Springer, 1999.

Stiller, Adolph (ed.), *Das Haus Tugendhat: Ludwig Mies van der Rohe, Brünn 1930,* Salzburg, Verlag Anton Pustet, 1999.

Miller, Wallis, *Tangible Ideas: Architecture and the Public at the 1931 German Building Exhibition in Berlin*, Ph.D. diss., Princeton, Princeton University, 1999.

Bergdoll, Barry and Riley, Terence (eds.), *Mies in Berlin,* New York, Museum of Modern Art, Munich, Prestel, 2001.

Lambert, Phyllis (ed.), *Mies in America*, Montreal, Canadian Centre for Architecture, New York, Whitney Museum for American Art, Abrams, 2001.

Safran, Yehuda, *Mies van der Rohe*, Barcelona, Gustavo Gili, 2001.

Bafna, Sonit, *A Morphology of Intentions: The Historical Interpretation of Mies van der Rohe's Residential Designs*, Ph.D. diss., Atlanta, Georgia Institute of Technology, 2001.

Wohlsdorf, Christian, *Mehr als der bloße Zweck, Mies van der Rohe am Bauhaus 1930–1933*, Berlin, Bauhaus-Archiv, 2001.

Blaser, Werner, *Mies van der Rohe: IIT Campus*, Basel, Birkhäuser Verlag, 2002.

Stemshorn, Max, *Mies und Schinkel. Das Vorbild Schinkels im Werk Mies van der Rohes*, Berlin, Ernst Wasmuth, 2002.

Hilpert, Thilo (ed.), *Mies van der Rohe im Nachkriegsdeutschland: Das Theaterprojekt Mannheim 1953*, Leipzig, E. A. Seemann Verlag, 2001.

Heuser, Mechthild, *Steel and Stone, Constructive Concepts by Peter Behrens and Mies van der Rohe*, Baden, Lars Müller Verlag, 2002.

Cuito, Aurora, *Mies van der Rohe*, Barcelona, TeNeues, 2002.

Vandenberg, Maritz, *Farnsworth House: Ludwig Mies van der Rohe*, London, Phaidon, 2003.

Blaser, Werner, *Mies van der Rohe: Crown Hall*, Basel, Birkhäuser Verlag, 2004.

Waldheim, Charles (ed.), *CASE: Hilberseimer/Mies van der Rohe, Lafayette Park, Detroit*, Munich, Prestel, Cambridge, Mass., Harvard University, Graduate School of Design, 2004.

Blaser, Werner, *Mies van der Rohe: Federal Center Chicago*, Basel, Birkhäuser Verlag, 2004.

Colomés, Enrique and Moure, Gonzalo, *Mies: Café de terciopelo y seda*, Madrid, Editorial Rueda, 2004.

Cramer, Johannes and Sack, Dorothée (eds.), *Mies van der Rohe, Frühe Bauten. Probleme der Erhaltung - Probleme der Bewertung*, Petersberg, Michael Imhof Verlag, 2004.

Zimmerman, Claire, *Modernism, Media, Abstraction: Mies van der Rohe's Photographic Architecture in Barcelona and Brno. (1927-1931)*, Ph.D. diss., New York, Graduate Center, City University of New York, 2005.

Kleinman, Kent and Van Duzer, Leslie, *Mies van der Rohe: the Krefeld Villas*, New York, Princeton Architectural Press, 2005.

Dzievior, Yilmaz, *Mies van der Rohe, Blick durch den Spiegel*, Cologne, Verlag der Buchhandlung Walther König, 2005.

Amaldi, Paolo, *Espace et densité. Mies van der Rohe: mur, colonnes, interférences*, Gollion, In folio, 2006.

Clemence, Paul, *Mies van der Rohe's Farnsworth House*, Atglen, Schiffer Publishing Ltd., 2006.

Berg, Ronald, *Denkmalkult: Mies' Denkmal - Rekonstruieren: ja oder nein?; Essays, Fragen, Dokumente*, Berlin, Mies van der Rohe Haus, 2005.

Colomés, Enrique and Moure, Gonzalo, *Mies van der Rohe; café de terciopelo y seda, Berlin 1920-27*, Madrid, Rueda, 2005.

Dodds, George, *Building Desire: Photography, Modernity and the Barcelona Pavilion*, London, Routledge, 2005.

Kries, Mateo and von Vegesack, Alexander, *Mies van der Rohe: architettura e design a Stoccarda, Barcellona e Brno*, Geneva, Skira, 2005.

Vandenberg, Maritz, *Farnsworth House: Ludwig Mies van der Rohe*, London, Phaidon, 2005.

Berger, Ursel and Pavel, Thomas, *Barcelona Pavilion: Mies van der Rohe & Kolbe: Architecture & Sculpture*, Berlin, Jovis Verlag, 2006.

Colman, Scott W., *Organism and Artefact: the Ludwig Mies van der Rohe Circle and the Chicago School: Architecture, Planning, and Sociology, circa 1944*, PhD dissertation, University of Sydney, 2006.

Friedman, Alice T., *Women and the Making of the Modern House: a Social and Architectural History*, New Haven, Yale University Press, 2006.

Lange, Christiane, *Ludwig Mies van der Rohe & Lilly Reich: Furniture and Interiors*, Ostfildern, Hatje Cantz, 2006.

Maruhn, Jan, and Mellen, Werner, *Haus Heusgen: Ein Wohnhaus Ludwig Mies van der Rohes in Krefeld*, Aachen, Mies van der Rohe-Haus Aachen, 2006.

Zimmerman, Claire, *Mies van der Rohe, 1886-1969: The Structure of Space*, Köln, Taschen, 2006.

Llobet i Ribeiro, Xavier, *Hilberseimer y Mies: la metrópoli como ciudad jardín*, Barcelona, Fundación Caja de arquitectos, 2007.

Montella, Concetta, *Mies van der Rohe e il teatro del Novecento: il teatro di Mannheim: dall'illusione all'astrazione*, Naples, Electa, 2007.

Sthamer, Ulf, *Ludwig Mies van der Rohe. Neue Nationalgalerie in Berlin*, Munich: GRIN Verlag GmbH, 2007.

Noack, Wita, *Konzentrat der Moderne. Das Landhaus Lemke von Ludwig Mies van der Rohe. Wohnhaus, Baudenkmal und Kunsthaus*, Munich: Deutscher Kunstverlag, 2008.

Reuter, Helmut, and Schulte, Birgit (eds.), *Mies and Modern Living. Interiors, Furniture, Photography*, Ostfildern, Hatje Cantz, 2008.

Bergdoll, Barry, Lange, Christiane, Maruhn, Jan, Neumann, Dietrich, Pogacnik, Marco, Reuter, Helmut, Sachsse, Rolf, Schulte, Birgit, and Wolf Tegethoff, *Mies van der Rohe: Raumkunst der Berliner Zeit*, Ostfildern, Hatje Cantz Verlag, 2008.

Curtis, Penelope, *Patio and Pavilion: the Place of Sculpture in Modern Architecture*, Los Angeles, J. Paul Getty Museum, 2008.

Blaser, Werner, *Ludwig Mies van der Rohe; gli arredi e gli spazi*, Milan, Electa, 2008.

Daza, Ricardo, *Looking for Mies*, Barcelona, Actar, 2008.

Lange, Christiane, *Die Zusammenarbeit von Lilly Reich und Ludwig Mies van der Rohe*, 2008.

Leoni, Giovanni, and Piot, Christine, *Ludwig Mies van der Rohe*, Arles, Actes Sud, 2009.

Chahil, André, *Stahlrohrstühle am Bauhaus (1925-1927). Entwürfe von Marcel Breuer und Ludwig Mies van der Rohe.* Munich, GRIN Verlag, 2009.

Cohen, Jean-Louis, Dachs, Sandra, Muga, Patricia de, and García Hintze, Laura, *Mies van der Rohe: Objects and Furniture Design*, Barcelona, Ediciones Polígrafa, 2010.

Jennings, Michael William, and Mertins, Detlef, *G: An Avant-Garde Journal of Art, Architecture, Design, and Film, 1923-1926*, Los Angeles, Getty Research Institute, 2010.

Riel, Robert van and Ezerman, Linda, *Ik Ben Gewoon Mies: Toronto Dominion Centre*, Haarlem, Van Riel, 2010.

Scotti, Francesca, *Lafayette Park, Detroit: la forma dell'insediamento*, Milan, Libraccio, 2010.

Bertig, Rudolf, *Ein Mies-Haus für Emil Nolde*, Aachen, Mies van der Rohe-Haus Aachen, 2011.

Girot, Christophe, Andritz, Inge, Ingersoll, Richard, Kirchengast, Albert, Köppler, Jörn, and Stoffler, Johannes, *Mies als Gärtner*, Zurich, gta Verlag, 2011.

Lange, Christiane and Wolfson, Michael, *Ludwig Mies van der Rohe: Architecture for the Silk Industry*, Berlin, Nicolai, 2011.

Jäger, Joachim, and Steinherz, Geoffrey, *Neue Nationalgalerie Berlin: Mies van der Rohe*, Ostfildern, Hatje Cantz, 2011.

Černá, Iveta and Černoušková, Dagmar, *Tugendhat: Ludwig Mies van der Rohe's Commission in Brno*, Brno, Brno City Museum, 2011.

Robbers, Lutz, *Modern Architecture in the Age of Cinema: Mies van der Rohe and the Moving Image*, PhD dissertation, Princeton University, 2012.

Papapetros, Spyros, *On the Animation of the Inorganic: Art, Architecture, and the Extension of Life*, Chicago, University of Chicago Press, 2012.

Reuther, Manfred and Bertig, Rudolf, *Nolde und Mies van der Rohe*, Neukirchen, Seebüll, Nolde Stiftung Seebüll, 2012.

Sedlák, Jan and Teplý, Libor, *The Tugendhat House: a Space for Art and Spirit*, Brno, Fotep, 2012.

Aubert, Danielle, Chandani, Natasha, and Cavar, Lana, *Thanks for the View, Mr. Mies: Lafayette Park, Detroit*, New York, Metropolis Books, 2012.

Ariu, Vincenzo, *Spazio, stile e tecnica in Mies van der Rohe*, Scandicci, Firenze Libri, 2012.

Hammer-Tugendhat, Daniela, Hammer, Ivo, and Tegethoff, Wolf, *Das Haus Tugendhat. Ludwig Mies van der Rohe.* Third expanded edition, Vienna, Ambra Verlag, 2012.

Neto, Pedro Leão and Bandeira, Pedro, *On the Surface: Images of Architecture and Public Space in Debate*, Porto, A.mag, 2012.

Fest, Karin, Rahman, Sabrina, and Yazdanpanah, Marie-Noëlle, *Mies van der Rohe, Richter, Graeff & Co.: Alltag und Design in der Avantgardezeitschrift G*, Vienna, Turia + Kant, 2013.

Lambert, Phyllis, *Building Seagram*, New Haven, Yale University Press, 2013.

Krohn, Carsten. *Mies van der Rohe - The Built Work*, Basel, Birkhäuser Verlag, 2013.

Llobet i Ribeiro, Xavier, *Hilberseimer y Mies: la metrópoli como ciudad-jardín*, PhD dissertation, Barcelona, Universitat Politècnica de Catalunya, 2013.

Colomina, Beatriz, *Manifesto Architecture: The Ghost of Mies. Critical Spatial Practice*, Berlin, Sternberg, 2014.

Sharoff, Robert, and Zbaren, William, *Last is More: Mies, IBM, and the Transformation of Chicago*, Victoria, Images Publ. Group, 2014.

Beitin, Andreas F., Eiermann, Wolf, Franzen, Brigitte, Elliott, Fiona et al, *Mies van der Rohe: Montage = Collage*, Köln, Verlag der Buchhandlung Walther König, 2017.

Noack, Wita, *Mies van der Rohe: schlicht und ergreifend: Landhaus Lemke*, Berlin, Form + Zweck, 2017.

Teixidor, Joana, Bonet, Llorenç, Lahuerta, Juan José, and Marín, Celia, *Mies van der Rohe, Barcelona 1929*, Barcelona, Tenov Books, 2017.

Černá, Iveta and Valdhansová, Lucie (eds.), *Villa Tugendhat: Zahrada/the Garden*, Brno, Muzeum města Brna, 2017.

Stach, Edgar, *Mies van der Rohe: Space, Material, Detail*, Basel, Birkhäuser Verlag, 2018.

Stierli, Martino, *Montage and the Metropolis. Architecture, Modernity, and the Representation of Space*, New Haven, Yale University Press, 2018.

Relevant essays from journals and references from other publications

Jaumann, Anton, "Vom künstlerischen Nachwuchs, Haus Riehl," *Innendekoration*, vol. 21, July 1910, p. 265-273.

"Architect L. Mies, Villa des Prof. Dr. Riehl in Neubabelsberg," *Moderne Bauformen*, vol. 9, 1910, p. 42-48.

Gottfried, Carl, "Hochhäuser," *Qualität*, vol. 3, no. 5-12, August 1922-March 1923, p. 63-66.

Behrendt, Walter Curt, "Skyscrapers in Germany," *Journal of the American Institute of Architects*, vol. 11, no. 9, September 1923, p. 365-370.

Richter, Hans, "Der neue Baumeister," *Qualität*, vol. 4, no. 1-2, January-February 1925, p. 3-9.

Westheim, Paul, "Das Haus eines Sammlers," *Das Kunstblatt*, no. 3, March 1926, p. 106-113.

Giedion, Sigfried, "Die Wohnung: Ein Rückblick auf Stuttgart," *Der Cicerone*, vol. 19, no. 24, 1927, p. 760-770.

Westheim, Paul, "Mies van der Rohe, Entwicklung eines Architekten," *Das Kunstblatt*, no. 2, February 1927, p. 55-62.

Hegemann, Werner, "Schräges oder flaches Dach," *Wasmuths Monatshefte für Baukunst*, May 1927, p. 120-127.

Hilberseimer, Ludwig, [s. t.], *Das neue Berlin*, February 1929, p. 39-41 (about the Alexanderplatz competition).

Lotz, Wilhelm, "Wettbewerb für ein Bürohaus am Hindenburgplatz in Stuttgart," *Die Form*, vol. 4, no. 6, 1929, p. 151-153.

Bier, Justus, "Mies van der Rohes Reichspavillon in Barcelona," *Die Form*, vol. 4, no. 16, 15 August 1929, p. 423-430.

Westheim, Paul, "Umgestaltung des Alexanderplatzes," *Bauwelt*, vol. 20, no. 13, 1929, p. 312-316.

Gravenkamp, Curt, "Mies van der Rohe: Glashaus in Berlin," *Das Kunstblatt*, no. 4, 1930, p. 111-113.

Cohen, Walter, "Haus Lange in Krefeld," *Museum der Gegenwart*, vol. 1, no. 4, first trimester 1931, p. 160-168.

Lotz, Wilhelm, "Die Halle II auf der Bauausstellung," *Die Form*, vol. 6, no. 7, 1931, p. 341-249.

"Deutsche Bauausstellung Berlin 1931," *Der Baumeister*, vol. 29, no. 7, July 1931, p. 261–268.

Bier, Justus and Riezler, Walter, "Kann man im Haus Tugendhat wohnen?," *Die Form*, vol. 6, no. 10, 1931, p. 392–394.

Bromberg, Paul, "De Berlijnsche Bouwtentoonstelling," *Binnenhuis*, vol. 13, no. 15, July 1931, p. 125–129.

Riezler, Walter, "Das Haus Tugendhat in Brünn," *Die Form*, vol. 6, no. 9, 15 September 1931, p. 321–332.

Ginsburger, Roger, "Zweckhaftigkeit und geistige Haltung," *Die Form*, no. 11, 15 November 1931, p. 431–437.

Tugendhat, Fritz, "Die Bewohner des Hauses Tugendhat äußern sich," *Die Form*, 1931, no. 11, 15 November 1931, p. 437–439.

Johnson, Philip, "The Berlin Building Exposition of 1931," *T-Square*, vol. 2, no. 1, January 1932, p. 17–19 and 36–37.

Eisler, Max, "Mies van der Rohe, eine Villa in Brünn," *Bau und Werkkunst*, no. 8, 1932, p. 25–30.

Hitchcock, Henry Russell and Johnson, Philip, *The International Style: Architecture since 1922*, New York, W. W. Norton, 1932.

Johnson, Philip, "Architecture in the Third Reich," *The Hound and Horn*, vol. 7, no. 1, October–December 1933, p. 137–139.

Paulsen, Friedrich, "Der Reichsbank-Wettbewerb," *Monatshefte für Baukunst und Städtebau*, vol. 17, 1933, p. 337–344.

"Der Wettbewerb der Reichsbank," *Deutsche Bauzeitung*, vol. 67, no. 607, 14 August 1933, p. 607–614.

Nelson, George, "Architects of Europe Today: 7 – Van der Rohe Germany," *Pencil Points*, vol. 16, no. 9, September 1935, p. 453–460.

Barr, Alfred H., *Cubism and Abstract Art*, New York, Museum of Modern Art, 1936, p. 156–157.

Behrendt, Walter Curt, *Modern Building: Its Nature, Problems and Forms*, New York, Harcourt, Brace, 1937.

"Metals and Minerals Research Building, Illinois Institute of Technology," *Architectural Forum*, vol. 79, no. 5, November 1943, p. 88–90.

Chermayeff, Serge, "Mondrian of the Perfectionists," *Art News*, vol. 44, no. 3, March 1945, p. 14–16.

Eames, Charles, "Museum of Modern Art Exhibit," *Arts and Architecture*, vol. 64, December 1947, p. 24–27.

Joseph Rykwert, "Mies van der Rohe," *The Burlington Magazine*, vol. 91, September 1949, p. 268–269.

Wachsmann, Konrad, "Mies van der Rohe, his Work," *Arts and Architecture*, vol. 69, no. 38, 1952, p. 16–31.

"Mies van der Rohe," *Architectural Forum*, vol. 97, no. 5, November 1952, p. 83–111.

Hitchcock, Henry Russell, "The Evolution of Wright, Mies and Le Corbusier," *Perspecta*, no. 1, Summer 1952, p. 8–15.

Curjel, Hans, "Die Mannheimer Theaterprojekte," *Das Werk*, vol. 40, no. 10, October 1953, p. 312–319.

"A Chapel by Mies van der Rohe," *Arts and Architecture*, vol. 70, no. 1, January 1953, p. 18–19.

"Mies van der Rohe, A Proposed National Theatre for the City of Mannheim," *Arts and Architecture*, vol. 70, no. 10, October 1953, p. 17–19.

Leitl, Alfons, "Anmerkungen zur Zeit. Mies van der Rohe in Deutschland," *Baukunst und Werkform*, no. 6, June 1953, p. 275–277.

Gordon, Elisabeth, "The Threat to the Next America," *House Beautiful*, April 1953, p. 126–130.

"Glass House Stones: Farnsworth House," *Newsweek*, vol. 41, 8 June 1953, p. 90.

Scully, Vincent, "Wright vs. the International Style," *Art News*, vol. 53, March 1954, p. 32–35.

Munro, Eleanor, "International Style Gone Native," *Art News*, vol. 54, May 1955, p. 36.

Blaser, Werner, "Mies van der Rohe, Chicago School 1938–56," *Bauen und Wohnen*, vol. 10, no. 7, July 1956, p. 217–229.

"Mies' Enormous Room," *The Architectural Forum*, vol. 105, August 1956, p. 104–111.

Rowe, Colin, "Chicago Frame: Chicago's Place in the Modern Movement," *The Architectural Review*, vol. 120, no. 718, November 1956, p. 285–289.

Lopez, Raymond, "Visite aux USA, la leçon de Mies van der Rohe," *L'Architecture d'aujourd'hui*, vol. 28, no. 70, February 1957.

Rogers, Ernesto N., "Problematica di Mies van der Rohe," *Casabella-continuità*, no. 214, February–March 1957, p. 5–6.

"Emergence of a Master Architect," *Life*, vol. 42, 18 March 1957, p. 60–68.

"The Miesian Superblock," *Architectural Forum*, vol. 106, March 1957, p. 128–133.

Blake, Peter, "The Difficult Art of Simplicity," *Architectural Forum*, vol. 108, May 1958, p. 126–131.

Drexler, Arthur, "Seagram Building," *Architectural Record*, vol. 124, July 1958, p. 139–147.

Mumford, Lewis, "The Lesson of the Master," *The New Yorker*, 13 September 1958, p. 141–148.

Zevi, Bruno, "Mies: là dove il razionale si logora nel classicismo," *L'Architettura-Cronache e Storia*, vol. 4, no. 37, November 1958, p. 439.

"L'œuvre de Mies van der Rohe," *L'Architecture d'aujourd'hui*, vol. 29, no. 79, September 1958 (special issue).

Jordy, William, "Seagram Assessed," *The Architectural Review*, vol. 124, December 1958, p. 374–382.

"Allarme per Mies van der Rohe," *Casabella-continuità*, no. 223, 8 January 1959.

Bronfman Lambert, Phyllis, "How a Building Gets Built," *Vassar Alumnae Magazine*, vol. 44, February 1959, p. 14.

Jordy, William H., "Seagram Building, New York, USA," *Architectural Design*, vol. 29, February 1959, p. 72–77.

"Seagram House Re-assessed Discussion," *Progressive Architecture*, vol. 40, no. 6, August 1959, p. 58, 64 and 192.

Bauen und Wohnen, vol. 14, no. 9, September 1959 (special issue).

"Siedlung Lafayette Park in Detroit," *Bauen und Wohnen*, vol. 15, no. 11, 1960, p. 392–399.

Blake, Peter, "Mies van der Rohe and the Mastery of Structure," in *The Master Builders*, New York, A. Knopf, 1960, p. 153–262.

"Wohnhochhäuser an der Commonwealth Promenade in Chicago," *Bauen und Wohnen*, vol. 15, no. 3, March 1960, p. 86–93.

Moholy-Nagy, Sibyl, "Ville tra i tuguri-2: per chi ricostruiamo?," *L'Architettura-Cronache e Storia*, vol. 6, no. 9, January 1961, p. 628–629, no. 10, February 1961, p. 700–701, and no. 11, March 1961, p. 772–773.

Jordy, William, "The Place of Mies van der Rohe in American Architecture," *Zodiac*, no. 8, June 1961, p. 28–33.

Banham, Reyner, "Mies van der Rohe on Trial: Almost Nothing is Too Much," *The Architectural Review*, vol. 132, no. 786, August 1962, p. 125–128.

Beasley, Elisabeth, *Designed to Live in*, London, George Allen and Unwin, 1962.

Four Great Makers of Modern Architecture: The Verbatim Record of a Symposium Held at the School of Architecture from March to May 1961, New York, Trustees of Columbia University, 1963.

Graeff, Werner, "Concerning the so-called G Group," *Art Journal*, vol. 23, no. 4, Summer 1964, p. 280–282.

Kuh, Katharine, "Mies van der Rohe: Modern Classicist," *Saturday Review of Literature*, 23 January 1965, p. 22–23 and 61.

"Modern Architecture Symposium," *Journal of the Society of Architectural Historians*, vol. 24, no. 1, March 1965, passim.

"Ludwig Mies van der Rohe 80 Jahre," *Bauen und Wohnen*, vol. 21, no. 5, May 1966, p. 163–206.

"Meinungen zu Mies," *Baumeister*, vol. 63, May 1966, p. 505.

Jordy, William, "The Aftermath of the Bauhaus in America: Gropius, Mies and Breuer," *Perspectives in American History*, vol. 12, Cambridge, Charles Warren Center for Studies in American History, Harvard University, 1968, p. 485–543.

Anderson, Stanford O., *Peter Behrens and the New Architecture of Germany, 1900–1917*, Ph.D. diss., New York, Columbia University, 1968.

Posener, Julius, "Eine Reise nach Brünn," *Bauwelt*, vol. 60, 1969, no. 36, p. 1244–1245.

Kuhne, Gunther, "Pure Form," *Architectural Design*, vol. 39, February 1969, p. 89–90.

Zoege von Manteuffel, Claus, "Die neue Nationalgalerie in Berlin," *Pantheon*, vol. 27, May 1969, p. 243–245.

50 Years Bauhaus, Stuttgart, Württembergischer Kunstverein, 1969.

Smithson, Alison and Peter, "Mies van der Rohe," *Architectural Design*, vol. 39, no. 7, July 1969, p. 363–366.

Berkeley, Ellen Ferry, "Westmount Square," *Architectural Forum*, vol. 131, September 1969, p. 82–89.

Tugendhat, Grete, "Zum Bau des Hauses Tugendhat," *Bauwelt*, vol. 60, no. 36, 1969, p. 1246–1247.

Jordy, William, "The Laconic Splendor of the Metal Frame: Ludwig Mies van der Rohe's 860 Lake Shore Drive Apartments and his Seagram Building," in *American Buildings and their Architects: The Impact of European Modernism in the Mid-Twentieth Century*, Garden City, New York, Doubleday and Co., 1972, p. 221–277.

"Mies' Toronto-Dominion Centre," *The Architectural Review*, vol. 151, January 1972, p. 48–55.

Winter, John, "Misconceptions about Mies," *The Architectural Review*, vol. 151, February 1972, p. 69 and 95–105.

Posener, Julius, "Absolute Architektur," *Neue Rundschau*, vol. 84, no. 1, 1973, p. 79–95.

Petras, Renate, "Drei Arbeiten Mies van der Rohes in Potsdam-Babelsberg," *Architektur der DDR*, vol. 23, no. 2, 1974, p. 120–124.

Futagawa, Yukio and Glaeser, Ludwig, "Mies van der Rohe: Farnsworth House, Plano, Illinois, 1945–50," *Global Architecture*, no. 27, 1974.

Rowe, Colin, "Neo-'classicism' and modern architecture II," in *The Mathematics of the Ideal Villa, and Other Essays*, Cambridge, Mass., MIT Press, 1976, p. 139–159.

Dal Co, Francesco and Tafuri, Manfredo, *Architettura contemporanea*, Milan, Electa, 1976.

Lüfkens, Karl Otto, "Die Verseidag-Bauten von Mies van der Rohe (1933 bis 1937), ein Dokument der Architektur des XX. Jahrhunderts," *Die Heimat, Zeitschrift für niederrheinische Kultur- und Heimatpflege*, vol. 48, December 1977, p. 57–61.

Damisch, Hubert (ed.), *Modern'Signe: Recherches sur le travail du signe dans l'architecture moderne*, Paris, Corda/Cehta, 1977, passim.

Beeby, Thomas Hall, "Vitruvius Americanus: Mies' Ornament," *Inland Architect*, vol. 21, no. 5, May 1978, p. 12–15.

Malcolmson, Reginald, "A Paradox of Humility and Superstar," *Inland Architect*, vol. 21, no. 5, May 1978, p. 16–19.

Schulze, Franz, "How Chicago got Mies – and Harvard didn't," *Inland Architect*, vol. 21, no. 5, May 1978, p. 23–24.

Honey, Sandra, "Mies at the Bauhaus," *Architectural Association Quarterly*, vol. 10, no. 1, 1978, p. 51–59.

Honey, Sandra, "Who and What Inspired Mies van der Rohe in Germany," *Architectural Design*, vol. 49, no. 3–4, 1979, p. 99–102.

Hoepfner, Wolfram and Neumeyer, Fritz, *Das Haus Wiegand von Peter Behrens in Berlin-Dahlem: Baugeschichte und Kunstgegenstände eines herrschaftlichen Wohnhauses*, Mainz, Philip von Zabern, 1979.

Buddensieg, Tilmann and Rogge, Henning, *Industriekultur. Peter Behrens und die AEG, 1907–1914*, Berlin, Gebr. Mann, 1979.

Serenyi, Peter, "Mies' New National Gallery: An Essay in Architectural Content," *Harvard Architecture Review*, no. 1, Spring 1980, p. 181–189.

Forster, Kurt W., "The Seagram Building Reconsidered," *Skyline*, February 1982, p. 28–29.

Von Beulwitz, Dietrich, "The Perls House by Mies van der Rohe," *Architectural Design*, vol. 53, no. 10–11, 1983, p. 63–71.

Tegethoff, Wolf, "Industriearchitektur und Neues Bauen, Mies van der Rohe, Verseidag-Fabrik in Krefeld," *Archithese*, no. 13, May–June 1983, p. 33–38.

"Mansion House Square Debate," *The Architect's Journal*, vol. 37, 1984, no. 28, 34, 36 and 37.

"Mansion House Square," *International Architect*, no. 3, 1984, p. 19–38.

Tegethoff, Wolf, "Orianda-Berlin: Das Vorbild Schinkels im Werk Mies van der Rohes," *Zeitschrift des deutschen Vereins für Kunstwissenschaft*, vol. 25, no. 1–4, 1985, p. 174–184.

Mislin, Miron, "Architekturtheorie und Architekturidee bei Mies van der Rohe: eine Kritik des positivistischen Architekturmythos," *Transparent*, vol. 16, 1985, no. 10–12, p. 46–60.

Frampton, Kenneth, "Mies van der Rohe: Avant-Garde and Continuity," in *Studies in Tectonic Culture*, Houston, Rice University, 1985 (Craig Francis Cullinan Lectures).

Hahn, Peter (ed.), *Bauhaus Berlin*, Berlin, Bauhaus-Archiv, 1985.

Šlapeta, Vladimír, *Die Brünner Funktionalisten, Moderne Architektur in Brno*, Innsbruck, Technische Fakultät der Universität Innsbruck, 1985.

Neumeyer, Fritz, "Neues Bauen in Wedding," in *Wedding im Wandel der Zeit*, Berlin, 1985, p. 26–34.

Culot, Maurice and Krier, Léon, "A European Perspective on the Mies van der Rohe Centennial," in *The Chicago Architecture Annual*, Chicago, Metropolitan Press Publications, 1986, p. 13–14.

Dal Co, Francesco, "Il centenario di Mies," *Domus*, no. 668, January 1986, p. 8–11.

Ruegenberg, Sergius, "Der Skelettbau ist keine Teigware," *Bauwelt*, vol. 77, no. 11, 14 March 1986, p. 346.

Stamper, John W., "Patronage and the City Grid: The High-Rise Architecture of Mies van der Rohe in Chicago," *Inland Architect*, vol. 30, no. 2, March–April 1986, p. 34–41.

Palumbo, Peter, "Farnsworth Impressions," *Inland Architect*, vol. 30, no. 2, March–April 1986, p. 43 and 46.

Rykwert, Joseph and Filler, Martin, "A Posthumous Mies: Two Views," *Art in America*, vol. 74, no. 4, April 1986, p. 152–156.

Laroque, Didier, "Le secret," *L'Architecture d'aujourd'hui*, no. 245, June 1986, p. V–XI.

Bonta, Juan Pablo, "The Analysis of Mies: A New Language or Old Clichés?," *Design Book Review*, no. 10, Autumn 1986, p. 20–29.

Tigerman, Stanley, "Mies van der Rohe: A Moral Modernist Model," *Perspecta*, no. 22, 1986, p. 112–135.

"Mies van der Rohe," Arquitectura Viva, no. 6, 1986 (special issue).

Dearstyne, Howard, *Inside the Bauhaus*, New York, Rizzoli, 1986, p. 226.

Menšík, Karel and Vodička, Jaroslav, *Vila Tugendhat Brno*, Brno, Odbor vnitrich veci Narodniho vyboru, 1986.

Šapák, Jan, "Vila Tugendhat," *Umení*, 1987, no. 1, p. 167–179.

Bonta, Juan Pablo, "Mies as Text," *Design Book Review*, 13, Autumn 1987, p. 20–25.

Jarzombek, Mark, "Mies van der Rohe's New National Gallery and the Problem of Context," *Assemblage*, no. 2, February 1987, p. 33–43.

Kirsch, Karen, *Die Weissenhofsiedlung: Werkbund-Ausstellung "Die Wohnung,"* Stuttgart 1927, Stuttgart, Deutsche Verlags-Anstalt, 1987.

Pommer, Richard (ed.), *In the Shadow of Mies: Ludwig Hilberseimer, Architect, Educator, and Urban Planner*, Chicago, The Art Institute of Chicago, Rizzoli, 1988.

Zimmermann, Florian (ed.), *Der Schrei nach dem Turmhaus. Der Ideenwettbewerb Hochhaus am Bahnhof Friedrichstraße Berlin 1921/1922*, Berlin, Argon-Verlag, 1988.

Nerdinger, Winfried, "Nachlese zum 100. Geburtstag: Neue Literatur zu Mies van der Rohe," *Kunstchronik*, vol. 41, no. 8, August 1988, p. 419–429.

Quetglas, Josep, "Fear of Glass," in Beatriz Colomina and Hays, K. Michael (eds.), *Architecture Production*, New York, Princeton Architectural Press, 1988, p. 122–151.

Šapák, Jan, "Das Alltagsleben in der Villa Tugendhat," *Werk, Bauen und Wohnen*, 1988, no. 12, p. 15–23.

Forster, Kurt W., "Four Unpublished Drawings by Mies van der Rohe: a Commentary," *Res*, no. 16, Autumn 1988, p. 5–8.

Cacciari, Massimo, "Mies's Classics," *Res*, no. 16, Autumn 1988, p. 9–16.

Guenther, Sonja, *Lilly Reich. Innenarchitektin, Designerin, Ausstellungsgestalterin*, Stuttgart, Deutsche Verlags-Anstalt, 1988.

Hartoonian, Gevork, "Mies van der Rohe: The Genealogy of Column and Wall," *Journal of Architectural Education*, vol. 42, Winter 1989, p. 43–50.

Newman, Lise, "Lafayette Park Detroit, Michigan: Mies van der Rohe and Ludwig Hilberseimer," *Modernist Visions and the Contemporary American City Center*, 5, 1989, p. 124–127.

Heuser, Mechthild, "Die Fenster zum Hof, die Turbinenhalle, Behrens und Mies van der Rohe," in Hans-Georg Pfeifer (ed.) *Peter Behrens: "Wer aber will sagen, was Schönheit sei?": Grafik, Produktgestaltung, Architektur*, Düsseldorf, Beton-Verlag, 1990, p. 108–121.

Brown, W. Gordon, "Form as the Object of Experience: Georg Simmel's Influence on Mies van der Rohe," *Journal of Architectural Education*, vol. 43, Winter 1990, p. 42–46.

Evans, Robin, "Mies van der Rohe's Paradoxical Symmetries," *Architectural Association Files*, no. 19, Spring 1990, p. 56–68.

Boyken, Immo, "Ludwig Mies van der Rohe and Egon Eiermann: The Dictate of Order," *Journal of the Society of Architectural Historians*, vol. 49, no. 2, June 1990, p. 133–153.

Constant, Caroline, "The Barcelona Pavilion as Landscape Garden: Modernity and the Picturesque," *Architectural Association Files*, no. 20, Autumn 1990, p. 46–54.

Otto, Christian and Pommer, Richard, *Weissenhof 1927 and the Modern Movement in Architecture*, Chicago, University of Chicago Press, 1991.

Neumeyer, Fritz, "Giedion en Mies van der Rohe: een paradox in de historiografie van het Moderne," *Archis*, no. 4, April 1992, p. 47–51.

Welter, Volker, "Landhaus Lemke in Berlin-Hohenschönhausen," *Bauwelt*, no. 12, 1991, p. 536.

Riley, Terence, *The International Style: Exhibition 15 and the Museum of Modern Art*, New York, Rizzoli, 1992.

Polano, Sergio, "I Kröller e i loro architetti: Spiritus e Materia Unum," *Domus*, no. 745, January 1993, p. 48–55.

Polano, Sergio, "Rose-shaped, Like an Open Hand, Helene Kröller-Müller's House," The Kröller-Müllers, Architectures for a Collection, *Rassegna*, vol. 15, no. 56, December 1993, p. 18–47.

Spaeth, David A., "Mies: Teaching Methods of Mies and Hilberseimer," *Inland Architect*, vol. 37, no. 4, July–August 1993, p. 49–52.

Kruse, Christiane, "Haus Werner – ein ungeliebtes Frühwerk Mies van der Rohes," *Zeitschrift für Kunstgeschichte*, vol. 56, 1993, no. 4, p. 554–63.

Mies van der Rohe à Montréal, Architecture/Québec, no. 71, February 1993 (special issue).

Ott, Randall, "Reflections on the Rational and the Sensual in the Work of Ludwig Mies van der Rohe," *Arris: Journal of the Southeast Chapter of the Society of Architectural Historians*, vol. 4, 1993, p. 38–53.

Neumeyer, Fritz, "Schinkel im Zeilenbau. Mies van der Rohes Siedlung an der Afrikanischen Straße in Berlin-Wedding," in Andreas von Beyer, Vittorio Lampugnani and Günter Schweikhart (eds.), *Hülle and Fülle: Festschrift für Tilmann Buddensieg*, Alfter, VDG, Verlag und Datenbank für Geisteswissenschaften, 1993, p. 415–431.

De Solà-Morales, Ignasi, "Mies van der Rohe e il grado zero," *Lotus*, no. 81, 1994, p. 20–27.

Tegethoff, Wolf, "Die Neue Nationalgalerie im Werk Mies van der Rohes und im Kontext der Berliner Museumsarchitektur," in Christian Hölz and Zentralinstitut für Kunstgeschichte, *Berlins Museen: Geschichte und Zukunft*, Munich, Deutscher Kunstverlag, 1994, p. 281–292.

Schulze, Franz, *Philip Johnson: A Biography*, New York, A. Knopf, 1994.

Smithson, Alison and Peter, *Changing the Art of Inhabitation*, London, Artemis, 1994.

Maruhn, Jan and Senger, Nina, "Ein Ort für Kunst," in Julian Heyden (ed.), *Ein Ort für Kunst/A Place for Art, Ludwig Mies van der Rohe, Haus Lange-Haus Esters, Krefeld*, Krefelder Kunstmuseen, Stuttgart, Gerd Hatje, 1995, p. 7–19.

Colomina, Beatriz, "Mies not," Columbia Documents of *Architecture and Theory*, vol. 5, 1996, p. 75–101.

Frampton, Kenneth, "Mies van der Rohe: Avant-Garde and Continuity," in Kenneth Frampton, *Studies in Tectonic Culture: The Poetics of Construction in the Nineteenth and Twentieth Century Architecture*, Cambridge, Mass., MIT Press, 1995, p. 159–207.

Morisset, Lucie K., "Monument d'Éternité: Le Seagram Building," *ARQ: La revue d'architecture*, no. 88, December 1995, p. 16-19.

Gregotti, Vittorio, "Res aedificatoria: dialogo con Massimo Cacciari," *Casabella*, vol. 59, no. 629, December 1995, p. 2-3.

Cacciari, Massimo, "Res aedificatoria: il 'classico' di Mies van der Rohe," *Casabella*, no. 629, December 1995, p. 3-7.

Northup, Dale, "Mies van der Rohe and Frank Lloyd Wright: A Dialogue," *Inland Architect*, vol. 40, July-August 1996, p. 12-15.

Lefaivre, Liane, "On the Road with Mies van der Rohe," in Michael Speaks (ed.), *The Critical Landscape*, Rotterdam, 010 Publishers, 1996, p. 172-185.

Lambert, Phyllis, "The Art of the Four Seasons," *ANY*, no. 13, 1996, p. 40-41.

Aparicio Guisado, Jesús Mariá, "La desmaterialización del muro, una evolución de lo tectónico: Gottfried Semper, Mies van der Rohe y la Casa Farnsworth," *Arquitectura*, no. 31, 1997, p. 16-21 and 116-119.

Hays, K. Michael, "Abstraction's Appearance (Seagram Building)," in Robert Somol (ed.), *Autonomy and Ideology: Positioning an Avant-Garde in America*, New York, The Monacelli Press, 1997, p. 277-291.

James, Kathleen, "Changing the Agenda: From German Bauhaus to U.S. Internationalism. Ludwig Mies van der Rohe, Walter Gropius, Marcel Breuer," in Stephanie Barron (ed.), *Exiles and Emigrés: The Flight of European Artists form Hitler*, Los Angeles, Los Angeles Museum of Art, 1997, p. 235-252.

Levine, Neil, "'The Significance of Facts:' Mies's Collages up Close and Personal," *Assemblage*, no. 37, 1998, p. 70-101.

Heuser, Mechthild, "Mies van der Rohes Rückkehr zum Textil," *Der Architekt*, no. 5, May 1998, p. 271-274.

Friedman, Alice T., *Women and the Making of the Modern House: A Social and Architectural History*, New York, Abrams, 1998, p. 126-159.

Waetzoldt, Stephen, "30 Jahre Mies van der Rohes Neue Nationalgalerie. Wie es dazu kam," *Jahrbuch Preußischer Kulturbesitz*, vol. 35, 1998, p. 77-94.

Waldheim, Charles, "Reviewing the Miesian Landscape," *Landscape Architecture*, vol. 89, no. 1, January 1999, p. 121 and 124.

Lambert, Phyllis, "Mies's Student Union: [IIT]," *ANY*, no. 24, 1999, p. 52-53.

Bohringer, Hannes, "The Absence of Architecture: Mies und die Moderne," *Arch plus*, no. 146, April 1999, p. 56-58.

Cêtre, Jean-Pierre, "Neue Nationalgalerie recto verso," *Faces*, no. 47, Winter 1999-2000, p. 34-40.

Beeby, Thomas H., "Toward a Technological Architecture?: Case Study of the Illinois Institute of Technology Commons Building," *Perspecta*, no. 31, 2000, p. 10-21 and 45.

Harrington, Kevin, "Table Talk: Ludwig Mies van der Rohe," *Chicago Architectural Journal*, vol. 9, 2000, p. 84-89.

Allen, Stan, "Mies's Theater of Effects, the New National Gallery," in Stan Allen, *Practice: Architecture, Technique and Representation, Essays*, Amsterdam, G+B Arts International, 2000, p. 71-85.

Kleinman, Kent and Van Duzer, Leslie, "Eisen und Mörtel: Anmerkungen zu Haus Lange und Haus Esters," *Bauwelt*, vol. 91, no. 41, 3 November 2000, p. 16-19.

Lahuerta, Juan Jose, "Su alcune fotografie di Mies (frammenti)," *Casabella*, vol. 64, no. 684-685, December 2000-January 2001, p. 38-43.

Tegethoff, Wolf, "La storia di un 'trono': l'archeologia della poltrona Barcellona," *Casabella*, vol. 64, no. 684-685, December 2000-January 2001, p. 44-49.

Conrads, Ulrich, "'Einfälle sind keine Ideen': Zurückgedacht an Mies' Fünfundsiebzigsten," *Bauwelt*, vol. 92, no. 47, December 2001, p. 36-39.

Dal Co, Francesco, "Mies van der Rohe: Grandezza della Modernità," *Casabella*, vol. 65, no. 692, September 2001, p. 4-5.

Dodds, George, "Body in Pieces: Desiring the Barcelona Pavilion," *Res*, no. 39, Spring 2001, p. 168-191.

Gänshirt, Christian, "Das Instrument neu schärfen: Zur großen Halle der Neuen Nationalgalerie in Berlin," *Bauwelt*, vol. 92, no. 39, 19 October 2001, p. 34-37.

Van der Rohe, Georgia, *La donna è mobile: Mein bedingungsloses Leben*, Berlin, Aufbau Verlag, 2001.

"Mies van der Rohe: Berlin/Chicago," *AV Monographs*, no. 92, November-December 2001.

Wolsdorff, Christian (ed.), "Mehr als der bloße Zweck," *Mies van der Rohe am Bauhaus 1930-1933*, Berlin, Bauhaus-Archiv, 2001.

Bergdoll, Barry, "Schinkel and Mies: Urban Perspective," *A+U*, no. 384, September 2002, p. 20-23, 26, 28-29 and 32-33.

Elwall, Robert, "My Kind of Town," *RIBA Journal*, vol. 109, no. 12, December 2002, p. 106.

Mayer, Jürgen and Vismann, Bettina, "The Perspiration Affair, or the New National Gallery between Cold Fronts," *Grey Room*, no. 9, Autumn 2002, p. 80-89.

Meier, Philippe, "L'importance de la pensée modulaire chez Ludwig Mies van der Rohe et Dominique Perrault," *Matières*, vol. 5, 2002, p. 90-101.

Gale, Adrian, "Mies and Me," *RIBA Journal*, vol. 109, no. 12, December 2002, p. 22-24.

Krausse, Joachim, Kuhnert, Nikolaus and Schindler, Susanne, "Miesverständnisse," *Arch plus*, no. 161, June 2002, p. 18-21.

Hilpert, Thilo, "Phantomschmerz Mies: Revision eines Klischees," *Arch plus*, no. 161, June 2002, p. 62-74.

Koolhaas, Rem, "Miesverständnisse," *Arch plus*, no. 161, June 2002, p. 78-83.

Hill, Jonathan, "Weathering the Barcelona Pavilion," *Journal of Architecture*, vol. 7, no. 4, Winter 2002, p. 319-327.

Kries, Mateo, "Pure Form Only?," *Architectural Design*, vol. 72, no. 4, July 2002, p. 14-16.

Jager, Markus, "Das Haus Warnholtz von Ludwig Mies van der Rohe (1914/15)," *Zeitschrift für Kunstgeschichte*, vol. 65, no. 1, 2002, p. 123-136.

Stankard, Mark, "Re-covering Mies van der Rohe's Weissenhof: The Ultimate Surface," *Journal of Architectural Education*, vol. 55, no. 4, May 2002, p. 247-256.

Steele, Brett, "Absolute Mies, Absolute Modern: Building Good Copy," *Architectural Association Files*, no. 48, Winter 2002, p. 2-14.

Watson, Victoria, "Mies van der Rohe: A Drawing and a Letter to a Client," *The Journal of Architecture*, vol. 7, no. 4, Winter 2002, p. 355-360.

Ungers, Oswald Mathias, "Endspiel [Neue Nationalgalerie, Berlin]," *Arch plus*, no. 161, June 2002, p. 88-91.

Georgiadis, Sokratis, "Mies' preußische Gefangenschaft," *Arch plus*, no. 161, June 2002, p. 84-87.

Bergdoll, Barry, "Schinkel and Mies: Nature's Perspective," *A+U*, no. 388, January 2003, p. 12-135.

Plummer, Henry, "Masters of Light: Ludwig Mies van der Rohe: Farnsworth House," "Masters of Light," in *A+U*, extra edition, November 2003, p. 262-267.

Curtis, Penelope, "The Modern Eye-Catcher: Mies van der Rohe and Sculpture," *ARQ: Architectural Research Quarterly*, vol. 7, no. 3/4, 2003, p. 361-370.

Carpo, Mario and Zancan, Roberto, "Mies à Montréal," *L'Architecture d'aujourd'hui*, no. 350, January-February 2004, p. 104-109.

Sayer, Derek, "The Unbearable Lightness of Building: A Cautionary Tale," *Grey Room*, no. 16, Summer 2004, p. 6-35.

De Michelis, Marco, "Sul monumento a Rosa Luxemburg e Karl Liebknecht di Ludwig Mies van der Rohe," in Jeffrey T. Schnapp (ed.), *In Cima, Giuseppe Terragni per Margherita Sarfatti, architetture della memoria nel'900*, Venice, Marsilio, 2004, p. 45-51.

Papapetros, Spyros, "Malicious Houses: Animation, Animism, Animosity in German Architecture and Film – From Mies to Murnau," *Grey Room*, no. 20, Summer 2005, p. 6-37.

Lambert, Phyllis, "Stimmung at Seagram: Philip Johnson Counters Mies van der Rohe," *Grey Room*, no. 20, July 2005, p. 38-59.

Mertins, Detlef, "Mies' Event Space," *Grey Room*, no. 20, Summer 2005, p. 60-73.

Wojcik, Marta, "Ludwig Mies van der Rohe and Chicago in the 1940s," in Sharp, Robert V., and Stepina, Elizabeth (eds.), *1945: Creativity and Crisis: Chicago Architecture and Design of the World War II Era*, Chicago, Art Institute of Chicago, 2005, p. 18-21.

Mertins, Detlef, "Goodness Greatness: the Images of Mies Once Again," *Perspecta*, vol. 37 2005, p. 112-121.

Watson, Victoria, "Mies van der Rohe – Drawing in Space," in van Eck, Caroline, and Winters, Edward (eds.), *Dealing with the Visual: Art History, Aesthetics, and Visual Culture,* Aldershot, Ashgate, 2005, p. 209-241.

James, Kathleen, "Proportions and Politics: Marketing Mies and Mendelsohn," *German Historical Institute Bulletin*, Supplement no. 2, 2005, p. 51-64.

Amaldi, Paolo, "Chairs, Postures, and Points of View: for an Exact Restitution of the Barcelona Pavilion," *Future Anterior*, vol. 2, no. 2, January 2005, p. 16-23.

Lambert, Phyllis, "'Stimmung' at Seagram: Philip Johnson Counters Mies van der Rohe," *Grey Room,* no. 20, July 2005, p. 38-59.

Newton, Clare, "The Phoenix Pavilion: Interpreting the Black and White Memory of the Barcelona Pavilion," *Fabrications*, vol. 15, no. 2, December 2005, p. 63-76.

Amaldi, Paolo, "Transparence et obstruction spatiale chez Mies van der Rohe," *Matières*, no. 8, 2006, p. 102-113.

Neumann, Dietrich, "Das Haus Ryder in Wiesbaden (1923) und die Zusammenarbeit zwischen Ludwig Mies van der Rohe und Gerhard Severain," *Architectura 36*, no. 2, 2006, p. 199-220.

Sunwoo, Irene, "Taming the Farnsworth House," *Thresholds*, no. 31, 2006, p. [66]-75.

Watson, Victoria, "How Henri Lefebvre Missed the Modernist Sensibility of Mies van der Rohe," *Journal of Architecture*, vol. 12, no. 1, February 2007, p. 99-111.

Gargiani, Roberto, "La Maison de campagne en briques de Mies van der Rohe: 'transfiguration esthétique' de l'espace de l'habitation bourgeoise," *Matières*, no. 9, 2008, p. 31-51.

Hartoonian, Gevork, "Mies: the Window Framed," *Fabrications*, vol. 18, no. 2, December 2008, p. 26-49.

Lohan, Dirk, Dal Co, Francesco, and Adams, Nicholas, "Mies van der Rohe, La Casa Farnsworth," *Casabella,* vol. 72, no. 767, June 2008, p. [90]-101.

Marx, Andreas, and Weber, Paul, "Zur Neudatierung von Mies van der Rohes Landhaus in Eisenbeton," *Architectura,* vol. 38, no. 2, 2008, p. 127-166.

Colomina, Beatriz, "The Endless Museum: Le Corbusier and Mies van der Rohe," *Log,* no. 15, January 2009, p. 55-68.

Eggler, Marianne, "Divide and Conquer: Ludwig Mies van der Rohe and Lilly Reich's Fabric Partitions at the Tugendhat House," *Studies in the Decorative Arts,* vol. 16, no. 2, April 2009, p. 66-90.

Grawe, Sam, and Mertins, Detlef, "Mies van der Rohe: Lafayette Park [Detroit]," *Dwell,* vol. 9, no. 2, January 2009, p. 114-121.

Kim, Ransoo, "The Tectonically Defining Space of Mies van der Rohe," *Arq: Architectural Research Quarterly,* vol. 13, no. 3-4, 2009, p. 251-260.

Madia, Enrique, "Edificios Bacardí En Miami," *Archivos de arquitectura antillana: AAA,* no. 32, January 2009, p. [296]-297.

Pogacnik, Marco, "Säule und Statue: Ludwig Mies van der Rohe und die Bildhauerei," *Werk, Bauen + Wohnen,* vol. 96, no. 4, 2009, p. 36-43.

Watson, Victoria, "Pictorial Grids: Reading the Buildings of Mies van der Rohe through the Paintings of Agnes Martin," *Journal of Architecture,* vol. 14, no. 3, June 2009, p. 421-438.

Colomina, Beatriz, "Mies Media," *L'Architecture d'aujourd'hui,* no. 378, June 2010, p. 40-45.

Pogacnik, Marco, "The Art of the Noblest Ornaments: the Statue and the Column in the Architecture of Mies van der Rohe," *Architectura,* vol. 40, no. 1, 2010, p. 21-54.

Stierli, Martino, "Mies Montage," *AA Files,* no. 61, 2010, p. 64-72.

Adams, Nicholas, "The Seagram Building: Thoughts on Context," *SOM Journal,* no. 7, 2011, p. 190-194.

Haps, Silke, "Zur Holzhaus - Fertigbauweise der Deutschen Werkstätten Dresden-Hellerau in der frühen Zwischenkriegszeit: das Gartenhaus von Haus Esters in Krefeld," *Architectura,* vol. 41, no. 2, 2011, p. 141-158.

Krohn, Carsten, "Unscheinbares in Fokus: Beobachtungen zu Mies," *Archithese,* vol. 41, no. 5, September 2011, p. 40-47.

Kuehn, Wilfried, "Appropriating Mies," *Bauwelt,* vol. 102, no. 44, November 18, 2011, p. 26-27.

Sánchez, Salvador Lizárraga, "Bacardí Breezer," *AA Files,* no. 62, 2011, p. 104-107.

Scott, Felicity D., "An Army of Soldiers or a Meadow: The Seagram Building and the 'Art of Modern Architecture'," *Journal of the Society of Architectural Historians,* vol. 70, no. 3, September 2011, p. 330-353.

Stierli, Martino, "Mies Montage: Mies van der Rohe, Dada, Film und die Kunstgeschichte," *Zeitschrift für Kunstgeschichte,* vol. 74, no. 3, 2011, p. 401-436.

Tietz, Jürgen, "Kultur auf's Forum: Berlin, zwischen Scharoun und Mies van der Rohe keimt Hoffnung auf," *Deutsche Bauzeitung,* vol. 145, no. 1, 2011, p. 12-13.

Aitchison, Mathew, "Finding the Context in Mies," *Fabrications,* vol. 22, no. 2, December 2012, p. 186-207.

Krohn, Carsten, "Ich baue um der Architektur Willen: zur Restaurierung des Hauses Tugendhat," *Archithese,* vol. 42, no. 6, November 2012, p. 12-16.

O'Rourke, Kathryn E., "Mies and Bacardi: Mixing Modernism, C. 1960," *Journal of Architectural Education* 66, no. 1, 2012, p. 57-71.

Wagner, Monika, "Mies van der Rohe's Tugendhat House - Weightless Living," *Docomomo Journal,* no. 46, 2012, p. 20-25.

Frohburg, Jan, "Freiraum: Ideas of Nature and Freedom in the Work of Mies van der Rohe," In Emmons, Paul, Lomholt, Jane, and Hendrix, John (eds.), *The Cultural Role of Architecture: Contemporary and Historical Perspectives,* London, Routledge, 2012, p. 114-122.

Černá, Iveta, Černoušková, Dagmar, and Wahla, Ivan, "Moderní dům jasných a jednoduchých tvarů - brněnska Vila Tugendhat," *Piranesi,* vol. 21, no. 33, January 2013, p. 16-31.

Šlapeta, Vladimír, "Vila Tugendhat - genese a ohlas: Ludwig Mies van der Rohe, Vila Tugendhat, Brno, Česká Republika, 1928-1930," *Piranesi,* vol. 21, no. 33, January 2013, p. 6-15.

Zappa, Alfredo, "Mies reloaded: una piccola opera dimenticata di Mies van der Rohe," *Casabella,* vol. 77, no. 4, April 2013, p. 8-15.

Ibelings, Hans, "Mies en Valeur," *Canadian Architect,* vol. 58, no. 8, August 2013, p. 26-30.

Arera-Rütenik, Tobias, "Mies van der Rohes Aufbruch in die Moderne: das Grabmal Laura Perls von 1919," *Architectura,* vol. 44, no. 2, 2014, p. 107-116.

Asendorf, Christoph, "Continually Renewed Contemporaneity: Ludwig Mies van der Rohe through the Lens of Different Ages," *Candide: Journal for Architectural Knowledge,* no. 8, August 2014, p. 57-88.

Cramer, Johannes, Sack, Dorothée, and Bergdoll, Barry, "Neues zu Mies van der Rohe," *Architectura,* vol. 44, no. 2, 2014, p. 97-100.

Bergdoll, Barry, "Fifteen Years of Publication on Mies van der Rohe, 2000-2015," *Architectura,* vol. 44, no. 2, 2014, p. 177-182.

Krohn, Carsten, "Haus Bueren: ein Unbekannter Bau von Mies van der Rohe in Berlin," *Architectura,* vol. 44, no. 2, 2014, p. 101-104.

Neumann, Dietrich, "Neue Überlegungen zu Mies van der Rohes Bürohausentwurf von 1925," *Architectura,* vol. 44, no. 2, 2014, p. 163-176.

Crippa, Maria Antonietta, "Romano Guardini, Rudolf Schwarz, Ludwig Mies van der Rohe: un dialogo amicale sull'architettura cristiana," *Palladio,* vol. 27, no. 53, January 2014, p. 83-98.

Shulman, Allan T., "Hormigón y transparencia: Bacardi en las Américas," *Summa+,* no. 138, September 2014, p. 94-101.

Chipperfield, David, "Notes on the New National Gallery," *Perspecta,* vol. 48 , 2015, p. 16-19.

Colombo, Luciana Fornari, "The Miesian Courtyard House," *ARQ: Architectural Research Quarterly,* vol. 19, no. 2, June 2015, p. 123-132.

Dreller, Sarah M., "Curtained Walls: Architectural Photography, the Farnsworth House, and the Opaque Discourse of Transparency," *ARRIS: Journal of the Southeast Chapter of the Society of Architectural Historians,* vol. 26, 2015, p. 22-39.

Dyja, Thomas, "The Place Between: a Modern Masterpiece Collides with a Literary Gem - that's Chicago," *Architectural Record,* vol. 203, no. 10, October 2015, p. 74-77.

Frohburg, Jan, "Regarding Mies's Courtyard Houses [Editorial]," *ARQ: Architectural Research Quarterly,* vol. 19, no. 3, September 2015, p. 198-201.

Gargiani, Roberto, "Truth and Disguises: Philip Johnson and the Non-Miesian Directions," *OASE: Architectural Journal,* no. 97, 2016, p. 61-70.

Lizondo Sevilla, Laura, Santatecla Fayos, José, and Salvador Luján, Nuria, "Mies in Brussels 1934: Synthesis of an Unbuilt Exhibition Architecture," *VLC Arquitectura,* vol. 3, no. 1, 2016, p. 29-53.

Luscombe, Desley, "Drawing the Barcelona Pavilion: Mies van der Rohe and the Implications of Perspectival Space," *Journal of Architecture,* vol. 21, no. 2 , 2016, p. 210-243.

Poppelreuter, Tanja, "Spaces for the Elevated Personal Life: Ludwig Mies van der Rohe's Concept of the Dweller, 1926-1930," *Journal of Architecture,* vol. 21, no. 2, 2016, p. 244-270.

Manferdini, Elena, "Grid and the Domain of Ink," *Journal of Architectural Education,* vol. 70, no. 1, 2016, p. 28-30.

Watson, Victoria, "Twentieth Century Modern Architecture and the Countryside: Ludwig Mies van der Rohe's Design for a Country Golf Clubhouse for the Krefeld Golf Club Association," *Transactions of the Ancient Monuments Society,* vol. 60, 2016, p. 80-93.

Bird, Winifred, "Icons of Design: Drawing on a Legacy [the Drawing Room, Arts Club of Chicago]," *Interior Design,* vol. 88, no. 3, March 2017, p. 68 and 70.

Christenson, Mike, "Critical Dimensions in Architectural Photography: Contributions to Architectural Knowledge," *Architecture Media Politics Society,* vol. 11, no. 2, February 2017, p. 1-17.

Hanenberg, Norbert and Lohmann, Daniel, "Master Plans and Deviations: Mies van der Rohe's Involvement in Urban Development at Verseidag Krefeld and IIT Chicago," *Docomomo Journal,* no. 56, 2017, p. 26-33.

Harboe, Gunny, "Restoring the 'God Box': Mies van der Rohe's Carr Chapel at IIT," *Docomomo Journal,* no. 56, 2017, p. 72-77.

Jaspers, Martijn, "The Neue Nationalgalerie: The Refurbishment of a Modern Monument," *Docomomo Journal,* no. 56, 2017, p. 78-85.

Martínez de Guereñu, Laura, "The Sequence of Mies van der Rohe in Barcelona: The German Pavilion as Part of a Much Larger Industrial Presence," *Docomomo Journal,* no. 56, 2017, p. 56-63.

Scholz, Maike and Lohmann, Daniel, "'Zur Neuen Welt' - Towards the New World: Ludwig Mies and his Architectural Youth in Aachen," *Docomomo Journal,* no. 56, 2017, p. 6-15.

Sexton, Mark, Bajor, Katherine, Kissinger, Bill, and Lee, Heidi, "Restoration of Crown Hall," *Docomomo Journal,* no. 56, 2017, p. 64-71.

Neumann, Dietrich, "Mies's Concrete Office Building and its Common Acquaintance," *AA Files,* no. 74, 2017, p. 70-84.

Jaspers, Kristina, "The Adam's Family Store," *AA Files,* no. 75, 2017, p. 20-27.

Lizondo Sevilla, Laura, "Mies's Opaque Cube: The Electric Utilities Pavilion at the 1929 Barcelona International Exposition," *Journal of the Society of Architectural Historians,* vol. 76, no. 2, June 2017, p. 197-217.

INDEX OF PERSONS
AND PROJECTS

Notes and Bibliography are not included.

Afrikanische Straße social housing scheme (Wedding, Berlin) 48, 50–52, 177, 179
Alexanderplatz competition project (Berlin) 81, 82, 177, 179
Algonquin Building (Chicago, Illinois) 180
Alumni Memorial Hall (Chicago, Illinois) 108, 109, 178, 180
Armour Institute campus plan (Chicago, Illinois) 177
Arp, Hans 31
Art Club (Chicago, Illinois) 124, 180

Baader, Johannes 30, 176
Bacardi headquarters building (Mexico) 178, 180
Bacardi office building (Santiago de Cuba) 160, 180
Baillie Scott, M. H. 8
Barcelona Pavilion, see German Pavilion at the 1929 International Exhibition
Barr, Alfred H. 94
Beckmann, Max 177
Behrendt, Walter Curt 32, 74
Behrens, Peter 6, 8, 11, 15, 17–22, 25, 27–30, 32, 34, 39, 42, 52, 56, 79, 81, 105, 161, 164, 166, 176
Benjamin, Walter 64
Bergdoll, Barry 46
Bergson, Henri 53
Berlage, Hendrik Petrus 8, 22–23, 25, 62, 71, 166, 176
Bestelmeyer, German 18
Bier, Julius 72
Blaser, Werner 70
Blossfeldt, Karl 100
Bonatz, Paul 52, 79
Bonta, Juan Pablo 64
Braque, Georges 92
Bremmer, Hendrik Peter 22
Broadacre City 100
Bronfman, Samuel 141, 144
Bruhn, Ada 16, 22, 176, 178
Bunshaft, Gordon 142, 146
Burckhardt, Jacob 21
Burnham, Daniel H. 30, 122, 146

Calder, Alexander 144, 148
Caldwell, Alfred 104, 134, 136, 146, 178
Carter, Peter 178

Cobb, Henry Ives 146
Cohen, Walter 63
Commonwealth Promenade (Chicago, Illinois) 129, 134, 181
Conrads, Ulrich 160
Convention Hall (Chicago, Illinois) 119, 122
Costa, Lucio 178
Crown Hall (Chicago, Illinois) 99, 118–122, 156, 160, 167, 178, 180

Dal Co, Francesco 31
Danforth, George 101, 176
Dearstyne, Howard 86
Dessauer, Friedrich 49, 100
Dessoir, Max 16
De Stijl 8, 32, 34, 38, 176
Dexel, Walter 16, 45
Diels, Rudolph 90
Döblin, Alfred 91
Döcker, Richard 52, 119
Drexler, Arthur 7
Duckett, Edward 177
Düttmann, Werner 161

Eichstädt House (Berlin) 25, 176, 179
Eliat, Ernst 16, 46
Eliat House 46, 179
Endell, August 29
Esters, Josef 8, 56, 90, 177
Esters House (Krefeld) 9, 60–61, 62, 79, 177, 179

Farnsworth, Edith 110, 115
Farnsworth House (Plano, Illinois) 8, 110–18, 178, 180
Federal Center (Chicago, Illinois) 146, 147, 148–49, 150, 178, 181
Feldmann House (Berlin) 25, 176, 179
Fischer, Max 14, 176
Foerster, Karl 16, 25
Francé, Raoul Heinrich 43, 100
Friedrichstraße skyscraper project (Berlin) 27–32, 140, 176, 179
Frobenius, Leo 42, 70
Fuchs, Eduard 46–47, 49, 72
Fuchs House 179
Fujikawa, Joseph 177

Garbe, Herbert 49
Gericke, Herbert 16, 88
Gericke House (Berlin) 88, 177, 180
German Pavilion at the 1929 International Exhibition (Barcelona) 13, 64–72, 88, 177, 179
Giedion, Sigfried 7, 102
Ginsburger, Roger 78
Glaeser, Ludwig 34
Goebbels, Ferries 20, 23, 176
Goebbels, Joseph 90–91
Goldberg, Bertrand 94, 146
Goldsmith, Myron 117, 178
Goodwin, Philip 94–95
Göring, Hermann 94
Gottfried, Carl 31
Graeff, Werner 34, 176
Graham, Ernest 30
Greenwald, Herbert 6, 124–25, 128–29, 134, 139, 166
Gropius, Ise 85
Gropius, Walter 8, 18, 22, 27, 32, 37, 52, 85, 86–87, 90–91, 94, 108, 124, 166
Gruen, Victor 134
Guardini, Romano 49, 100

Harden, Maximilian 14
Häring, Hugo 30, 45, 52, 74, 87, 118
Hausmann, Raoul 32, 176
Heald, Henry Townley 100, 102
Heide, Helmut 90
Henke House (Essen) 88
Henny House (The Hague) 22
Herzog, Oswald 32
Hesse, Fritz 85
Heusgen House (Krefeld) 7, 90, 180
Hilberseimer, Ludwig 30, 42, 52, 81, 86–87, 90, 92, 100, 102–03, 134, 136, 165, 178
Hirche, Herbert 177
Hitchcock, Henry-Russell 88
Hitler, Adolf 91–92, 97, 101, 177
Höch, Hannah 32, 176
Hoffmann, Josef 56
Holabird, John 102–03, 181
Hubbe, Margaret 92–93, 177
Hubbe House (Magdeburg) 95, 178, 180
Hudnut, Joseph 94

IBM Regional Office Building (Chicago, Illinois) 146, 151, 178, 181

Illinois Institute of Technology buildings (Chicago, Illinois) 18, 100–08, 118–19, 122, 176, 180–81

Jaeger, Werner 16
Jaques-Dalcroze, Émile 16, 176
Jeanneret, Albert 16
Jeanneret, Charles-Édouard, see Le Corbusier
Johnson, Lyndon 179
Johnson, Philip 7, 72, 86, 91, 94, 101, 110, 141, 142–43, 177–78, 180–81

Kahn, Albert 102
Kahn, Louis I. 165
Kandinsky, Wassily 90, 176
Katzin, Samuel 128
Kelly, Richard 142
Kempner House (Charlottenburg, Berlin) 25, 46, 179
Kennedy, John F. 178
Kiehl, Reinhold 14
Klee, Paul 96–97, 177
Kleinmotorenfabrik (Berlin) 17, 18
Kolbe, Georg 68, 70–71, 88
Kollwitz, Käthe 91
Koolhaas, Rem 104
Korn, Arthur 31
Kornacker, Frank J. 118
Kracauer, Siegfried 29
Kreis, Wilhelm 18
Kremmer, Martin 104
Kröller-Müller House (The Hague) 22–25, 27, 37, 176
Kropotkin, Piotr 100

Lafayette Park row houses and tower (Detroit, Michigan) 134–35, 137, 178, 181
Lake Shore Drive apartments (Chicago, Illinois) 125–30, 143, 178, 181
2400 Lakeview apartments (Chicago, Illinois) 138–39, 181
Lambert, Phyllis 105, 141
Lange, Hermann 6, 9, 56, 62, 64, 90, 93, 97, 177
Lange (Hermann) House (Krefeld) 9, 56, 62, 177, 179
Lange, Ulrich 97, 177
Lange (Ulrich) House (Krefeld) 178

Larkin Building (Chicago, Illinois) 39
Le Corbusier 6–8, 11, 16, 18, 35, 50, 52, 56, 71–72, 76, 83, 165–66
Lehmbruck, Wilhelm 25, 70, 176
Lemke, Karl 88
Lemke House (Berlin) 88, 177, 180
Liebknecht, Karl 46
Liebknecht, Karl, and Rosa Luxemburg monument 46–48, 92, 177–79
Lindner, Werner 100
Lippold, Richard 142–43
Lissitzky, El 32, 34, 36–37, 39, 42
Lohan, Dirk 160, 164, 166, 178
Luckhardt, Hans and Wassili 81, 87
Luckman, Charles 141
Lurçat, André 177
Luther, Hans 91
Lutyens, Edwin L. 8
Luxemburg, Rosa 46, 49, see also Liebknecht

Mächler, Martin 29
Mackintosh, Charles Rennie 8
Manglano-Ovalle, Iñigo 56, 60, 62
Mann, Heinrich 91
Mannesmann Building (Düsseldorf) 20–21, 35
Mansion House Square tower (London) 152, 178, 181
Martens, John 14
Marx, Lora 101, 177–78
May, Ernst 56
May, Karl 96
Mebes, Paul 15–16, 23
Meier-Graefe, Julius 22
Mendelsohn, Erich 49, 52, 82, 91–92, 99, 104, 128
Mertins, Detlef 53, 100
Messel, Alfred 8, 16, 23
Meyer, Adolf 18, 32, 108
Meyer, Hannes 85–86, 177
Mies, Ewald 11, 18, 176
Mies, Michael 11, 13, 176
Moholy-Nagy, László 102, 118
Moholy-Nagy, Sybil 85
Möhring, Bruno 28–29
Mondrian, Piet 39
Moreau-Vauthier, Paul 47

Mosler House (Neubabelsberg, Potsdam) 15, 25, 38–39, 45, 176, 179
Mumford, Lewis 144
Museum of Fine Arts, (Houston, Texas) 159, 178, 181
Muthesius, Hermann 15–16

National Theater (Mannheim) 119, 178, 180
Nelson, George 91
Neue Nationalgalerie (Berlin) 108, 160–64, 178, 181
Neufert, Ernst 104
Neumeyer, Fritz 16, 50
Niemann, Wilhelm 64
Nierendorf, Karl 96
Nolde, Emil 16, 78–79, 93, 177
Nolde House (Berlin) 78, 177, 180

Oechslin, Werner 36
Olbrich, Joseph Maria 8, 52
One Illinois Center (Chicago, Illinois) 146, 151
Orlik, Emil 15
Osthaus, Karl Ernst 36
Oud, J.J.P. 52, 72, 94

Paepke, Walter Paul 102
Palladio, Andrea 16, 21, 25
Palumbo, Peter 117, 152
Panaggi, Ivano 91
Paul, Bruno 13–15, 17, 34, 122, 176
Pechstein, Max 20
Perls, Hugo 18, 20, 46
Perls House (Zehlendorf, Berlin) 11, 19–20, 23, 25, 46, 49, 72, 179
Perret, Auguste 8
Peterhans, Walter 86, 100
Picasso, Pablo 101
Pieck, Wilhelm 47
Poelzig, Hans 79
Pompidou Center (Paris) 160
Popp, Joseph 15–16, 176
Posener, Julius 72, 164
Priestley, William Turk 94
Prinzhorn, Hans 177
Promontory Apartments (Chicago, Illinois) 109, 125, 126–27, 142, 178, 180

Rathenau, Emil 17
Rathenau, Walther 16, 28, 32
Reich, Lilly 56, 64, 78, 86–88, 90, 97, 176–77, 179
Reichsbank (Berlin) 91–93, 97, 177, 180
Resor, Helen and Stanley Burnet 94, 96, 176
Resor House (Wilson, Wyoming) 95–97, 101, 110, 177, 180
Reuther, Walter 134
Richter, Hans 32, 34, 39, 43, 176
Riehl, Alois and Sofie 15, 16, 28
Riehl House (Neubabelsberg, Potsdam) 14–16, 20, 25, 46, 161, 176, 179
Rimpl, Herbert 104
Rodgers, John Barney 94, 100, 177
Rodin, Auguste 47
Rohe, Amalie 11, 176
Rosenberg, Alfred 90–91, 97
Rowe, Colin 118
Rückriem, Ulrich 162
Ruegenberg, Sergius 47, 70, 78, 92, 176
Ruff, Ludwig 92
Ruhtenberg, Jan 94
Rukser, Udo 30
Ryder House (Wiesbaden) 7, 179
Rykwert, Joseph 104

Sagebiel, Ernst 94
Schacht, Hjalmar 91
Schäfer, Georg 160, 181
Schäfer Museum (Schweinfurt) 160, 178, 181
Schaper, Hermann 13
Scharoun, Hans 52, 74, 119, 160
Scheerbart, Paul 31
Scheffler, Karl 29, 32, 35, 82–83
Schinkel, Karl Friedrich 8, 18, 20–21, 23, 25, 27, 37, 39, 70, 85–86, 88, 108–10, 161, 166, 176, 178, 180
Schmitthenner, Paul 52
Schneider, Albert 14, 176
Schnitzler, Georg von 70
School of Social Service Administration (Chicago, Illinois) 156, 158, 181
Schultze-Naumburg, Paul 23, 90–91
Schupp, Fritz 104
Schwarz, Rudolf 49–50, 52, 119, 136, 165
Schweizer, Otto Ernst 119

Schwitters, Kurt 32, 127 176
Seagram Building (New York) 139, 141–45, 178, 181
Sennett, Richard 111
Silk Café 64, 177, 179
Sitte, Camillo 146
Smithson, Alison and Peter 164
Sörgel, Hermann 35
Speer, Albert 91
Spranger, Eduard 16
Stam, Mart 52
Storonov, Oscar 134
Straumer, Heinrich 79
Sullivan, Louis 101, 126
Summers, Gene 122, 144, 178

Tafuri, Manfredo 31
Taut, Bruno 29–31, 49, 50, 52, 83, 100, 176
Taut, Max 52
Tegethoff, Wolf 39
Tessenow, Heinrich 52, 87
Thiersch, Paul 17, 176
Toronto Dominion Center (Toronto) 9, 146–52, 178, 180
Tugendhat, Grete and Fritz 8, 72, 74, 78
Tugendhat House (Brno) 13, 72–78, 88, 110, 177, 180

Urbig, Franz 25
Urbig House (Neubabelsberg, Potsdam) 15, 25, 176, 179

Van der Rohe, Georgia 92, 97, 166, 176–77
Van Doesburg, Theo 32, 34, 36, 39, 56, 178
Venturi, Robert 6
Verseidag factory (Krefeld) 56, 90, 97, 177
Viollet-le-Duc, Eugène 8, 35, 164
Voysey, Charles Annesley 8

Waldhausen, W. von 176
Wagner, Martin 50, 81, 91
Wagner, Otto 43
Warnholtz House (Charlottenburg, Berlin) 7, 23, 179
Weber, Gerhard 119
Weber, Hugo 166, 167
Weidemann, Hans 91
Weissbourd, Bernard 139
Werner House (Zehlendorf, Berlin) 23–24, 176, 179

Westheim, Paul 18, 27, 76
Westmount Square (Montreal) 141, 151, 153–54, 178, 181
Wiegand, Theodor 21
Wiegand House (Peter Behrens; Dahlem, Berlin) 19, 20–21, 23, 37
Winslow House (Frank Lloyd Wright; River Forest, Illinois) 25
Wolf, Erich 16, 46,
Wolf House (Guben) 46–47, 56, 63, 78, 177, 179
Wölfflin, Heinrich 16
Wright, Frank Lloyd 8, 25, 37, 39, 46, 63, 71, 95, 99–102, 134, 136, 166, 177

Yamasaki, Minoru 134

ILLUSTRATION CREDITS

Headstone of Mies van der
Rohe, Graceland cemetery,
Chicago.